DATE DUE

SE 09 95			
SE 22 95			
SE 23 95			
JE 13 95			
JE 27 95			
SE 15 95			
FE 12 96			

DEMCO

REDEFINING
THE FIRST
FREEDOM

REDEFINING
THE FIRST
FREEDOM

The Supreme Court
and the Consolidation of State Power

Gregg Ivers

Transaction Publishers
New Brunswick (U.S.A.) and London (U.K.)

Library of Congress Catalog Number: 91-42998
ISBN: 1-56000-054-6
Printed in the United States of America

Library of Congress Cataloging-in-Publication-Data
Ivers, Gregg
Redefining the first freedom: the Supreme Court and the consolidation
of state power/Gregg Ivers.
    p. cm.
    ISBN 1-56000-054-6
    1. Freedom of religion—United States. 2. United States. Supreme
Court. 3. Religion and politics—United States. I. Title.
    KF4783.I94 1992
    342. 73'0852—dc20
    [347.302852]

                                                            91-42998
                                                            CIP

Contents

Acknowledgments

I wish I could thank all the people who helped me write this book. I have been fortunate to receive the advice and counsel of numerous individuals, who gave generously of their time; to have excellent research assistance from talented and conscientious students; and to have received financial support that enabled me to research and write without the pressure of additional responsibilities.

I profited from discussion and dialogue with several people, some academics, some not, but all were constructive in their effort to make this book better. Erwin Chemerinsky, Bette Novit Evans, Nancy Maveety, Ronald Shaiko, and Brent Walker all helped me at different junctures and in different ways. I sometimes differed with the advice or criticism I was offered; on some points, we had to agree to disagree. That is inevitable when discussing religion and politics. But each person made me think about what I had written and forced me to account for it. I also learned much from simply listening to what other people had to say. Alyscia Roach, Maria Menor and Timothy Evanson provided excellent research assistance. Paula Nix and Valerie Tate provided first-rate administrative and word-processing assistance. Neil Kerwin, dean of the School of Public Affairs at American University, made available generous research support that enabled me to have the time I needed to concentrate on this book.

At last count, I owe my wife, Janet Krell, somewhere around a zillion thanks for enduring all the unpleasantries that researchers immersed in their work inflict on people who lead normal lives. So here they are—all one zillion and then some. Scott Diener, as usual, did nothing to help this project along. But because he is my best friend, and because he provided two tickets to the 1991 World Series so that I could watch my hometown team, the Atlanta Braves, and because he listens to me when Janet cannot take it anymore, I must thank him for his support and friendship. I also would like to thank Karen O'Connor for her bottomless well of support, encouragement, and friendship.

Some of the material in this book is taken from chapters 2 and 4 of *Lowering the Wall*, a monograph I wrote for the Anti-Defamation League of B'nai B'rith (1990). I also presented papers and addresses at conferences sponsored by the American Political Science Association, the Midwest Political Science Association, Creighton University and Ripon College, where some of the arguments presented in this book first took shape.

I dedicate this book to Joyce Brady Krell and Ethel Chester Cohen, whose courage, intelligence, wit, and charm inspire all those who are fortunate enough to know them.

Introduction

For reasons that had little to do with the law, the United States Supreme Court decided in March 1991 to accept for oral argument an obscure church-state case involving the constitutionality of religious invocations at high school graduation ceremonies. The Court's decision to hear *Lee v. Weisman*[1] did not result from irreconcilable conflict among the lower federal courts or the presentation of novel constitutional questions previously undecided. In fact, *Weisman* did not appear on first glance to raise issues of the slightest constitutional significance. The Court has ruled on numerous occasions over the past three decades that state-sponsored religious exercises in the public schools are unconstitutional.[2] Two lower federal courts, following the Court's line of precedents banning such practices in public schools, struck down the religious devotionals challenged in *Weisman*, and did so in rather routine fashion.[3]

But the Providence, Rhode Island, high school appealing the case received a tremendous boost when the United States Department of Justice filed an *amicus curiae*, or friend-of-the-court, brief asking the High Court to accept the case. In the brief, the solicitor general, acting on behalf of the Bush administration, asked the Court not just to reverse *Weisman* on the merits, but to use the Rhode Island case to reconsider a fundamental and long-standing component of its establishment clause jurisprudence. The Department of Justice's brief was not directed toward the narrow school prayer issue, but instead asked the Court to discard a jurisprudential rule it adopted two decades ago in *Lemon v. Kurtzman* (1971),[4] a case involving government financial aid to parochial schools. In *Lemon*, the Court held that for a statute touching upon the establishment clause to survive constitutional review, such policies must have a secular purpose, neither advance nor inhibit religion, and not create excessive entanglement between religious and state institutions.

In *Weisman*, the Bush administration asked the Court to jettison the analytical framework developed in *Lemon* in favor of what it calls a "noncoercion" standard. Under this mode of establishment clause inquiry, government support for private religion is permissible as long as it does not favor one religion over another or require individuals to repudiate their religious conscience through state-coerced observance of

1

certain religious beliefs. For the Court to use *Weisman* to abandon the wall of separation metaphor that has stood as the constitutional foundation of its church-state jurisprudence since its landmark decision in *Everson v. Board of Education* (1947)[5] and replace it with the Bush administration's "noncoercion" standard will render the establishment clause toothless. In a perverse sense, an adverse ruling in *Weisman* will complement the Court's disastrous decision in *Employment Division of Oregon v. Smith* (1990),[6] which emasculated the law of religious free exercise. But however *Weisman* turns out, and there is no guarantee the Court will adopt the Bush proposal, and whether *Smith* does indeed have portentious consequences for religious free exercise, as it appears it will, one thing is for sure: church-state separation and religious freedom are not privileged occupants in the contemporary Court's constellation of constitutional values.

Weisman and *Smith* provide closure to a decade in which the church-state jurisprudence of the Court underwent a profound and important alteration. The ascent of the Reagan administration to political power in 1980 was accompanied—and indeed supported—by an energetic movement on the Christian evangelical and fundamentalist right to reorder the place of religion in American public life.[7] President Reagan, supported by this amalgam of conservative religious lobbies, used the power and prestige of his office to press the political process to legislate on issues of importance to these constituencies. Having brought the first Republican Senate to Washington in over twenty-five years on his political coattails, President Reagan used that leverage to press Congress to enact a constitutional amendment overturning the Court's historic decisions making state-sponsored religious exercises in the schools unconstitutional. The Reagan administration also took the lead in promoting other legislative initiatives that offered advantages to private religion, including federal block grants for religious institutions and tax relief for the parents of parochial school children.

President Reagan used the power and prestige of his office to encourage state legislatures around the nation to legislate on behalf of religious values. He also intervened on behalf of several states that had religious preference statutes challenged in the courts. On the national and state level, the Reagan administration encouraged the political process to use its collective will to reintroduce majoritarian religious values into the civic culture. Never mind that Reagan had been elected president of the

United States; and never mind that the nation was more religiously plural and diverse than ever before; his administration was determined to lead the charge on behalf of this social agenda, even though it excluded the needs and interests of religious minorities and casually dismissed their hard-fought efforts to overcome their historical place on the political and constitutional margins of the American polity.

But President Reagan did not view the political process as the sole agent of social change; he also maintained that the Supreme Court had been a co-conspirator, if not the principal force, in leading the generational transition of the United States from an era in which a common religious heritage influenced and cultivated our private and public mores to one in which secular values had emerged triumphant in our social and political institutions. President Reagan continually emphasized that the decisions of the Warren Court and the early Burger Court had resulted in a moral climate hostile to religious values. To heal the Constitution from the deep wounds inflicted on it by the Court, President Reagan pledged to reshape the Court in his own image. The Constitution should not be held hostage by the Court and the personal philosophies of the Justices, argued the president; rather the Court should allow the people, through their elected representatives, to decide the boundaries between religion and public life.

More so than any other president since Franklin D. Roosevelt, President Reagan made the Court an extension of presidential power.[8] The Reagan administration took great care to ensure that appointees to the Court, as well as to the lower federal courts, reflected the values set forth during the presidential campaign.[9] It did not want to repeat the mistake of President Dwight D. Eisenhower, whose appointments to the Court included Earl Warren and William J. Brennan, both of whom represented the judicial and constitutional values that the Reagan administration had targeted for reform and reconsideration. When President Eisenhower was later asked to name the biggest mistakes of his presidency, he replied that there were two, and they were both sitting on the Supreme Court.[10] No such error would befall the Reagan administration. President Reagan promised to appoint justices to the Court who held conservative views on civil rights and civil liberties and on the extent to which the Constitution compelled judicial intervention to uphold claims brought under the Bill of Rights. This included justices who would allow greater government accommodation of religion in American public life, who would prefer religious values to secular values, and who would correct the constitutional excesses wrought by the Court under Earl Warren and then later, under the de facto leadership of Justice Brennan.

Perhaps because President Reagan was so determined to use the Court to embark on a wide-scale program of judicial and legal reform, his wishes came true. From 1980 to 1987, President Reagan appointed three distinctly conservative associate justices to the Court, and elevated a sitting justice, William H. Rehnquist, the Court's most conservative member, to chief justice. Sandra Day O'Connor replaced Justice Potter Stewart; Antonin Scalia replaced Chief Justice Warren Burger; and Anthony Kennedy replaced Justice Lewis Powell. As I shall argue in this book, Chief Justice Rehnquist and Justices O'Connor, Scalia, and Kennedy have each taken lead roles in reshaping the religion clause jurisprudence of the Court. Indeed, at one point or another since 1980, each has written an opinion suggesting that the Court either revisit or abandon settled constitutional jurisprudence governing church-state law;[11] and, in one case, the Court took such a step.[12] With the addition of Justices Scalia and Kennedy, Chief Justice Rehnquist was able to obtain with greater consistency majorities that reflected the constitutional and judicial values he had long espoused. By the close of the 1988–89 term, a Rehnquist Court had consolidated, with the chief justice and Justices Scalia, Kennedy, O'Connor, and Byran R. White forming a consistent, working majority, especially in cases involving civil rights and civil liberties.[13]

Since 1989, Justices Brennan and Marshall have resigned, all but depleting the Court's constitutional jurisprudence of any liberal marrow. President Bush replaced the Court's two remaining liberals from the Warren era with David Souter and Clarence Thomas. Although neither has been on the Court long enough to reveal a judicial philosophy, it borders on the fantastic to believe that President Bush will abandon President Reagan's commitment to conservative legal and judicial reform and nominate justices in the Brennan-Marshall mold. When one considers the Department of Justice's *amicus curiae* brief in *Weisman*, the desire of the Bush administration to continue President Reagan's drive to use government leverage to reintroduce majoritarian religious values into the civic culture is apparent. More than ever before, the Court is now positioned to redefine the judicial role in the separation of powers; the obligation of the Justices to confine themselves to the constitutional text; the methodologies applicable in the interpretation of statutes and constitutional provisions; and the relevance of historical intent and social evolution in constitutional jurisprudence. In sum, the Court is now positioned to fulfill the aspirations that Ronald Reagan had envisioned for it as candidate and president.

Outline of the Book

The central objective of this book is to describe and analyze the enormous changes that have taken place in the church-state jurisprudence of the Supreme Court from 1980 to 1990. As I described above, President Reagan was fortunate to have three opportunities to appoint justices to the Court and to name a new chief justice. President Bush has had two opportunities to fill vancancies on the Court. Since 1980, conservative Republican presidents have appointed two-thirds of the Court. Law and politics do not operate independent of one another, but are intertwined. Here, as I will argue, the Court has become an extension of the political process. The Court no longer embraces the countermajoritarian function, but places among the highest of judicial and consitutional values respect for majoritarian bodies. That argument has been made elsewhere to describe with considerable sophistication and power the Court's overall approach to constitutional jurisprudence.[14] I will argue that the Court's interpretation of the religion clauses has been consistent with this shift in constitutional jurisprudence.

Chapter 1 of this book examines the Court's decisions on religion and public education, and focuses on three major areas: religious doctrine, including school prayer; Bible reading and other religious devotionals; and equal access and public school curriculum. Chapter 2 discusses the financial relationship between government and private religion, including aid to parochial schools and noneducational institutions. I also examine the Court's decisions on tax exemption for religious institutions and individuals. Chapter 3 examines religion and public places, with particular emphasis on the constitutionality of religious symbols on public land and government support for religious displays on private property. This chapter concludes with a discussion of legislative chaplaincies and other state action on behalf of religion. Chapter 4 concludes substantive treatment of the Court's religion clause decisions with an examination of religious free exercise and related issues. Particular areas covered include religious discrimination in employment, religion-based exemptions from laws having general application, and the Court's dichotomous standards on religious belief and religious conduct. Finally, I conclude with a summation of my thesis on the Court and the religion clauses.

Notes

1. 908 F.2d 1090 (1st Cir. 1990), *cert. granted*, 111 S.Ct. 1305 (1991).
2. E.g., *Jager v. Douglas County School District*, 862 F.2d 824 (11th Cir. 1989), *cert. denied*, 109 S.Ct. 2431 (1989); *Wallace v. Jaffree*, 472 U.S. 38 (1985); *Abington v. Schempp*, 374 U.S. 203 (1963); *Engel v. Vitale*, 370 U.S. 421 (1962).
3. *Weisman v. Lee*, 728 F.Supp. 68 (D.R.I. 1990), *aff'd*, 908 F.2d 1090 (1st. Cir. 1990).
4. 403 U.S. 602 (1971).
5. 330 U.S. 1 (1947).
6. 110 S.Ct. 1595 (1990).
7. For excellent accounts of the sources, strategies and objectives of religious political involvement during the 1980s, see, for example, Matthew C. Moen, *The Christian Right and Congress* (Tuscaloosa, Ala.: University of Alabama Press, 1989); Charles W. Dunn, ed., *Religion in American Politics* (Washington, D.C.: Congressional Quarterly Press, 1989); Allen D. Hertzke, *Representing God in Washington* (Knoxville, Tenn.: University of Tennessee Press, 1988); A. James Reichley, *Religion in American Public Life* (Washington, D.C.: The Brookings Institution, 1985).
8. For a discussion of the judicial appointments of President Reagan and their impact on the federal courts and public law, see David O'Brien, "The Reagan Judges: His Most Enduring Legacy?" in *The Reagan Legacy* (Chatham, N.J.: Chatham House, 1988), 60–101.
9. Id., 62.
10. Henry J. Abraham, *Justices and Presidents* (New York: Oxford University Press, 1974), 246.
11. E.g., *County of Allegheny v. ACLU*, 109 S.Ct. 3086, 3134–46 (Justice Kennedy, concurring in part and dissenting in part) (suggesting that the Court replace *Lemon* with a noncoercion standard); *Wallace v. Jaffree*, 372 U.S. 38, 91–118 (Justice Rehnquist, dissenting) (Court should overrule *Lemon* and *Everson* and engage in a nonpreferential interpretation of the establishment clause); *Lynch v. Donnelly*, 465 U.S. 668, 674–688 (Justice O'Connor, concurring) (suggesting that the Court adopt an endorsement standard in place of *Lemon*).
12. *Employment Division of Oregon v. Smith*, 110 S.Ct. 1595 (1990).
13. For a persuasive argument that a Rehnquist Court has emerged, see Erwin Chemerinsky, "The Vanishing Constitution," 103 *Harvard Law Review* 44 (1989).
14. Id.

1

Religion and Public Education

Proponents of a government-endorsed religious presence in American public life have generally viewed with contempt the historic Supreme Court decisions of *Engel v. Vitale* (1962)[1] and *Abington v. Schempp* (1963),[2] which outlawed state-sponsored prayer and other religious devotional exercises in the public schools. In this view, *Engel* and *Schempp* personified the determined effort of the Warren Court to build what Reverend Richard John Neuhaus has called a "naked public square," or a public life exclusive of the moral force of religion.[3] Initial reaction to these decisions was generally favorable among secular and religious Jewish agencies,[4] as well as the major mainline Protestant representative bodies, such the National Council of Churches and the Baptist Joint Committee on Public Affairs.[5] But most Catholic[6] and conservative Protestant groups,[7] whose reaction was much closer to public opinion,[8] were outraged by *Engel* and *Schempp*, and along with other conservative organizations, have since sought to have them over-turned.[9]

Since *Engel* and *Schempp*, Congress has attempted on several occasions to overturn the Court's ban on state-sponsored religious devotionals in the public schools, but has failed either to pass legislation or to muster enough votes for a constitutional amendment.[10] Subsequent to these historic decisions the Court has reaffirmed that states cannot require students to recite state-composed prayers or permit school-sponsored religious exercises in the public education system.[11] But these setbacks only served to strengthen the determination of politicians and private

7

interests resolved to win government support for religion in the public schools. After a generation of frustration on the part of religious conservatives, sheer dint of persistence merged with political fate in 1980 when Ronald Reagan, who made support for a constitutional amendment to overturn *Engel* and *Schempp* a campaign pledge,[12] was elected president.

The Reagan administration created a much more receptive political and legal climate for advocates of the restoration of government-endorsed religion in public life, especially Christian evangelicals and fundamentalists, to advance their interests than did his predecessors. President Reagan spoke often and forcefully of the need for government to work actively to lower the metaphorical wall separating church and state, and pledged that his administration would support this goal through initiatives of its own and by assisting similar efforts of state governments and private organizations, which it did.[13] Having the obtained the power and prestige of the president to back their assault on church-state separation, conservative organizations with religious and secular ties made government support for religious practices in the public schools a leading component in this reenergized drive to reshape the law of church and state. From the dawn of the modern constitutional era, the public schoolhouse has traditionally been at the center of the debate over the meaning of the religion clauses. Indeed, over the last four decades, the Court's decisions interpreting the establishment clause have, with some exceptions,[14] turned on the constitutional limits of sectarian influence in public education and government financial assistance to parochial schools.

State and federal legislation enacted during the 1980s to permit public schools to integrate religious exercises and support for student religion clubs into their educational mission, most of which ran counter to the settled establishment clause doctrine of the Court, reflected the new wave of religious revivalism sweeping the country and the emerging political forces behind it. Instrumental in bringing these issues before the legislatures and the courts were organizations whose support came from conservative religious evangelicals and fundamentalists determined to redefine the contours of establishment clause law. These organizations, such as the Moral Majority, the Christian Legal Society, the National Association of Evangelicals, and the National Legal Foundation, had acquired a new political sophistication in the period between the demise of the separationist impulses of the Warren Court and the early Burger

Court and the election of Ronald Reagan, and now understood how to pull the levers of American politics to their advantage.[15]

In a reprisal of the arguments that greeted its landmark decisions in *Engel, Schempp* and *Epperson v. Arkansas* (1968)[16] a generation before, the Court again found itself caught in the middle of a political crossfire between competing visions of the proper place of religion in the public schools. The Court faced the unenviable task of trying to resolve through constitutional adjudication what the legislative process could not—the limit the Constitution places on religion as a moral and pedagogical component in the public school system. The debate centered on three areas: religious doctrine, equal access, and curriculum reform.

Religious Doctrine

Shortly into the 1980 term, the Supreme Court revisited the question of whether public schools can use state-provided religious texts and materials for the purpose of teaching and promoting sectarian religious doctrine. The Court has never held that public schools are forbidden from teaching *about* religion in the historical and literary context.[17] Rather, the Court has ruled that public schools are enjoined from conducting religious exercises or preaching religious doctrine in their classrooms and environs.[18] The Court has also ruled that public school officials are prohibited from distributing religious literature on school grounds, even if such materials are provided by private contributors.[19]

In *Stone v. Graham* (1980),[20] the Court reaffirmed these holdings. In a 5-4 *per curiam* opinion, the Court declared unconstitutional a Kentucky state statute requiring elementary and secondary public schools to post copies of the Ten Commandments in their classrooms. The High Court reversed the Kentucky Supreme Court, which had found the statute to have the secular purpose of advancing an historical and literary understanding of the Bible. The Court held that the Kentucky law failed to satisfy the secular-purpose prong of the *Lemon* test. Drawing upon *Schempp*, which struck down state-endorsed and teacher-led recitation of biblical scripture and verse in the public schools, the Court in *Stone* held that

the preeminent purpose for posting the Ten Commandments on schoolroom walls is plainly religious in nature. The Ten Commandments are undeniably a sacred text in the Jewish and Christian faiths, and no legislative recitation of a supposed secular

purpose can blind us to that fact. . . . This is not a case in which the Ten Commandments are integrated into the school curriculum, where the Bible may consitutionally
be used in an appropriate study of history, civilization, ethics, comparative religion,
or the like. Posting of religious texts on the wall serves no such educational purpose.[21]

The Court's opinion in *Stone* injected needed life into the separationist
principles articulated in the foundational *Schempp* and *Engel* decisions.
But *Stone* is really an easy case. A more complex question that had failed
to reach the Court in the ensuing period after *Engel* was whether state
statutes setting aside a moment-of-silence at the beginning of each school
day for meditation or voluntary prayer violated the establishment clause.
Unlike *Engel*, these statutes did not involve the state's hand in composing
the content of classroom devotionals. On one occasion, the Court had
affirmed without opinion a lower federal court's ruling striking down a
blatant effort to circumvent *Engel*,[22] but had otherwise not felt compelled
to address the issue. In *Wallace v. Jaffree* (1985),[23] the Court received the
chance to address the multi-faceted debate over permissible school
prayer laws.

From 1978 to 1982, the Alabama state legislature enacted three
separate statutes authorizing public school authorities to provide a moment of silence at the beginning of each school day for student meditation, reflection or prayer. The first law, passed in 1978, required
elementary school teachers to provide a minute of silence "for meditation" before the first morning class.[24] In 1981, the Alabama legislature
enacted a second statute authorizing elementary and secondary school
teachers to provide "a period of silence not to exceed one minute in
duration . . . for meditation or voluntary prayer."[25] One year later,
Alabama passed the most comprehensive of its three back-to-back legislative attempts aimed at restoring school prayer. The 1982 Alabama
statute gave "any teacher or professor . . . in any public educational
institution within the state of Alabama" the right to lead "willing students" in specifically worded prayer that expressly recognized "Al-
mighty God . . . Creator and Supreme Judge of the World."[26]

In May 1982, Ishmael Jaffree, a Mobile County, Alabama, resident,
with three children in the local school system, filed a complaint against
the Mobile County School Board requesting the cessation of these
religious practices. In his complaint, Jaffree also alleged that two of his
children had been coerced into taking part in school religious exercises.
Additionally, his children had been subjected to continuous religious

proselytizing by other students and, in some cases, their teachers. Jaffree's frequent attempts to have schools officials put an end to these coercive religious practices had failed. Finally, Jaffree argued that the presence of ongoing religious exercises in the public schools, which received the full support of the Mobile school board, violated the First and Fourteenth Amendments to the United States Constitution.

Less than a week after filing his first complaint, Jaffree amended it to include a challenge the constitutionality of the three Alabama prayer laws. At the federal hearing to consider the motions brought by Jaffree, Alabama State Senator Donald G. Holmes, the leading sponsor of the 1981 bill, testified that the purpose of the statute was to "return voluntary prayer to our public schools. . . . It is a beginning and a step in the right direction . . . *with no other purpose in mind.*"[27]

The trial court handed down its ruling. It held that Jaffree would in all likelihood prevail on the merits of his complaint because none of the Alabama prayer statutes, and in particular the 1981 and 1982 laws, met the secular legislative purpose requirement of the *Lemon* test. However, in November 1982, after a full trial on the merits, Judge Brevard Hand, who had just issued the order enjoining the state school system from continuing its religious practices, issued a startling opinion reversing his earlier decision.

Ignoring long-standing and unchallenged fundamental principals of modern constitutional jurisprudence, Judge Hand held that the Alabama prayer statutes did not violate the First Amendment because the establishment clause did not apply to the states. After a lengthy review of what he termed newly uncovered historical evidence, Judge Hand wrote that the "Establishment Clause of the First Amendment to the United States Constitution does not prohibit the state from establishing a religion."[28] Judge Hand ruled that the establishment clause banned the federal government from establishing religion, but left the states free to do so if they wished.[29]

Judge Hand's decision was reversed by the Eleventh Circuit Court of Appeals, which did not consider the constitutional challenge to the 1978 statute that permitted teachers to allow a moment of silence "for meditation," but did find the 1981 and 1982 laws "to advance and encourage religious activity."[30] Alabama petitioned the Eleventh Circuit for a rehearing *en banc*, but it was denied. However, four judges dissented from this decision, arguing that the court should have agreed to decide whether the 1981 Alabama statute permitting public schools to set aside moments of silence for "meditation or voluntary prayer" violated the establishment clause.[31] The Supreme Court considered the disagreement among the Eleventh Circuit judges important enough to accept *Wallace v. Jaffree* for review during the 1984–85 term. But it also decided to limit argument to just those provisions of the three separate Alabama laws dealing with voluntary prayer.

In a 6–3 decision, the Court found the 1981 Alabama statute to violate the purpose prong of the *Lemon* test.[32] In his opinion for the Court, Justice John Paul Stevens relied extensively on the legislative record developed during the drafting and passage of the statutes. Justice Stevens held that the Alabama state legislature enacted the 1981 law

> for the sole purpose of expressing the State's endorsement of prayer activities for one minute at the beginning of each school day. The addition of "or voluntary prayer" [to the 1978 law] indicates that the State intended to characterize prayer as a favored practice. Such an endorsement is not consistent with the established principle that the Government must pursue a course of complete neutrality towards religion.[33]

Wallace gave nervous separationists some reassurance that the Court, especially after its recent decisions in *Lynch v. Donnelly* (1984),[34] *Marsh v. Chambers* (1983)[35] and *Mueller v. Allen* (1983)[36] that weakened settled establishment clause jurisprudence, still retained the judicial backbone to strike down such brazen attempts as Alabama's to circumvent the line of decisions from *Engel* through *Stone* outlawing state-supported religious practices in the public schools. The Court openly dismissed Judge Hand's conclusion that the establishment clause meant simply that the federal government was barred from establishing or supporting an official state church. Justice Stevens said that Judge Hand's conclusion was "remarkable [in finding] that the Federal Constitution imposes no obstacle to Alabama's establishment of a state religion."[37] The Court, in fact, seemed somewhat miffed by this attack on its legitimacy:

> [W]hen the Constitution was amended to prohibit any State from depriving any person of liberty without due process of law, that Amendment imposed the same substantive limitations on the States' power to legislate that the First Amendment had always imposed on the Congress' power. This Court has confirmed that elementary principle time and time again.[38]

However, Justice Stevens' opinion declined to address the question simmering underneath the "voluntary prayer" debates: Did the establishment clause mandate the same categorical ban on "moment of silence" statutes constructed without references to religious observances? In her concurring opinion, Justice Sandra Day O'Connor concluded from the legislative record that "little doubt" existed that Alabama intended to use the statute as a vehicle to "endorse and sponsor voluntary prayer in the public schools."[39] But, in crucial *dicta*, Justice O'Connor also wrote that moment-of-silence statutes "drafted and implemented so as to permit prayer, meditation and reflection . . . without endorsing one alternative over the others," would not necessarily "manifest the same infirmity."[40] In a separate concurrence, Justice Lewis Powell endorsed this view as well.[41]

But the most spectacular and perhaps prophetic opinion in *Wallace* came from Justice Rehnquist. Mounting the most substantial and wide-ranging attack on the Court's church-state jurisprudence from the bench since *Everson v. Board of Education* (1947),[42] Justice Rehnquist called on the Court to abandon the "unnecessary" wall-of-separation metaphor as the fixed star guiding its constitutional decision making in establishment clause cases.[43] Justice Rehnquist argued that the establishment clause only prohibited the federal government from designating an official church, or providing assistance to some religious denominations at the expense of others, but did not require the government to remain "neutral between religion and irreligion."[44] The Court's flawed and unworkable establishment clause jurisprudence since *Everson*, wrote Justice Rehnquist, had resulted from a misplaced understanding of Thomas Jefferson's wall-of-separation metaphor, which, in his view, provided no basis for the contemporary "theory of rigid separation."[45]

Justice Rehnquist's clarion call for the Court to discard the *Lemon* test as its core analytical device in reviewing establishment clause cases,[46] to cast Justice Black's *Everson dicta* into the dustbin of constitutional jurisprudence,[47] and to reassess the permissible role of government in supporting religion in both the private and public spheres[48], received a greater reception off the Court than among his colleagues.[49] Neither Justice White, who urged "a basic reconsideration of our precedents" in his dissent[50] nor Chief Justice Burger, who also dissented,[51] joined Justice Rehnquist's opinion. But it might well be the new Chief Justice who ultimately triumphs in the battle over the Court's future establishment clause jurisprudence. Since *Wallace*, two of the Court's four new members, Antonin Scalia and Anthony Kennedy, have supported Chief Justice Rehnquist's call for a passive, nonpreferentialist jurisprudence, and in terms no less stark.[52] *Lee v. Weisman*, argued in the Fall 1991 Supreme Court term, will determine if Justice Rehnquist's once-derided *Wallace* dissent will become law. The Court has decided to use *Weisman* to reconsider the *Lemon* test's application in establishment clause cases.

Wallace did not extinguish the school prayer debate. While the Court's 9–0 decision striking down the 1982 Alabama statute permitting public school personnel to lead students in state-composed vocal prayer leaves almost no doubt that *Engel* will remain good law,[53] the present constitutional ban on moment-of-silence statutes and similar vehicles to permit voluntary prayer in public schools appears to stand on more tenuous ground. The Court's several opinions in *Wallace* striking down the 1981 Alabama statute leave unclear the latitude of public school authorities in permitting or prohibiting moments-of-silence in their classrooms. Since *Wallace*, the Court has ruled that verbal religious exercises conducted under the auspices of school officials or policies that allow state supervision over the content of student devotionals are unconstitutional.[54] But Justice O'Connor's concurring *dicta* suggests that moment-of-silence laws, neutral in construction and lacking an incriminating legislative record, that permit silent meditation, reflection, or prayer but do not mention them as such in the statutory text, are acceptable constitutional alternatives to the Alabama statutes invalidated in *Wallace*.[55] In fact, Justice O'Connor's *Wallace* concurrence is all but a blueprint for legislatures wishing to enact constitutional moment-of-silence statutes.

Two years later, the Court heard such a case. In *Karcher v. May* (1987), the Court was asked to decide whether a New Jersey statute authorizing a moment-of-silence in public schools "for quiet and private contemplation or introspection"[56] violated the establishment clause, but dismissed the case for lack of standing.[57] The New Jersey statute's history was a troubled one. First passed in 1982, vetoed by Governor Thomas P. Kean the bill was, but the veto was overridden the following term. A coalition of New Jersey public school students, their parents, and a secondary school teacher challenged the law almost immediately after the legislative override. To complicate matters, the New Jersey attorney general refused to defend the statute in court, calling it a thinly veiled attempt by the legislature to reintroduce prayer in the public school system.[58] The state legislature decided to hire outside counsel to press the case.

In October 1983, a federal court ruled the New Jersey moment-of-silence statute to violate all three prongs of the *Lemon* test.[59] First, the district court found the statute to have an impermissible religious purpose—"to mandate that all students assume the posture of one traditional form of prayer."[60] Second, the court ruled that the law had the dual effect of advancing and inhibiting religion, an unusual departure from traditional analysis under *Lemon*. Under the effect test in *Lemon*, the question centers on whether the statute has advanced *or* inhibited religion, but not managed a simultaneous violation on both counts.[61] The court nonetheless concluded that the state advanced religion by designating "a time and place when children and teachers may pray if they do so in a particular manner,"[62] and inhibited religion because such coercive measures drained the vitality of other students' religious observances.[63] Finally, the court found the statute to violate the excessive-entanglement prong of *Lemon* because it fostered divisiveness among religious and nonreligious groups in a manner that threatened the school's daily agenda.[64]

Hearing the legisature's appeal, the Third Circuit Court of Appeals affirmed the lower court decision, but it disagreed with the method in which it applied *Lemon* in reviewing the statute.[65] The appeals court instead ruled that both the effect and entanglement provisions of the *Lemon* test were intended to determine whether the statute resulted in neutrality toward religion.[66] Still, the Third Circuit concluded that because the law lacked a clear secular purpose, the lower court decision must be sustained.[67] The Third Circuit followed the guidelines laid down in *Wallace v. Jaffree*, which the Supreme Court had decided just months before its decision. Like the High Court in *Wallace*, the Third Circuit ruled that the legislative record made evident the religious purpose behind New Jersey's enactment of the statute. While incorporating no direct reference to prayer in the text of the moment-of-silence statute, the Third Circuit nonetheless struck it down on the basis that the legislative record was replete with evidence of the law's religious purpose.

Clearly, *Wallace* and *May* are the two most important cases elucidating the constitutional limitations on state-sponsored religious devotionals in the public schools since the landmark decisions of *Engel* and *Schempp* over twenty-five years ago. Unfortunately, the failure of the Court to reach the constitutional question in *May* means that a large element of uncertainty currently exists as to how it and other courts will view the legislative purpose behind the enactment of facially neutral moment-of-silence statutes challenged in future litigation. If the Court relies on

Wallace and continues to scrutinize the legislative histories of similar laws, a chance exists that it will continue to consider *Wallace* controlling under those circumstances. However, if the *Wallace* concurrences of Justices Powell and O'Connor, both of whom indicated that "some moment-of-silence statutes may be constitutional,"[68] assume a more central place in the approach of the Court to subsequent school prayer cases, the future portends a quite different outcome. New constitutional challenges to the Court's rules in *Wallace* and attempts to sustain "pure" moment-of-silence statutes could succeed or fail depending upon the resolution of two questions. First, is the religious purpose driving the enactment of such laws appropriately camouflaged in the legislative record? Second, will the accommodationist wing of the Court follow Justice Scalia's stated preference to ignore legislative history in interpreting the intent of a law, but rely instead on a "plain view" understanding of the statutory text?[69]

The answer to the first question is clear: the Court demonstrated in *Wallace* that it is sympathetic to moment-of-silence laws that are constructed in neutral language. Support for these statutes came from Justice O'Connor and Justice Powell, both of whom joined the *Wallace* majority. While *Wallace*, for now, remains good law, the majority that decided the case has dissipated. Justice Powell has since left the Court, but there is no need to speculate on his replacement's leanings. Justice Kennedy is a solid fourth vote, along with Justices Scalia, White, and Chief Justice Rehnquist, on the anti-*Lemon*, nonpreferentialist wing of the Court. Justice Kennedy certainly would have joined the *Wallace* dissenters, as his opinion in *County of Allegheny v. ACLU* (1989) has indicated.[70] Justice Scalia, who expressed his initial contempt for the Court's establishment clause jurisprudence in his *Edwards v. Aguillard* (1987) dissent,[71] would have been with the *Wallace* dissenters as well. But Justice Scalia replaced another *Wallace* dissenter, Chief Justice Burger, while Justice Kennedy replaced Justice Powell, who voted with the separationist wing of the Court in *Wallace* and *Aguillard*, making the latter more significant in the Court's realignment on establishment clause cases.

Justices Brennan and Marshall have also since retired, taking their reliable separationist votes with them. In their respective careers on the Court, neither Justice Brennan nor Justice Marshall voted to sustain state statutes designed to introduce prayer in the public schools. Their replacements, Justices Souter and Thomas, are *tabula rasa* on the establishment clause. *Weisman* is the first chance for the two newest members of the Court to express their views on the establishment clause and, for Justices Kennedy and Scalia, their first occasion to address the school prayer issue directly. A decision to permit or prohibit state-sponsored religious exercises at public school commencement ceremonies will give a first glimpse into the Rehnquist Court's understanding of the establishment clause's limits in this area. *Weisman,* because it involves religious practices not required through state statute, will not give Justice Scalia, should he get to write the opinion, the opening he wants to extend his "plain view" method of reviewing statutes and constitutional provisions to the establishment clause area. That will have to wait until the Court addresses the moment-of-silence issue again. Perhaps then we will see how Justice Thomas and Justice Souter interpret the language of more sophisticated statutory proposals designed to introduce religion into the public schools.

Equal Access

The tension inherent in attempting to reconcile the constitutional promises of church-state separation, religious free exercise, and freedom of speech embodied in the First Amendment is nowhere better illustrated than in the long-running debate over equal access policies that permit student religious organizations to meet in the public schools. In 1984, Congress passed the Equal Access Act,[72] which requires that public high schools permitting noncurriculum student clubs to meet on school grounds must allow religious organizations "equal access" to its facilities. Due largely to a persistent lobbying effort by an unusual coalition of mainline, evangelical, and fundamentalist Protestant religious organizations, Congress passed the Equal Access Act, although not without persistent and vocal opposition from a small, but influential, coalition of religious and secular organizations, after several previous legislative proposals were unable to win wide-scale support.[73]

The Supreme Court has since rejected a constitutional challenge brought against the Equal Access Act,[74] but this has not put the issue to rest, as school boards continue to grapple with its implementation at the local level. Organizations representing educators and school boards, in fact, opposed the Equal Access Act when it was being debated in Congress[75] and later urged the Court to rule it unconstitutional.[76] The opposition to the Equal Access Act manifested itself on two levels. On one level, numerous school boards believed that permitting religious clubs to hold meetings in public school facilities placed schools in the tenuous position of appearing, if not actually, to endorse student religious beliefs.[77] School administrators also feared that Congress, having found a constitutional opening through the free speech clause to circumvent the Court's prohibition on state-led religious exercises, had brushed aside the genuine establishment clause problems in the Equal Access Act. If schools were required to treat student-initiated religious clubs the same as the French club or chess club, how could their meetings be supervised without risking just the kind of on-going, pervasive government surveilliance of private religion that the Court had ruled in previous cases was unconstitutional?[78]

Second, several of these same school boards also believed that, on a practical level, the Equal Access Act would be impossible to implement in a manner satisfactory to the organizations that had championed it, as well as to those that had not.[79] School boards also feared that construing the act in sweeping, expansive terms would remove local discretion in deciding whether partisan, controversial, and unwanted student-initiated organizations could meet in their classrooms,[80] a fear that was realized in the Court's decision in *Board of Westside Schools v. Mergens* (1990).[81] Even supporters of the Equal Access Act, including those whose scholarship was influential in the Court's decision in *Mergens*, acknowledge that the legislation is poorly drafted and open to abusive implementation.[82]

But these arguments raised against equal access are, for now, beside the point. In June 1990, the Supreme Court, 8-1, ruled in *Mergens* that the Equal Access Act of 1984 required public high schools receiving federal funds to permit student religious clubs to meet in their classrooms if other student groups whose activities were not directly related to school curriculum were extended such privileges. On the establishment clause issue, the Justices determined that the Equal Access Act was not unconstitutional, but could not put together an opinion for the Court explaining this conclusion.[83] It appears that the Justices were not comfortable with the establishment clause problems raised by the Equal Access Act. Recognizing that rigorous treatment of the establishment clause issues might expose the constitutional infirmities of the Equal Access Act, the Court in *Mergens* decided to avoid, rather than to address, these problems.

Critical in the Court's approval of equal access was its willingness to accept without question the legislation's chief constitutional argument—that organized religious exercises in public schools, violative of the establishment clause when teacher-led, become just another form of speech protected from content-based prohibition when such practices are student-initiated. In *Mergens*, the Court never questioned the dubious legislative record built during the congressional debates over the Equal Access Act, a record replete with references to equal access as an acceptable back-door alternative to the failed attempt to pass a constitutional amendment to permit prayer in public schools.[84] One of the Equal Access Act's leading backers, Senator Mark Hatfield (R-Ore.), made clear that his support for the bill rested on securing the right of students to engage in religious speech, and that such protection did not extend to organized student worship services, even if these services were student-initiated.[85] This distinction did not trouble the Equal Access Act's supporters, who claim that religious worship and religious speech cannot be separated, and therefore, neither can their constitutional adjudication.[86] In this view, the Constitution does not recognize a distinction between a government-created forum for organized religious exercises in public schools and protection for private student religious speech, as long as students, and not public school personnel, are the initiators of such speech.[87] Equal access advocates have argued that public schools are public fora, like public parks and sidewalks, and therefore open to all privately initiated speech.[88]

This argument is disingenuous, but not new. It received initial endorsement in the Court's first equal access case, *Widmar v. Vincent* (1981),[89] which served to reignite a diligent effort on the part of religious conservatives to bring similar protection down to the high school level.

Widmar v. Vincent: *Establishing the Conceptual Framework*

In *Widmar*, the Court ruled that once public universities made their campus facilities available to noncurriculum student clubs, they had created an "open forum" accessible to all student organizations regardless of their stated purpose or activities. *Widmar* grew out of a challenge brought by a campus religious group to a University of Missouri Board of Regents regulation banning the use of "university buildings or grounds . . . for purposes of religious worship or religious teaching."[90] The

University of Missouri-Kansas City argued that it was required under the Missouri Constitution and the establishment clause of the federal Constitution to prohibit student religious clubs from using its facilities.

Claiming that the regulation violated the free exercise and free speech clauses of the First Amendment, Cornerstone, a Christian evangelical student organization, filed suit against the university. Cornerstone argued that its right to meet on campus grounds was not an establishment clause matter; rather, the students claimed that the speech clause required the university to allow religious clubs to meet on campus grounds.[91] Otherwise, the school would be making its decision to exclude Cornerstone on content-based grounds, which the students argued was unconstitutional. Cornerstone also argued that universities, because of their moral commitment to intellectual pluralism, must permit religion equal access to the marketplace of ideas as an essential component in an enlightened and educated campus discourse.[92]

The federal district court agreed with the university, ruling that state universities were barred by the establishment clause from permitting student organizations to meet on campus if their purpose was to engage in religious worship.[93] The court did not decide the free speech issue. But the Eighth Circuit Court of Appeals reversed, holding that student-initiated religious speech falls squarely within the protection of the speech clause.[94] The appellate court also ruled that the University of Missouri-Kansas City had created an "open forum" because it permitted other student groups to use its facilities and therefore could not exclude religious groups.[95] Rejecting the district court's conclusion, the Eighth Circuit instead found that allowing student religious clubs access to campus had "the primary effect of advancing the university's admittedly secular purpose—to develop students' social and cultural awareness as well as their intellectual curiosity."[96]

The Supreme Court, in an 8–1 opinion written by Justice Powell, affirmed the Eighth Circuit's decision. The Court said that the free speech clause, not the establishment clause, controlled the issue of student access to university fora in *Widmar*.[97] For universities to ban student speech because it is religious is impermissible. When universities allow all other student organizations to meet on campus grounds, it has created an "open forum" that prohibits denial on content-based grounds.[98] The Court flatly rejected UMKC's establishment clause defense that religion received state endorsement under the equal access rule, even though it required the university to accommodate student religious clubs. In two major respects, the Court found the benefits that accrued to religion incidental. First, the "open forum" policy of the university did not constitute state endorsement or advancement of religion, but the proper application of speech clause principles.[99] Second, campus life encompassed such a broad, diverse range of student organizations that religious clubs stood little chance of achieving a position of dominance that would result in the appearance of state endorsement.[100]

But in an important footnote, the Court repeated its long-standing opinion that college students are less impressionable than their "younger, secondary school" counterparts and more capable of treating religious speech as but one component of the intellectual environment associated with academic life.[101] The Court reasoned that a college environment, traditionally rich in intellectual diversity, attenuated the likelihood that student religious organizations would become a state-endorsed, coercive force in campus life, a problem that had long concerned the Court at the high school level.[102] Given the strong line that the Court had taken against state support for religious exercises in public secondary schools, even separationists managed to accept the distinction outlined in Justice Powell's opinion between college and high school students, and remained reasonably confident that equal access would not find its way into high schools.

This appeared at first to be the case. After *Widmar*, equal access policies implemented at the high school level were generally struck down in the lower federal courts as unconstitutional under the establishment clause,[103] although there were some exceptions.[104] Not even the Equal Access Act, passed in 1984, which covers all public high schools receiving federal funds, saved two such local policies from the judicial guillotine.[105] But the Court's decision in *Board of Westside Schools v. Mergens*,[106] which held that the Equal Access Act required public schools to permit student religious clubs to assemble on school grounds if such access was available to other noncurriculum student organizations, has reordered the entire debate over equal access.

On the constitutional issue, the Court did not reach an opinion. Justice O'Connor, joined by Chief Justice Rehnquist and Justice White, concluded under her "endorsement" test that the Equal Access Act did not violate the establishment clause.[107] Concurring, Justices Kennedy and Scalia concluded that because the Equal Access Act involved no coercive governmental pressure to engage in religious activities, the establishment clause was not violated.[108] In a separate concurrence, Justices Marshall and Brennan concluded that the Equal Access Act did not constitute a facial violation of the establishment clause, but suggested that improper implementation of the legislation could well produce a different result.[109] Only Justice Stevens dissented. While concerned about the establishment clause issues implicated by the Equal Access Act, Justice Stevens seemed more disturbed by the statute's intrusive reach into the traditional policy-making authority of local school boards to order their educational environment.[110]

In *Mergens*, both the Court and the Eighth Circuit declined to reach a definitive constitutional interpretation of the Equal Access Act. Both courts decided the case on statutory grounds and limited, for the most part, their scope of inquiry to the facts of the case. *Mergens* thus represented a point of departure from previous equal access litigation. Given the importance that *Mergens* will have in shaping the implementation of the Equal Access Act, it is important to review the doctrinal evolution of the equal access issue in the federal courts.

The Resolution of the Early Cases

In *Nartowicz v. Clayton County* (1984)[111] and *Lubbock Civil Liberties Union v. Lubbock Independent School District* (1983),[112] two federal appeals courts struck down different equal access policies as violative of the establishment clause. Both cases involved the question of whether student groups, either before or after class hours, could meet on school grounds. In each case, student religious organizations held prayer meetings and spiritual consultations that received the schools board's endorsement and approval.

The equal access policies at issue in *Lubbock* involved religious meetings conducted under teacher supervision. Since 1971, a Texas school district permitted its classroom teachers to lead a number of religion-based exercises. These included the recitation of teacher-led prayers and morning Bible readings, the distribution of Gideon-provided Christian Bibles to fifth and sixth grade students, and school assemblies featuring evangelical Christian speakers.[113] The Lubbock school board continued to permit these government-endorsed religious exercises even after the Lubbock Civil Liberties Union (LCLU) filed a complaint to enjoin them. In 1980, the LCLU filed suit in federal district court asking for a constitutional ruling on the school board's policies. The school board then amended its policies to require that all religious exercises conducted in its schools must be student-initiated. Unsatisfied, the LCLU pressed its establishment clause challenge against the Lubbock school board policies, arguing that the school board's amendment to its earlier policies would still result in the authorization of unconstitutional religious exercises. The lawsuit focused on the following provision:

> The School Board permits students to gather at the school with supervision either before or after regular school hours on the same basis as other groups as determined by the school administration to meet for any educational, moral, religious or ethical purposes so long as attendance at such meetings is voluntary.[114]

The district court found the pre-1980 religious activities unconstitutional,[115] but upheld the facial validity of the school board's 1980 amendment.[116] Thus, the court continued to permit the Lubbock board to encourage its schools to engage in religious exercises, so long as they were conducted under the post-1980 rule. On appeal, the Fifth Circuit reversed the lower court's decision on the 1980 amendment. Using the *Lemon* test, the appeals court ruled that the Lubbock policies had the primary effect of "imply[ing] recognition of religious activities and meetings as an integral part of the District's extracurricular program [which] carries with it implicit approval by school officials of those programs."[117] The Fifth Circuit also rejected the school board's argument that because the religious exercises were student-initiated and the language of the equal access policies facially neutral, the establishment clause arguments were nullified. The court held that the "critical factor [was] the [District's] compulsory education machinery . . . and its implicit support and approval of the religious meetings."[118]

But the Fifth Circuit rejected the LCLU's request for an injunction enjoining the religious exercises, based on its view that these practices were not likely to continue. The Supreme Court denied the school board's request for an appeal.[119]

One year later, the Eleventh Circuit Court of Appeals, in *Nartowicz*, held unconstitutional similar equal access policies instituted by a suburban Atlanta school district. *Nartowicz* involved a challenge to four separate religious practices taking place in the Clayton County public schools. A parents group filed suit against the school board, alleging that its support for the following practices violated the establishment clause:

(1) allowing the student group "Youth for Christ" to hold meetings on school grounds after school; (2) permitting school assemblies featuring speakers who discussed, but also preached, religious doctrines; (3) permitting religious groups to use classrooms and other school common areas to advertise local worship services and other church-related events; (4) and using the school public address system to allow announcements of local church and church-sponsored events.[120] The federal court ruled that each challenged practice violated the establishment clause and enjoined the school from continuing them.[121] The school board admitted that the student assemblies involved religious teachings and that they allowed school property to be used to promote them, but it appealed that part of the ruling that prohibited student religious clubs from meeting on school grounds and posting advertisements for church and church-spon-sored events.[122]

In a brief *per curiam* opinion, the Eleventh Circuit affirmed the lower court on both questions. The appeals court concluded that the court's injunction prohibiting the Youth for Christ club from meeting on school premises under faculty approval and supervision was correct when considered "in light of the district's apparent support of religious assem-blies, religious signs and announcements of church-sponsored activities via bulletin boards and public address systems."[123] The court also ruled that Clayton County's policy of allowing the use of school facilities to promote local church and church-related events was unconstitutional because it fostered excessive entanglement between religion and govern-ment prohibited by the establishment clause.[124]

Rather than discouraging school boards from experimenting with equal access programs, these adverse decisions provided proponents of such policies with an idea of what courts might find appropriate and what they might not. The lower federal courts issued several other important decisions in this area, each of which continued to shape the judicial parameters of viable equal access policies. In some cases, such as *Bell v. Little Axe* (1985)[125] and *May v. Evansville* (1986),[126] appeals courts in two separate federal circuits struck down two poorly designed equal access plans that had greater resemblance to pre-*Abington* school-spon-sored religious exercises than more recent and sophisticated, but still flawed, proposals emphasizing student, not state, control over their content. *Mergens* and *Garnett v. Renton School District* (1989)[127] are indicative of the latter efforts, which were based squarely on the Equal

Access Act. The differences among the equal access policies at issue in these cases, as we shall see, are quite apparent.

In *Little Axe*, the Tenth Circuit declared unconstitutional an equal access policy implemented by the Little Axe School District in Cleveland County, Oklahoma. *Little Axe* began when the parents of two local high school students initiated a constitutional challenge to the Oklahoma Voluntary Prayer Act, which authorized the board of education of each school district to permit willing students and teachers to engage in voluntary prayer.[128] Soon thereafter the school board decided to amend the time and manner in which such religious exercises could be held. The relevant section of the new guidelines held that

> [a]ll students, whether as school sponsored clubs, nonsponsored student associations or individuals shall have equal access to school facilities. . . . Student use of school facilities shall not be regulated on the basis of the content of the students' meetings. . . . Religious speech shall receive the same rights and protections as political and all other speech, including private voluntary prayer, reading from religious or political books and speaking about political or religious topics.[129]

The teacher-student religious devotionals continued to take place on school premises prior to the start of the school day. These meetings were also advertised on classroom bulletin boards and devoted to "prayers, songs and 'testimony' concerning the benefits of knowing Jesus Christ and . . . Christianity."[130] Unsatisfied with the amended statute, the parents amended their lawsuit to challenge both the Little Axe School Board policies permitting student prayer meetings and the Oklahoma Prayer Act as violative of the establishment clause.

A federal court struck down the Little Axe policies permitting teacher-student prayer meetings as violative of the establishment clause. The court ruled that the school board policies failed to satisfy the effects prong of the *Lemon* test. It ruled that because "the Board provided religious services on school grounds during the school day, with teachers or school officers attending, monitoring or participating, [and] providing . . . governmental support, it can hardly be doubted that the sessions were of a religious nature and content and second, that their principal or primary effect was to advance religion."[131] While the district court struck down the prayer sessions as unconstitutional in effect, it limited the scope of its decision to that narrow question. The court did not find the school board policies unconstitutional on their face.[132] Nor did it address the constitutional arguments raised over the Oklahoma Voluntary Prayer Act because the plaintiffs had disclaimed reliance upon the statute in their complaint.[133]

The Tenth Circuit Court of Appeals upheld the trial court decision enjoining the school board from sponsoring student prayer meetings on school premises. The appeals court also held that the amended "equal access" plan implemented by the school district was unconstitutional on the grounds that it endorsed in-school religious activities during regular hours.[134] But the Tenth Circuit failed to address the constitutional status of the Oklahoma prayer statute, which was just as egregious an establishment clause violation as the school board's equal access policies, for the same reasons articulated by the trial court. Still, by any measure, *Little Axe* was a resounding defeat for those in the Oklahoma legislature who sought to evade the law prohibiting state-supported religious exercises in the public schools through a deceptive equal access plan. Even the Tenth Circuit's decision not to address the constitutional merits of the Oklahoma prayer statute does not diminish *Little Axe*, since the Supreme Court in *Wallace* rendered invalid an almost identical Alabama statute.[135]

In a departure from previous equal access cases, the question facing the Seventh Circuit Court of Appeals in *May v. Evansville* (1986)[136] did not concern whether student-initiated religious meetings were permissible on public school grounds, but rather whether teachers could organize religious clubs and hold meetings on school premises. *May* began when a small group of teachers at Harper Elementary School in Evansville, Indiana, began meeting before regular classes began in their classrooms to hold religious devotionals. These meetings included prayer, Bible recitation, and the singing of religious hymns. After receiving numerous complaints from other teachers and students, the school banned the teacher-led religious meetings from campus. Mary May, representing the evangelical teachers, sued the school board seeking to obtain an injunction against the school-imposed ban on their religious meetings. In her complaint, May argued that the school's prohibition against teacher-conducted religious exercises violated her constitutional right to free speech.

The district court first ruled out the claim that the school qualified as a public forum and dismissed the corollary argument that the teachers had a right to school facilities under the free speech clause. The court emphasized that the school board lacked a policy authorizing other teacher- or student-led organizations to meet on campus, noting that "no evidence [existed] that teachers met at Harper School, or in any other

EVSC school, in a consistent, formal, patterned way other than to conduct business necessary to the operation and administration of this school."[137] The court disagreed with the plaintiffs that because Harper had no written policy prohibiting teacher-led religious meetings the school had given implicit recognition and approval to them.[138] But the court's most significant legal confrontation came with the free speech component of the plaintiff's arguments: Did the free speech clause require public schools to permit teacher-initiated religious meetings on school grounds as a condition of equal access?

The district court held in clear and convincing terms that the free speech clause did not require public schools, under the rubric of equal access, to allow such an obviously unconstitutional arrangement. With little fanfare, the court said that nothing in the plaintiff's arguments even hinted that public schools had a constitutional obligation to accomodate teacher-led religious meetings during the day.[139] On the establishment clause issue, the court ruled that permitting public schools to allow teacher-initiated religious clubs to meet on campus would result in a "significant risk of creating an improper imprimatur of state approval for religious activity.[140] The court also held that placing on school administrators the burden of supervising the religious meetings risked fostering excessive entanglement between religion and government.[141]

The Seventh Circuit Court of Appeals affirmed the lower court judgment, ruling that the free speech clause did not grant teachers a constitutional right to conduct religious meetings on campus.[142] In his opinion for the court, Judge Richard Posner dismissed the plaintiff's argument that Harper had created a public forum open to all noncurriculum student and teacher-initiated organizations.[143] Since no public forum existed, the school's decision to exclude teacher-led religious meetings from school grounds did not constitute content-based discrimination violative of the free speech clause. Judge Posner also ruled that personal discussion between individuals, regardless of the topic, were of no interest to the school, whereas teacher-initiated organizations that used school facilities on a regular basis were classifiable as school-related activities, thus falling within the school administration's legitimate power to regulate its internal affairs.[144]

Prior to *Mergens*, the most recent pronouncement on the equal access question came from the Ninth Circuit Court of Appeals. In *Garnett v. Renton School District* (1989),[145] the Ninth Circuit heard arguments brought by students of a Renton, Washington, high school that contested the school board's policy prohibiting student religious organizations from meeting on the premises of its public schools. The student club's stated purpose was to engage in Bible reading, to discuss how the lessons of spiritual life could be applied to the problems students faced in their personal lives, and to provide a forum in which students could pray together and provide support and encouragement to one another.[146] The student plaintiffs relied on the Court's opinion in *Widmar*, arguing that the free speech and free exercise clauses of the First Amendment and similar provisions in the Washington state constitution required the school to recognize their right to assemble on school grounds. Furthermore, the students argued that the Equal Access Act required the school to accommodate student religious clubs because the act's provisions recognizing the existence of open forum meant that all student-initiated organizations, not just those of which the school approved, were allowed to meet on school grounds.

The district court did not decide the federal statutory or constitutional questions raised under the Equal Access Act, even though the parties had requested that it reach those issues.[147] But the court did hold that the Washington state constitution, which contained "much stricter" prohibitions on government support for religion in the public schools,[148] prevented student religious clubs from meeting in the public schools.[149] On appeal, the Ninth Circuit Court of Appeals agreed with the district court that permitting such meetings in the public schools was unconstitutional, but ruled that the establishment clause of the First Amendment, not the Washington state constitution, controlled the question.[150] The appeals court held that to permit student religious clubs whose activities encompassed evangelism and proselytization to assemble on school grounds would violate the effect and entanglement prongs of the *Lemon* test.[151] In plain language, the Ninth Circuit held that "[t]he school district's refusal to approve a student religious group as a district activity is, therefore, not only reasonable, but required."[152]

The Ninth Circuit also dismissed the students' reliance on the free speech clause to support their equal access claim, a crucial component in their argument.[153] Unpersuaded by the students' argument, the court concluded that Lindbergh High School did not constitute a traditional public forum under speech clause doctrine.[154] The court distinguished public schools, which are not to open to the larger public for conventional

First Amendment activities, from traditional public fora such as public parks and other public properties, which are available to private speakers and groups, whose access is limited to content-neutral time, place, and manner regulations. Public schools have greater discretion, the court said, in regulating the conditions upon which student organizations can form and have access to campus facilities, a principle long recognized in First Amendment law.[155]

The students and the school board, as well as the numerous organizations that submitted *amicus* briefs in the case, including the United States Department of Justice, had urged the Ninth Circuit to use *Garnett* to address the constitutionality of the Equal Access Act.[156] But the Ninth Circuit avoided the constitutional question because it found the school's policy towards student groups not to trigger the Equal Access Act. To trigger the "limited open forum" provision of the Equal Access Act, which would then compel the school to accommodate student clubs, the school would have had to already permit noncurriculum student organizations to meet on campus.[157] The Ninth Circuit did not conclude that Lindbergh High School had created a "limited open forum"[158] as defined in the Equal Access Act, thus making it unnecessary to decide the constitutional issue.

The Ninth Circuit took the easy way out. It could have addressed the constitutional question had it wanted, but it chose instead to take the back exit by focusing on the statutory construction of the Act. The Ninth Circuit held that public schools were "required" to refuse student religious clubs access to campus facilities because to permit such access would violate the establishment clause.[159] In the same sentence, the appeals court also said that it could see no other "reasonable" conclusion other than to prohibit student religious clubs in public schools.[160] But the court declined to extend that same rationale to the constitutional arguments brought against the Equal Access Act, which requires schools to accommodate such clubs, even though the principal litigants and *amici* said the constitutional issue was ripe.[161]

It is quite conceivable that the Ninth Circuit, sensing that the plaintiffs would appeal, simply wanted to defer to the Supreme Court responsibility for initial interpretation of the Equal Access Act. Or perhaps it thought the Eighth Circuit, having just heard *Mergens*, would decide the constitutional question. The Ninth Circuit's decision does implicitly conclude that the Equal Access Act is unconstitutional. Surely, if the court could find that the establishment clause requires public schools to forbid student religious organizations from using school facilities because it has the unconstitutional effect of endorsing certain religious beliefs, then it would seem to follow that federal legislation mandating that public schools accommodate such clubs is unconstitutional. But rather than take a step toward resolving the problem, the Ninth Circuit's decision added another knot around the equal access issue. How were local school districts supposed to respond to demands from student religious organizations for equal access to their facilities when the federal courts, which had held most state and local level equal access plans unconstitutional, were refusing to address the constitutional arguments mounted on behalf of and against the Equal Access Act? How were public schools to define the "limited open forum" provision of the Equal Access Act, since the courts had taken pains to avoid statutory interpretation? What were school boards to make of the Ninth Circuit's decision concluding that to permit student religious clubs to meet in public schools would violate the establishment clause, but that federal legislation requiring the same raised different considerations?

These problems were compounded just one month later, when the Eighth Circuit Court of Appeals held, in *Mergens v. Westside Community School Board*, that an Omaha, Nebraska, school board's refusal to permit student religious clubs to meet in public school buildings violated the Equal Access Act, which the court also found not to violate the establishment clause.[162] With two separate federal circuits now in conflict over a major piece of federal legislation, the Court had little choice but to resolve the problematic statutory and constitutional issues that had emerged in this ponderous sequence of litigation involving the Equal Access Act.

Board of Westside Schools v. Mergens: *Equal Access Approved*

The progression of events that led to the Supreme Court's decision in *Mergens* began in February 1985. Bridget Mergens, a student at Westside High School in Omaha, Nebraska, asked her principal to grant formal recognition to the Christian Bible Club that she and some friends had formed so that the group could meet on school grounds to discuss religion and to pray together. Westside had no written regulation that covered the use of school facilities by noncurriculum-related student organizations.

When such an occasion arose, Westside required the students to present a petition stating their purpose and objective in forming the organization to school officials. Mergens's request for official school recognition was turned down, which meant that her club could not meet on campus. Mergens then appealed to the superintendent of Westside Schools, who agreed with her principal that for the school to give formal recognition to a Christian Bible club would violate the establishment clause.[163] The Westside School Board ruled that since its regulations permitted official recognition solely for student organizations engaged in "school-sponsored, curriculum-related activities," it could not allow meetings of a religious club to take place in school facilities.[164]

Bridget Mergens decided to bring suit in federal district court to argue that the Westside School Board's rule prohibiting equal access to the Christian Bible Club violated the Equal Access Act as well as her constitutional rights under the free exercise, free speech, and freedom of assembly provisions of the First Amendment. But to Mergens' dissapointment, the court entered judgment on behalf of the Westside School Board. The court ruled that Westside High School did not maintain a "limited open forum," and thus failed to trigger the requirement of the Equal Access Act.[165] Second, the court ruled that, even without the Equal Access Act, Westside had no affirmative obligation under the First Amendment to accommodate a student-initiated religious organization's request for the use of campus facilities because of the legitimate establishment clause concerns involved.[166]

But a unanimous three-judge panel for the Eighth Circuit Court of Appeals reversed. Focusing first on the statutory construction of the Equal Access Act, the appeals court ruled that Westside High School did indeed maintain a "limited open forum" as defined in the legislation because it permitted several other noncurriculum-related student organizations, including the chess club and scuba diving club, to use school facilities for their meetings. The Eighth Circuit also said that Westside High had sought to avoid meaningful compliance with the Equal Access Act by defining all of its student clubs as "curriculum related."[167] While it did acknowledge that Congress's failure to define what a "non-curriculum-related" club was did make implementation of the Equal Access Act more problematic than one might hope, the court held that Westside's interpretation of the legislation rendered it "meaningless."[168] The Eighth Circuit also determined that Westside High, by denying

Bridget Mergens' Christian Bible Club a right accorded to other "non-curriculum" clubs, had "reach[ed] exactly the result that Congress sought to prohibit by enacting the EAA"—the withholding of approval to "disfavored student club[s] based [on their] speech content."[169]

On the constitutional issues, the Eighth Circuit ruled that the Equal Access Act codified the rationale that the Supreme Court used in *Widmar* to find in favor of the student plaintiffs that challenged similar policies at the university level. In *Widmar*, the Court ruled that student-initiated religious organizations must be allowed to meet in campus facilities if the school maintained a limited open forum.[170] The Eighth Circuit, in commenting on the parallels between the two cases, said that "the only difference between the EAA and *Widmar* is the EAA's express extension of the equal access principle to public secondary school students."[171] In conclusion, the Eighth Circuit held that a

> constitutional attack on the EAA must therefore be predicated upon the difference between secondary school students and university students. We reject this notion because Congress considered the difference in maturity level of secondary students and university students before passing the EAA. We accept Congress' fact-finding.[172]

In conclusion, the Eighth Circuit said that had Congress "never passed the EAA, our decision would be the same under *Widmar* alone."[173]

The Supreme Court, 8-1, affirmed. For the Court, Justice O'Connor held that Westside High School was required under the Equal Access Act to recognize Bridget Mergens' Christian Bible Club because it granted recognition to other noncurriculum clubs and allowed them to use school facilities. Since Westside had created a "limited open forum" as Congress had defined it in the statute, its refusal to grant the Christian Bible Club the same right as the Chess Club to meet on school grounds violated the Equal Access Act.[174] To Justice O'Connor, the compelling obstacle preventing local school boards from implementing the Equal Access Act was not the establishment clause, but lack of a definitive interpretation of the statute's meaning with respect to "noncurriculum club" and when the legislation's "limited open forum" provision was triggered.[175]

In contrast, the Court showed little concern for the establishment clause arguments raised by the Westside school board and its *amici*.[176] The Court rejected Westside's arguments that the Equal Access Act violated the establishment clause because it required those schools covered under the statute to incorporate religious activities into their educational mission, and because such a relationship gave off the appearance, if not the effect, of school endorsement of student religious beliefs. But the Court was unable to agree on the rationale supporting its judgment on the establishment clause issue. Incorporating her endorsement standard into the *Lemon* test, Justice O'Connor, joined by Justices Blackmun, Justice White, and Chief Justice Rehnquist, ruled that the Equal Access Act did not on its face violate the establishment clause.[177] Justice O'Connor noted that the Court had already held in *Widmar* that universities were prohibited under the free speech clause from discriminating against student-initiated religious clubs that wished to use their facilities for organized meetings.[178] In *Widmar*, the Court found the establishment clause arguments without merit and ruled instead that ensuring a content-neutral application of free speech principles for a "broad spectrum of groups [was] an important index of secular effect," as well as an adequate measure of secular purpose.[179] Justice O'Connor concluded that those same principles inspired Congress when it passed the Equal Access Act. In reaching a decision on the constitutional merits, Justice O'Connor held that "the logic of *Widmar* applie[d] with equal force to the Equal Access Act."[180]

On the constitutional issues, Justice O'Connor's plurality opinion drew several analogies between *Widmar* and *Mergens*. Justice O'Connor wrote that Westside High School, like the University of Missouri-Kansas City, was open to a "broad spectrum of officially recognized student clubs . . . and . . . that [its] students are free to initiate and organize additional student clubs" in order to "counteract any possible message of official endorsement or preference for religion or a particular religion."[181] The opinion also equated the Equal Access Act's "limited open forum" proviso and its application to Westside with the "important index of secular effect" that equal access for private speakers had to the facts in *Widmar*.[182] Justice O'Connor determined that the net result in each case produced unlimited access for student-initiated groups. This made it unlikely that religious organizations would dominate nonreligious organizations in the extracurricular environment.[183] The plurality also extended the Court's analysis in *Widmar* of excessive entanglement to the Equal Access Act, although not in a manner that makes much sense. In *Mergens*, Justice O'Connor concluded that denying "equal access to religious speech might well create greater entanglement problems in the form of pervasive monitoring to prevent religious speech at meetings at which such speech might occur."[184]

How Justice O'Connor's conception of unconsitutitonal entanglement squares with the Court's line of decisions, beginning in *Lemon* and continuing through *Grand Rapids v. Ball* (1985)[185] and *Aguilar v. Felton* (1985),[186] invalidating state and federal funding schemes for parochial schools is not clear. The Court, in *Lemon*, had said that just such supervision violated the establishment clause when it held unconstitutional a Rhode Island statute that provided supplemental salaries to public school teachers who taught secular courses in parochial schools. The Court rejected Rhode Island's plan to ensure that no state-subsidized teacher inculcated religion in the parochial school in which he or she taught. Here is Chief Justice Burger, for the Court, in *Lemon*:

> A comprehensive, discriminating, and continuing state surveillance will inevitably be required to ensure that these restrictions are obeyed and the First Amendment otherwise respected. Unlike a book, a teacher cannot be inspected once so as to determine the extent and intent of his or her personal beliefs and subjective acceptance of the limitations imposed by the First Amendment. These prophylactic contacts will involve execessive and enduring entanglement between state and church.[187]

Two terms later, in *PEARL v. Nyquist* (1973),[188] the Court did not consider the entanglement dimension when it invalidated a New York parochaid scheme under the effect prong of the *Lemon* test. But Justice Powell, in important *dicta*, said that "the importance of the competing societal interests implicated here prompts us to make the further observation that, apart from any specific entanglement of the State in particular religious programs, assistance of the sort here involved carries grave potential for entanglement in the broader sense of continuing political strife over aid to religion."[189] *Lemon* and *Nyquist* cemented the Court's position on excessive entanglement between religion and the state with respect to parochaid statutes. These two decisions also served to articulate a broader application of that principle—religious institutions were barred from access to governmental funds if the result was to produce an ongoing, intimate relationship between church and state. Nothing in *Lemon* or *Nyquist*, or the cases decided after them that struck down similar statutory schemes involving the transfer of public funds to church schools,[190] informs Justice O'Connor's peculiar understanding of the Court's previous no-entanglement requirement.

Justice O'Connor concluded that in order to avoid excessive entanglement between government and religion it is incumbent upon public school administrators to permit equal access for private, organized religious meetings in their schools. Even though the Equal Access Act permits school administrators, teachers, or other school employees to attend such meetings for supervisory, but not participatory, purposes,[191] and even though the act contains no measure to ensure compliance with its nonparticipation requirement, and even though the legislation contains no independent provision to protect against an abusive interpretation of the school-affiliated supervisor's role in student meetings, Justice O'Connor found much worse the prospect that disallowing "equal access to religious speech might well create greater entanglement problems in the form of invasive monitoring to prevent religious speech at meetings at which such speech might occur."[192] This interpretation of the Court's no-entanglement requirement ignores Chief Justice Burger's admonition in *Lemon* that, "unlike a book, a teacher cannot be inspected once so as to determine the extent and intent of his or her personal beliefs and subjective acceptance of the limitations imposed by the First Amendment."[193]

In *Mergens*, the Court has come full circle. For some reason, the Court believes that having teachers charged with supervising the on-site meetings of student religious clubs in public schools raises no question of government endorsement or advancement of religion, but having public school teachers teach math and science to parochial students in church schools does.[194] How the Court can conclude, on the one hand, that, even assuming no "bad faith or any conscious design to evade the limitations imposed by the statute and the First Amendment" exists on the part of public school teachers who teach in parochial schools, such statutes are unconstitutional,[195] but then rule, on the other hand, that teacher supervision of student religious meetings is permissible "custodial oversight . . . merely to ensure order and good behavior" and does not foster unconstitutional advancement of religion or entangle government with religion.[196] Justice O'Connor's perfunctory analysis of the excessive entanglement problems posed by the Equal Access Act's implementation does not dismiss the problem. If anything, Justice O'Connor's opinion in *Mergens* turns the Court's previous definition of entanglement on its head.

But the Court in *Mergens* expressed, at best, a tangential concern with the establishment clause problems of the Equal Access Act. What the Court wanted to do—and did do—was to resolve the conflict among the lower federal courts on the statutory meaning of the Equal Access Act.

Prior to *Mergens*, the lower federal courts were in discord over the statutory meaning of the act. In contrast to the Courts of Appeals for the Fifth,[197] Seventh,[198] Ninth,[199] Tenth[200] and Eleventh Circuits,[201] each of which had read the Equal Access Act's statutory requirements quite narrowly, the Eighth Circuit construed the conditions creating a "limited open forum" in public schools, which triggers the legislation's application, in broad, general terms. The Court agreed with the Eighth Circuit that, with respect to defining noncurriculum clubs, "Congress inten[ded] to provide a low threshold for triggering the Equal Access Act's requirements,"[202] although the phrase is nowhere defined in the legislation. Alternative interpretation of congressional intent, the Court held, would permit schools that wished to avoid compliance to describe all their student clubs as curriculum-related. The Court ruled that to permit such clever circumvention on the part of resistant public schools would "render the [Equal Access] Act merely horatory."[203]

Mergens does not close the door on equal access. The Court's construction of the Equal Access Act is so broad and all-encompassing that confusion over its application at the high school level is unavoidable. If Justice O'Connor meant what she said in *Mergens*, then public high schools, once having established a "limited open forum," can no longer prohibit student organizations whose activities are not related to the school's curriculum from using their facilities. This means that federal law now prohibits local level school administrators from distinguishing between a Christian Bible group, the chess club or a student-founded organization advocating racial intolerance or anti-Semitism when considering requests for classroom time. If public school classrooms are made available to one student organization, then they must remain open to all groups, regardless of a group's stated goals. No other result can be reached without violating the free speech clause. Justice Stevens, in his dissent, was right to ask if Congress ever intended such a "bizzare" result when it enacted the Equal Access Act.[204] Indeed, there exists conflicting evidence for the Court's conclusion in *Mergens* that Congress, in conceiving the Equal Access Act, intended to divest school officials of their discretion in governing extracurricular student affairs.[205] But, like the numerous other defects of the Act, the Court chose to ignore it.

On the constitutional issues, *Mergens* is inconsistent with the Court's previous decisions on student rights in the public schools. Supporters of equal access argue that the First Amendment requires public schools to accommodate student religious clubs, because schools are prohibited from requiring students to surrender held or professed political or religious beliefs and cannot punish them for exercising legitimate constitutional rights.[206] The cases that equal access advocates[207] have cited as controlling on the question of students' First Amendment rights in the public schools, *Tinker v. Des Moines* (1969)[208] and *West Virginia v. Barnette* (1943),[209] do not provide a plausible foundation from which to create a "right" of equal access. *Tinker* and *Barnette* were not about providing student dissenters with public fora in which to express their views, but, as one distinguished commentator has pointed out, about the use of administrative power to exclude individual student viewpoints deemed unacceptable or potentially disruptive.[210] *Tinker* and *Barnette* protect without question, and *Engel, Schempp*, or *Wallace* do not even come close to prohibiting, the rights of students to engage in religious speech, to read religious materials, or to wear jewelry featuring religious symbols while in public schools.[211] But the Court has never said, in these cases and in others, that First Amendment protection for individual religious and political speech in the public schools means that school administrators are constitutionally required to create a forum for the expression of student views, whether political, religious, or other.

When placed against the backdrop of the Court's recent decisions involving the constitutional rights of students in public schools, *Mergens* is even more anomalous. One does not even have to agree with the Court's student-rights decisions to see the disparities. The Court has ruled that students in public schools are not entitled to the same Fourth Amendment protection against unreasonable searches and seizures as they are outside of school walls,[212] that administrators can exercise "editorial control" of content of student-run newspapers funded and supported by the public school system,[213] and that a student could be punished for using sexual metaphors in a speech given on behalf of a student government candidate during a school assembly.[214] In the latter cases, *Hazelwood v. Kuhlmeier* (1988) and *Bethel School District No. 403 v. Fraser* (1986), the Court held that such power could be exercised over curriculum-related materials. Seen in this light, no plausible reason exists to explain why "noncurriculum" student organizations are entitled to greater constitutional rights than students whose claims are linked to the curriculum. But in *Mergens*, whether it meant to or not, that is precisely what the Court said. If *Mergens* prohibits school administrators

from controlling access to "limited open fora" and regulating the conduct
of student-initiated meetings, then the Court's decisions in *Hazelwood*
and *Bethel* do not stand up against this new standard. Schools cannot pick
and choose among popular and unpopular viewpoints. No constitutional
basis exists for the exercise of governmental authorities of content-based
control over student political speech, but not over the regulation of
student religious exercises. It makes even less sense to argue that compelled school accommodation of student religious exercises is *required*
under the Constitution, but similar treatment of other student-rights
claims are not.

In the end, the successful struggle for federal legislation guaranteeing
student-initiated religious clubs the right to organize and meet in the
public schools and its vindication in *Mergens* was not about restoring
student free speech rights. Nor was—and is—equal access about prohibiting government from discriminating against religious speech. From the
beginning, the political and legal efforts to create through federal statute
and then to constitutionalize an affirmative right of equal access have
been about securing a forum for student religious exercises in the public
schools. To insist that equal access is about saving student religious
speech from the yoke of hostile public school authorities is nonsense.
Full constitutional protection for religious speech, like other classes of
protected speech, lies at the heart of the First Amendment's promise.[215]
Nothing in the Court's decisions interpreting the free speech rights of
students has ever suggested that the verbal or nonverbal expression of
religious conscience deserves substandard protection.[216] Indeed, it is
almost impossible to envision *how* public school authorities could regulate or even censor student religious speech. Such private, personal
speech, religious, political, or otherwise, is ungovernable. Government
is powerless to control the content of opinions and to regulate conversa-
tion between individuals. For equal access supporters to argue that
governmental authorities have engaged in the unconstitutional censor-
ship of the religious speech of high school students because public school
administrators have refused to create a forum for organized student
religious exercises is to misrepresent what the Court's precedents on
religious doctrine in the public schools have held.

What the Court has held since *Engel* is that public schools cannot
support or encourage religious activities in the public schools, and neither
the free exercise nor the free speech clauses trump the establishment

clause in holding fast to this fundamental principle.[217] The Court has heard arguments challenging this rationale and rejected them.[218] But rather than recognize the substantive constitutional distinctions between what student speech rights the free speech clause protects and what the establishment clause forbids with respect to student religious activities in the public schools, advocates of equal access have collapsed these categories into a single classification in an effort to blur them. Prior to *Mergens*, the Court had underscored the principle that government action intended to accommodate private religious beliefs is permissible only when "the manifest objective of a statute is to facilitate the free exercise of religion by lifting a government-imposed burden."[219] Otherwise, such government action risks advancing religion in violation of the establishment clause.[220] But in *Mergens*, equal access advocates were successful in persuading the Court to juxtapose the meaning of the free speech, free exercise, and establishment clauses to find an affirmative right for student-initiated religious exercises to take place in public schools. Their arguments were framed so that religious conduct otherwise classifiable under the free exercise clause is instead a free speech issue,[221] even though these asserted "rights" interfere with the special obligation of public schools to enforce the establishment clause, and even though such a posture lends the government's prestige and support to religion in an unconstitutional manner.

Mergens might well handcuff all tax-supported institutions, not just public schools, which attempt from now on to invoke the establishment clause against private efforts to secure compelled access to their facilities for the purposes of religious speech. Public institutions will now have to accommodate all privately held and initiated expressions of religious belief, including religious symbols and regalia, if their constitutional obligation is, as equal access advocates argue, to remain absolutely neutral toward religion. The sole requirement for individuals who desire the public square or the public school as a platform to engage in religious exercise is that the originator of such conduct be a private individual, not the government. It matters not whether government encouraged or supported religious exercise as long as the government remains silent. If the government prohibits religious cermonies from taking place at high school graduation exercises, or bans religious symbols from public places, the government engages in content-based discrimination against religious speech. That is just one example. But there are more egregious possibilities, with far greater threats for religious freedom, than this inversion of the free speech and establishment clauses. One is that courts will simply absolve themselves of their basic adjudicating function in cases involving facially neutral statutes that encourage, support, or aid religion, consolidating futher power in the hands of transient majorities to advance the interests of some religious denominations over others. These arguments are beginning to appear in establishment clause cases since *Mergens*.[222] Given the Court's new disposition toward the establishment and free speech clauses, such claims will be difficult to counter if they become woven into the mosaic of constitutional law.

Worse, the Court could adopt the position that facially neutral statutes that result in government financial aid that benefits religion, or assists some religions and not others, are not deserving of searching judicial inquiry, even if religious motives are behind such a statute's enactment, since such legislation does not contain textual references to religion. In two establishment clause cases decided just prior to *Mergens*, the Court had either ruled, or dropped hints, that such statutes are constitutional, even while it acknowledged the inequitable benefits that some religious denominations did or would receive over others.[223] In *Mergens*, the Court accelerated this alarming trend. The Court invoked the majoritarian paradigm on the assumption that some consensus had been reached regarding the purpose of the Equal Access Act because it had been passed by a wide margin, even though no such evidence of this consensus can be derived from the legislative debates over the statute.[224]

If the Court will uphold neutral legislation that confers benefits upon religious majorities to use the public schools to advance and disseminate their religious beliefs, then what will prevent it from upholding "neutral" government funding schemes that benefit religious institutions? This is not a result that several of the religious organizations that fought hardest to obtain federal legislation guaranteeing equal access would welcome, because several of the more prominent and influential among them, including the Baptist Joint Committee on Public Affairs and the National Council of Churches, are staunch opponents of federal and state parochaid programs. These organizations also vigorously oppose traditional government-sponsored prayers in public schools. But this is the jurisprudential dilemma that equal access hath wrought. For those religious organizations caught in the middle, time will tell if mortgaging the establishment clause for the sake of creating a right of student religious worship in public schools will have been worth this Faustian bargain.

Curriculum

Equal access emerged as the dominant, but not the sole, issue concerning the place of religion in public education during the 1980s. Conservative religious organizations also were responsible for bringing another contentious issue to the forefront of this debate—the treatment of religion in public school curricula. The constitutional arguments made on behalf of including religious doctrine in science and literature courses taught in the public schools, like those for student-initiated religious exercises, are couched in the free exercise and free speech clauses of the First Amendment. But the similarities end there. Whereas the equal access cases confined themselves to questions involving school endorsement or sponsorship of student-inititated religious clubs that meet before or after regular classroom hours, the textbook and curriculum cases decided in the federal courts have raised the issue of direct government support for religious doctrine as a pedagogical component in public education. Eschewing the establishment clause difficulties associated with incorporating religious doctrine into the curricula of the public schools, religious fundamentalists succeeded in resurrecting the first great public debate over the place of religion in the schools since the "Scopes" monkey trial of 1925[225] and returning it to the courts albeit in a more sophisticated form.

Epperson v. Arkansas (1968), the swan song of the landmark series of church-state decisions handed down by the Warren Court holding government-sponsored religious doctrine in the public schools unconstitutional, struck down a 1927 Arkansas statute that prohibited the public schools from teaching "that mankind ascended or descended from a lower order of animals" or from using textbooks that supported evolution theory.[226] Writing for a unanimous Court, Justice Abe Fortas analogized the plight of Susan Epperson, who was fired from her job as a high school biology teacher and then convicted and fined under the statute by an Arkansas court, to that of John Scopes, who had suffered a similar fate in Tennessee forty years before.[227] The Court, in comparing the statutes, concluded that the Tennessee and Arkansas statutes were both products "of the 'fundamentalist' religious fervor of the twenties."[228] Said the Court:

> [there is] no doubt that Arkansas sought to prevent its teachers from discussing the theory of evolution because it is contrary to the belief of some that the Book of Genesis must be the exclusive source of doctrine as to the origin of man. It is clear that fundamentalist sectarian conviction was and is the law's reason for existence.[229]

The Court held, with no signs of dissension, that the Arkansas statute criminalizing the teaching of evolution violated the establishment clause in a "plain" manner.[230] While *Scopes* doused the fundamentalist flame for antievolution statutes in the states for decades, the Court's unequivocal decision in *Epperson* was thought to have quelled the desire on the part of their generational successors to work for similar measures that compelled the public schools to teach their students a biblical version of human origin. But religious fundamentalists, determined to reintroduce creationism into the public school curriculum, decided to pursue a new line of constitutional attack. Rather than attempt to overcome an almost unsurmountable establishment clause barrier, religious fundamentalists decided instead to frame the problem as a free speech issue. In addition, advocates of creationism argued that requiring schoolchildren to attend class and to read instructional materials that affronted their religious beliefs constituted a violation of the free exercise clause.[231]

In this view, for students that held sincere, devout religious beliefs, having to choose between being obedient to school rules or remaining true to their religious faith gave rise to a problematic issue of religious freedom. Religious and parental groups that formed to challenge the public school curricula argued their dilemma in a fashion reminiscent of the arguments proffered by the Jehovah's Witness schoolchildren in *The Flag Salute Cases*.[232] Like their forebearers of an era gone past, these well-organized advocates turned to the legislatures and the courts in their fight to force public schools to incorporate sectarian religious doctrine into their curriculum. But the federal courts, as well as the Supreme Court, have not yet found their arguments persuasive.

Scopes *Redux:* Edwards v. Aguillard

While the Court's splintered opinions in *Wallace* indicated a equivocal posture on the issue of religious exercises in the public schools, no such vacillation haunted its decision in *Edwards v. Aguillard* (1987),[233] which held unconstitutional a Louisiana statute requiring teachers to allocate "equal time" to teach creationism if their courses also included instruction in evolution. *Aguillard* involved a constitutional challenge to the 1981 Louisiana Balanced Treatment for Creation-Science and Evolution-Science Act, which prohibited public schools from teaching evolution as part of their science curriculum unless they also incorporated "creation-science" into their instruction.[234] The Balanced Treatment Act's passage consummated a decade of persistent lobbying by organized religious fundamentalists to persuade the Louisiana state legislature that "scientific creationism" was entitled to a place in the science curriculum of the public schools. In contrast to earlier attempts to influence school curriculum, these advocates insisted that creationism was not rooted in a theological understanding of human origin, but that new evidence showed the theory to be based on scientific fact. Following Justice Hugo Black's *dicta* in *Epperson*, which asked whether statutes such as Louisiana's were permissible since their requirements left the schools "in a neutral position toward these supposedly competing religious and anti-religious doctrines," advocates of the Balanced Treatment Act argued that the free speech clause allowed teachers to include all theories in their courses touching upon these subjects.

Rather than wait for opponents to challenge the Louisiana statute in court, the Creation Science Legal Defense Fund, which the Lousiana attorney general had deputized to represent the state in the expected lawsuits that would be filed against the Balanced Treatment Act, asked a federal district court to enter a declaration on the legislation's constitutionality after its passage in December 1981. It anticipated correctly. The next day, the American Civil Liberties Union asked the court to declare unconstitutional the Balanced Treatment Act. But the court dismissed the suit on procedural grounds.[235]

In 1985, a citizen coalition of parents, teachers, and clergy initiated a second lawsuit in federal district court challenging the statute. This time the court ruled that the Balanced Treatment Act violated the establishment clause.[236] On apppeal, the Fifth Circuit Court of Appeals affirmed, holding that the statute's purpose and effect was "to discredit evolution by counterbalancing its teaching at every turn with the teaching of creationism, a religious belief."[237]

In a forceful and muscular opinion, the Supreme Court, 7-2, ruled in clear and uncompromising terms that it had no intention of backing off

from the principles that it had articulated in *Epperson* twenty years
before. The Court's decision implied tones of astonishment. For the
Court, Justice Brennan held that the legislative record made clear the
Louisiana state legislature's purpose in drafting and passing the statute.
That objective was "to advance the religious viewpoint that a supernatural being created humankind."[238] While acknowledging that the Court's
traditional practice was to show deference to a challenged statute's
purpose as stated in the text, the Court also said that legislative materials
were relevant to judicial review to ensure that the legislative objective is
"sincere and not a sham."[239] Here, the Court found it impossible to
conclude otherwise.

Concurring, Justice Powell agreed with the Court's inclusion of the
legislative record to determine the statute's religious purpose. For Justice
Powell, the issue was not whether the Louisiana state legislature had
acted with a religious purpose, but whether a religious motive was the
sole purpose behind the statute. Here, Justice Powell believed that here
the analogies to *Epperson* were quite clear.[240] The Louisiana statute's
legislative record and purpose was "strikingly similar" to the Arkansas
antievolution statute held unconstitutional in *Epperson*.[241] The Tennessee
and Louisiana legislatures each "acted with the unconstitutional purpose
of structuring the public school curriculum to make it compatible with a
particular religious belief: 'the divine creation of man.'"[242] These similarities, plus suggestions from the Court that Louisiana's record was even
worse, provided an ample basis for Justice Powell to join the Court's
opinion holding unconstitutional the Balanced Treatment Act under the
purpose-prong of the *Lemon* test.

Justice Scalia, joined by Chief Justice Rehnquist, lit into the Court's
decision with a caustic and acerbic dissent. Taking his cue from the Chief
Justice's dissent in *Wallace*, Justice Scalia called on the Court to engage
in a wholesale reexamination of the Court's establishment clause jurisprudence. Justice Scalia also used *Aguillard* to fire the first in a continuous line of judicial blasts calling for the Court to abandon the *Lemon*
test in favor a nonpreferentialist interpretation of the establishment
clause. Justice Scalia believed that *Lemon*'s stringent analytical framework had little relevance to the religion clauses, and instead had the
harmful result of keeping legislative bodies from promoting social welfare legislation that had "untoward consequences" for religion.[243]
Aguillard provided a model case of *Lemon*'s unreasonableness. Justice

Scalia said that Louisiana had crafted the Balanced Treatment Act not to advance fundamentalist religious doctrine, but to promote a more comprehensive understanding of human orgin.[244] For the Court to impugn the motives of the legislature on the basis of an incomplete legislative record was an improper use of judicial power. Judges, said Justice Scalia, should construe a statute based on text and not by assessing the subjective intent of what some legislators intended.[245]

Aguillard marked Justice Scalia's inaugural encounter with the establishment clause since his elevation to the Court, but his open contempt for the Court's church-state jurisprudence came as no surprise. Justice Scalia's *Aguillard* dissent attracted little support, but it served as an important benchmark for his views on the establishment clause and constitutional method. On the establishment clause, Justice Scalia indicated that he was prepared to follow Chief Justice Rehnquist's call in *Wallace* to abandon the *Lemon* test as the Court's core analytical framework in establishment clause cases,[246] and added that he also viewed the Court's establishment clause jurisprudence as "embarrassing . . . and lacking in principled rationale."[247] One term into his appointment, Justice Scalia left little doubt about where he stood on the establishment clause. Since *Aguillard*, Justice Scalia has voted against claims alleging establishment clause violations in each such case to come before the Court.[248]

Justice Scalia also used *Aguillard* to express his distaste for the Court's methodological approach to constitutional interpretation. Concern for a precise understanding of the constitutional text and judicial fidelity to that text, not an unscientific assessment of legislative intent, should guide the Court's interpretative approach. Justice Scalia argued that the Court, in establishment clause cases and in others, should refine its interpretative method to adopt a "plain view" meaning of constitutional provisions and statutes.[249] For the Court to interpret legal text based on nontextual sources was inconsistent with the judicial role, regardless of whether such sources informed the meaning of a constitutional provision or federal and state statutes. This criticism, combined with the vigorous endorsement given to the principles articulated in Chief Justice Rehnquist's *Wallace* dissent, foreshadowed the gradual transition in the Court's methodological approach to establishment clause cases, as its post-*Aguillard* decisions have illustrated.

The Textbook Cases

While evangelical and fundamentalist forces in Louisiana attempted to advance their transparent agenda of requiring, through the Balanced Treatment Act, religion-based instruction to be included in the biological and life sciences taught in public schools, like-minded organized religious interests in Tennessee and Alabama launched even more ambitious constitutional challenges to the public school curriculum in their respective states. In each case, much more was at stake than the revisionist *Scopes* legislation at issue in *Aguillard*. The Tennessee and Alabama cases also differed from *Aguillard* in another important respect. Whereas *Aguillard* centered on the narrow issue of creationism versus evolution in the biological science curriculum, the Tennessee and Alabama cases were much more encompassing challenges to the liberal arts curriculum and other nonacademic course offerings in the public schools, such as home economics. In each instance, federal appellate courts were asked to consider far more than just small objections from fundamentalist parents to the content of certain books or course offerings because the compelled use of these materials offended the religious beliefs of their children. For the first time, federal courts were asked to decide whether certain books, course plans, and even entire academic tracks should be removed from the curriculum because these materials advanced the official state religion of secular humanism.

The Alabama case: is secular humanism a religion?

When Ishmael Jaffree filed suit against the school board of Mobile County, Alabama, in 1981 asking it to discontinue state-sponsored religious observances in the local schools, he had no idea that his case would become the vehicle for Christian fundamentalist parents to challenge large parts of the public school curriculum as violative of the establishment and free exercise clauses of the First Amendment. In an attempt to thwart Jaffree's challenge to a series of Alabama statutes permitting religious observances in the public schools, a citizen's coalition asked Judge Brevard Hand, a staunch judicial and political conservative who was presiding over Jaffree's case, to allow it to intervene in the litigation. This coalition, with strong ties to the religious right, including television evangelist Pat Robertson's National Legal Foundation, which funded and

supported the intervenors' effort, wanted Judge Hand to declare unconstitutional under the establishment clause a textbook series used in the
Alabama public schools on the grounds that it promoted the "religion"
of "secular humanism."[250] Thus began the strange but true saga of *Smith
v. Board of Commissioners* (1987).[251]

Smith evolved out of the original Jaffree lawsuit after Judge Hand
decided to sever the intervenors' challenge to the textbooks from the
prayer issues and hear the case separately. But Judge Hand did not take
up the fundamentalists' challenge to the curriculum and textbooks until
after he had ruled on the constitutionality of the Alabama prayer statutes.
In August 1985, Judge Hand commenced the trial to decide whether the
educational materials cited by the fundamentalists promoted the religion
of "secular humanism." Three months into the trial, the intervenors
received an encouraging signal from state authorities when Governor
George Wallace announced that his office and the Mobile school board
signed a consent decree empowering Judge Hand to approve new textbook selection standards. The consent decree also declared that "Humanism is a religion" and that the presence of such material in state-purchased
textbooks used in class censored the contributions of the Christian
religions to American culture.[252] The intervenors charged that these
improprieties violated the establishment and free speech clauses of the
federal Constitution.[253]

In March 1987, Judge Hand issued a 169-page opinion agreeing with
the fundamentalists' contention that the forty-four textbooks and miscel-
laneous other materials at issue used in the Mobile County schools
violated the establishment clause because they promoted an official state
"religion of secular humanism."[254] Judge Hand first ruled that secular
humanism constituted a religion because it represented a systematic body
of thought resting on a reasoned world view rooted in well-defined moral
and ethical precepts. Second, Judge Hand determined that secular humanism was distinct from Western theistic religion because "the most
important belief of this religion is its denial of the transcendent and/or
supernatural."[255] Because the textbooks did not discuss theological alternatives to the "secular" reasoning these materials taught, Judge Hand
concluded that Alabama had preferred secular humanism to theistic
religion in violation of the establishment clause.

The Eleventh Circuit did not react with the same visible disbelief to
Judge Hand's *Smith* opinion declaring "secular humanism" a state-spon-

sored religion as it did to his earlier ruling in *Wallace* that the establishment clause of the First Amendment did not apply to state and local governments. Perhaps after *Wallace*, the Eleventh Circuit had come to expect almost anything from Judge Hand. In *Smith*, Judge Hand just about outdid even himself in declaring that home economics, social science, and literature textbooks promoted the "systematic belief system" of "secular humanism" that denigrated theistic religion.[256] So when the Eleventh Circuit confronted Judge Hand's eccentric views on the establishment clause, it exhibited no hesitation in overruling him, unanimously, for the second time in less than five years. Writing for a unanimous court, Judge Frank M. Johnson ruled that Judge Hand held a "misconception of the relationship between church and state mandated by the establishment clause,"[257] and that nothing about the "textbooks evidence[d] an attitude antagonistic to theistic belief. The message conveyed by these textbooks is one of neutrality: the textbooks neither endorse theistic religion as a system of belief, nor discredit it."[258] For the second time in five years, the Eleventh Circuit saved the establishment clause and religious freedom from Judge Hand's historical revisionism. But more trouble lurked across the Alabama state line.

The Tennessee case: are religion-based exemptions from public school curriculum required?

On the surface, the issues in *Mozert v. Hawkins County Board of Education* (1987)[259] might bear some resemblance to those raised and decided in *Smith*, but in fact the constitutional challenge brought against the Tennessee State Textbook Committee by a fundamentalist parents' group contending that certain materials used in the public school curriculum violated the religious beliefs of their children posed a much more legitimate and difficult series of questions. Unlike the Alabama case, the Tennessee parents parents' group did not ask the courts to remove books and related materials from the public school curriculum. Instead, the parents' group, Citizens Organized for Better Schools (COBS), asked the courts to require public schools to provide either alternative curricula for the objecting religious students or permit them to "opt out" of classes in which such materials were used.[260] COBS argued that to require their children to participate in classes in which objectionable material was used violated the free exercise clause because the public schools were coercing them into affirming repugnant beliefs.[261]

Prior to filing suit, COBS had attempted to persuade the Hawkins County school board at the outset of the 1983–84 school year to provide their children with an alternative reading series to the state-approved Holt, Rinehart and Winston basic reading series used in grades 1 through 8. The parents were successful in persuading one school to create an alternative reading series; in two others, the parents were able to have their children excused from reading objectionable material.[262] In November 1983, the Hawkins County school board voted to eliminate both these options that had been set aside for religious students and to require them to attend classes using the standard reading series, despite the hardship that would result. When COBS was unable to reach an agreement with Hawkins County, it persuaded Concerned Women for America, a Washington, D.C.-based conservative legal and educational foundation with strong fundamentalist convictions, to file suit alleging that the Hawkins County school board's educational policies violated the free exercise rights of their children.[263] The school board in turn contacted People for the American Way (PAW), a liberal research and educational lobby also headquarted in Washington that had formed in 1980 to combat the influence of religious fundamentalists in politics, to defend it against COBS's challenge on the grounds that to tailor its curriculum to the needs of religious students would violate the establishment clause. PAW persuaded the prestigious Washington law firm of Wilmer, Cutler and Pickering to represent the Hawkins County school board.[264] Thus, as is so often the case in constitutional litigation, the stakes in *Mozert* involved much more than the narrow issue of the obligation that the Hawkins County schools had to accommodate their curriculum to meet the objections of a handful of Christian fundamentalist students. Each side, backed by powerful national interest groups, saw *Mozert* as a case that could determine the power of school boards to define the contours of the public school curriculum and the place of the establishment and free exercise clauses in making that determination.

In February 1984, a federal district court ruled in favor of the school board. While the court found that the "plaintiffs' religious beliefs were sincere and that certain passages in the Holt series might be offensive to them . . . because the books appeared neutral on the subject of religion, they did not violate the plaintiffs' constitutional rights."[265] On appeal, a

unanimous Sixth Circuit panel found the district court in error for
dismissing COBS's challenge because it had not considered all the facts
relevant to the case. The Sixth Circuit instructed the court to reconsider
several of the issues presented to them, foremost among them the
question of whether requiring the students to use the standard Holt
reading series placed an unconstitutional burden on their religious beliefs.[266] On remand, the lower court held that the school board had placed
an undue burden on the free exercise rights of the students because their
participation in the reading series "required that the student[s] either read
the offensive texts or give up their free public education."[267] But the court
did not rule that Hawkins County was required to provide an alternative
reading series for the fundamentalist students, holding that such a requirement would force the school board to act in violation of the establishment clause. The court did not, however, so rule on the "opt out"
option. Students objecting to material on religious ground were permitted
to excuse themselves from class to read their own materials.[268]

COBS appealed this ruling, but this time it met with a reversal of
fortune. The Sixth Circuit overruled the entire judgment of the lower
court and rejected *in toto* the arguments on which Concerned Women for
America had relied to support the claim that public schools were required
to provide alternative curriculum and "opt out" privileges for those
students whose religious beliefs prevented them from reading and com-
prehending objectionable educational materials. COBS had argued that
the Supreme Court's series of free exercise rulings in *Sherbert v. Verner*
(1963),[269] *Thomas v. Indiana Review Board* (1981)[270] and *Hobbie v.
Unemployment Appeals Commission* (1987)[271] required the school board
to create a religion-based exemption for those students so affected. The
Sixth Circuit rejected that claim on the grounds that *Sherbert, Thomas,*
and *Hobbie* all involved "governmental compulsion to engage in conduct
that violated the plaintiff's religious convictions,"[272] whereas in *Mozert*
no such compulsion existed. In fact, the court rejected that claim outright,
holding that "students [who] read the assigned materials and attend
reading classes, in the absence of a showing that this participation
entailed affirmation or denial of a religious belief, or performance or
non-performance of a religious exercise of practice," were not subject to
an undue burden on their rights of religious free exercise.[273]

COBS also was unsuccessful in persuading the Sixth Circuit to consider their plight as analagous to the historic *Flag Salute Cases*,[274] where

the children of Jehovah's Witnesses faced the choice of having to salute the flag, which violated their religious beliefs, or face expulsion from the public schools. The Court also saw no relationship between *Mozert* and *Wisconsin v. Yoder* (1972),[275] in which the Amish were successful in securing a constitutional exemption for their children from compulsory state school attendance laws.[276] In rejecting these arguments, the Sixth Circuit again held that the "critical elements of compulsion to affirm or deny a religious belief or to engage or refrain from engaging in a practice forbidden or required in the exercise of a plaintiff's religion were missing.[277] The Sixth Circuit concluded that the free exercise clause did not afford students a constitutional right to refrain from participating in the established public school curriculum simply because some material might offend their religious beliefs.[278]

Mozert did not involve the same flights of eccentric fancy as *Smith* that made that case so difficult to take seriously. *Mozert* involved a legitimate assertion of rights under the free exercise clause that ultimately did not outweigh the governmental interest in ordering and maintaining the public education system. Judge Thomas G. Hull, a Reagan appointee, who presided over *Mozert* at the trial stage, did not engage in a dogged pursuit of "secular humanism" and seek to banish it from Earth, but approached the case from the vantage point of the litigants without concocting bizarre theories on new religious movements. When *Mozert* was decided, there was a chance that similar claims brought in the federal courts might receive more sympathetic treatment in the future as more and more Reagan appointees donned judicial robes. But a Reagan appointee, this time on the Supreme Court, soon eliminated the basis for whatever free exercise claim might succeed in creating a religion-based exemption from objectionable public school curriculum. In *Employment Division of Oregon v. Smith* (1990), Justice Antonin Scalia held that governmental bodies were no longer required to demonstrate a compelling interest when neutral statutes or policies applicable to the general population burdened religious free exercise. Since educational curriculum falls under the umbrella of neutral regulation, students having religion-based objections to what their public schools teach no longer have recourse. Religious fundamentalists recognize this dilemma and are now concentrating on forcing school boards to incorporate religious materials into their curriculum as a way of fufilling the free speech and free exercise clauses.[279] As an alternative, religious fundamentalists have begun pulling their children out of public schools altogether and establishing "home school" programs in order to free their children from what they believe are religious burdens imposed by secular school systems.[280]

Conclusion

Since the Warren Court first ruled in *Engel* and *Schempp* that governmental authorities were prohibited from sponsoring religious observances in the public schools, the desire of conservative religious denominations and their corporate representatives to undo the imprint of these decisions on establishment clause law has never ebbed. Conservative organized religious interests have been persistent and tireless in their judicial and legislative efforts to remove the constitutional constraints on government power to use the public schools to inculcate sectarian religious values. But until Ronald Reagan assumed the presidency in 1980, their campaign to return the public schools to a period in which pan-Christian values dominated educational curriculum as well as the choice of instruments through which to transmit majoritarian religious values had been thwarted.

President Reagan was not successful in securing federal legislation or a constitutional amendment that would have overturned *Engel* and *Schempp*, but, through fate and skill, he was able to reshape the Court with justices who shared his values. While religious fundamentalists and their allies in the White House were not able to claim absolute victories on all fronts in the battle over religion in the public schools, the Court did hint that reasons for celebration are forthcoming. The Court said that government cannot write and then require students to recite religious devotionals, but it did rule that students are free to engage in such activities in the public schools on their own volition. More ominous was the Court's declaration that moment-of-silence statutes might be constitutional, even if their design and purpose reflects a transparent effort to secure a teacher-led forum for religious devotionals.

These shifts, some of which have already occurred and more of which are on the horizon, shadow the fundamental changes at work in the Court's jurisprudence in cases involving religious doctrine in the public schools. In *Mergens*, the Court gave the first indication that the establishment clause is undergoing a remedial conceptual transformation, one that is coming at the urging of conservative, primarily fundamentalist, religious organizations. For example, religious activities, religious worship and prosyletization, once thought unconstitutional under the establishment clause if taking place in the public schools, are now required under the free speech clause. Similar arguments are now being advanced to enable religious fundamentalists to reorder public school curricula and to permit government-sponsored religious devotionals during ceremonial occasions. If the Court decides that religious exercises such as these in the public schools are free speech rights, will the establishment clause still have a role in securing religious freedom for those too powerless to overcome majoritarian dominance, not just for students in the public schools, but for anyone at all?

Notes

1. 370 U.S. 421 (1962).
2. 374 U.S. 203 (1963).
3. Richard John Neuhaus, *The Naked Public Square* (Grand Rapids, Mich.: Eerdmans Publishing, 1984).
4. Rabbi Joachim Prinz, president of the American Jewish Congress, welcomed *Engel* and *Schempp* as decisions that "will prove of significant benefit to the cause of religion and religious freedom in America," *Washington Post*, 18 June 1963, p. A6; A.M. Sonnabend, president of the American Jewish Committee, responded that the rulings "affirmed that prayer in our democratic society is a matter for the home, synagogue, and church, and not for state institutions," *New York Times*, 26 June 1962, p. 17; The New York Board of Rabbis, The Rabbinical Council of America, Central Conference of American Rabbis, the Union of American Hebrew Congregations and the United Synagogue of America also endorsed *Engel* and *Schempp*. See *New York Times*, 18 June 1963, p. 29.
5. Dr. C. Emanuel Carlson, executive director of the Baptist Joint Committee on Public Affairs, said that he "was not disturbed by the elimination of 'required prayers' from schools because he had never felt that recital of such prayers had any real religious value for children," *New York Times*, 27 June 1962, p. 20; Dean Kelley, Director of Department of Religious Liberty, National Council of Churches, said "many Christians will welcome the decision [because] it protects the rights of minorities and guards against the development of public school religion which is neither Christianity nor Judaism but something less than neither," *New York Times*, June 26, 1962, p. 17. Kelley also said that "neither the church nor the state should use the public school to compel acceptance of any creed or conformity to any specific religious practice," *New York Times*, 18 June 1963, p. 29.
6. For a sample of Catholic reaction, see the editorial reaction of the Jesuit magazine *America*: "To Our Jewish Friends," 107 *America* 665 (1962); "The Main Issue," 107 *America* 13 (1962); "P.S.—To Jewish Friends," 107 *America* 768. See also, William Bentley Ball, "The Forbidden Prayer," 77 *Christian Century* 419 (1962). See also, Robert F. Drinan, *Religion, the Courts and Public Policy* (New York: McGraw Hill, 1963), 52–56.

7. See, for example, the response of Stanley Mooneyham, director of information, National Association of Evangelicals. Calling *Engel* and *Schempp* regrettable, Mooneyham said that "the only way left for the majority to express their opinion on this matter is to have the majority push for a constitutional amendment," *New York Times*, 18 June 1963, p. 17; Bishop Fred Pierce Corson, president, World Methodist Council, said *Schempp* "penalized religious people who are very definitely in the majority in the United States," *New York Times*, 18 June 1963, p. 29.

8. In a Gallup Poll taken one month after the Court decided *Engel*, respondents were asked, "Do you approve or disapprove of religious observances in public schools?" The results: 79 percent approved of religious observances, 14 percent did not, and 7 percent had no opinion. The response of parents of public school children was almost identical: 80 percent approved of religious observances, 14 percent did not, and 6 percent had no opinion. See *The Gallup Report*, 25 July 1962.

9. For a description of these efforts, see, for example, Steven K. Green, "Evangelicals and the Becker Amendment: A Lesson in Church-State Moderation," 32 *Journal of Church and State* 541 (1991); Edward Keynes and Randall Miller, *The Court vs. Congress: Prayer, Busing and Abortion* (Durham, N.C.: Duke University Press, 1989); Matthew C. Moen, *The Christian Right and Congress* (Tuscaloosa, Ala.: University of Alabama Press, 1989); Allen D. Hertzke, *Representing God in Washington* (Knoxville, Tenn.: University of Tennessee Press, 1988).

10. A comprehension discussion of congressional response to overturn the Court's school prayer decisions through federal statute, constitutional amendment, and legislation stripping the federal courts of jurisdiction in such cases is contained in Keynes and Miller, *The Court vs. Congress*, 187–205; see also Green, "Evangelicals and the Becker Amendment."

11. *Wallace v. Jaffree*, 466 U.S. 924 (1985).

12. "Reagan Tells Broadcasters He'll Press for Laws Granting Voluntary School Prayers," *Los Angeles Times*, 4 October 1980.

13. In addition to working with organized religious interests on the Christian evangelical and fundamentalist right in the 1983–84 battle for a constitutional amendment authorizing school prayer in Congress, the Reagan administration submitted *amicus curiae* briefs in several church-state cases urging the Supreme Court to adopt more permissive rules allowing government sponsorship and support of private religious practices, including *County of Allegheny v. ACLU*, 109 S.Ct. 3086 (1989); *Bowen v. Kendrick*, 108 S.Ct. 2562 (1988); *Grand Rapids v. Ball*, 473 U.S. 373 (1985); *Wallace v. Jaffree*, 472 U.S. 38 (1985); *Lynch v. Donnelly*, 465 U.S. (1984); *Marsh v. Chambers*, 463 U.S. 783 (1983).

14. E.g., *Bowen v. Kendrick*, 108 S.Ct. 2562 (1988) (holding federal funding scheme that provided cash grant to religious institutions for sex education counseling not to violate the establishment clause); *Lynch v. Donnelly*, 465 U.S. 668 (1984) (ruling that display of city-owned creche in private park did not violate establishment clause); *Marsh v. Chambers*, 463 U.S. 783 (1983) (state-funded legislative chaplaincies are "historical exception" under establishment clause and constitutionally permitted); *U.S. v. Seeger*, 380 U.S. 163 (1965) (broadening categories of religious exemption from selective service laws); and *Torcaso v. Watkins*, 367 U.S. 488 (1961) (holding compelled religious oaths as a qualification to assume public office unconstitutional).

15. For an excellent discussion of the causes and effect of the rise of conservative religious lobbies to political power in the early 1980s, see Moen, *The Christian Right and Congress*; Hertzke, *Representing God in Washington*; and A. James

Reichley, *Religion in American Public Life* (Washington, D.C.: The Brookings Institution, 1985).

16. 393 U.S. 97 (1968) (ruling that public schools could not teach religion-based theories in secular classroom instruction).

17. See *Edwards v. Aguillard*, 482 U.S. 578, 603 (1987) (Justice Powell, concurring); *Abington v. Schempp*, 374 U.S. 203 (1963); *Engel v. Vitale*, 370 U.S. 421 (1962).

18. Id. See also, *Wallace v. Jaffree*, 472 U.S. 38 (1985); *Epperson v. Arkansas*, 393 U.S. 421 (1968).

19. *Gideons International v. Tudor*, 100 A.2d 857 (1953), *cert. denied*, 348 U.S. 816 (1954).

20. 449 U.S. 39 (1980).

21. Id. at 41–42.

22. See *Karen B. v. Treen*, 653 F.2d 897 (5th Cir. 1981), *aff'd mem*, 455 U.S. 913 (1982).

23. 472 U.S. 38 (1985).

24. Id. at 40.

25. Id.

26. Id.

27. Id. at 43 (emphasis added).

28. *Jaffree v. James*, 554 F.Supp. 1130, 1132 (S.D. Ala. 1983).

29. Id.

30. *Jaffree v. Wallace*, 705 F.2d 1526, 1535–36 (11th Cir. 1983).

31. *Jaffree v. Wallace*, 713 F.2d 614 (11th Cir. 1983).

32. *Wallace*, 472 U.S. at 56.

33. Id. at 60.

34. 465 U.S. 668 (1984).

35. 463 U.S. 783 (1983).

36. 463 U.S. 388 (1983).

37. *Wallace*, 472 U.S. at 48.

38. Id. at 49.

39. Id. at 77 (Justice O'Connor, concurring).

40. Id. at 76, 67.

41. Id. at 62–67 (Justice Powell, concurring).

42. 330 U.S. 1 (1947).

43. *Wallace*, 472 U.S. at 91–114, 112 (Justice Rehnquist, dissenting).

44. Id. at 113.

45. Id. at 106.

46. Id. at 112.

47. Id. at 106-7.

48. Id. at 108-114

49. See, for example, Robert L. Cord, "Church-State Separation: Restoring the 'No Preference' Doctrine of the First Amendment," 9 *Harvard Journal of Law and Public Policy* (1986).

50. Id. at 90–91 (Justice White dissenting).

51. Id. at 84–90 (Chief Justice Burger dissenting).

52. See *County of Allegheny v. ACLU*, 109 S.Ct. 3086, 3134–46 (1989) (Justice Kennedy, concurring in part and dissenting in part); *Edwards v. Aguillard*, 482 U.S. 578, 627–40 (1987) (Justice Scalia, dissenting).

53. *Wallace v. Jaffree*, 466 U.S. 924 (1984).

54. Four years after *Wallace*, the Court declined to review an Eleventh Circuit decision, *Jager v. Douglas County School District*, 862 F.2d 824 (11th Cir. 1989), *cert.*

denied, 109 S.Ct. 2431 (1989) (holding that a Georgia high school's practice of recruiting Protestant ministers to give a religious invocation before football games violated the establishment clause).

55. *Wallace*, 472 U.S. at 76 (Justice O'Connor, concurring).
56. 484 U.S. 72, 75, (1987).
57. 780 F.2d 240 (3rd Cir. 1985), *appeal dismissed, sub nom Karcher v. May*, 484 U.S. 72 (1985).
58. See *May*, 780 F.2d at 242.
59. *May v. Cooperman*, 572 F. Supp. 1561 (D.N.J. 1983).
60. Id. at 1574.
61. *Lemon v. Kurtzman*, 403 U.S. 610, 612–13 (1971).
62. *May*, 572 F. Supp. at 1574.
63. Id.
64. Id.
65. *May*, 780 F.2d 240, 247 (1985).
66. Id. at 247–50.
67. Id. at 253.
68. See *Wallace*, 472 U.S. at 62 (Justice Powell, concurring).
69. Justice Scalia has argued that when interpreting federal and state statutes, the Court should adopt a "plain view" method of judicial review that relies on language and text rather than on historical record, social science research, and other nontextual materials in addition to text. On this point, see Antonin Scalia, "Originalism: The Lesser Evil," 57 *Cincinnati Law Review* 849 (1989). Justice Scalia has also expressed this view in several opinions since coming to the Court. See, e.g., *Chisom v. Roemer*, 111 S. Ct. 2354, 2369–76 (1991) (Justice Scalia, dissenting); *I.N.S.V. Cardoza-Fonseca*, 480 U.S. 421, 452–455 (1987) (Justice Scalia, dissenting).
70. 109 S.Ct. 3086, 3138–46 (1989) (Justice Kennedy, concurring in part and dissenting in part).
71. 482 U.S. 578, 610–40 (1987) (Justice Scalia, dissenting).
72. The Equal Access Act of 1984, Pub.L. 98–377, 98 Stat. 1302, 20 U.S.C. 4071–74.
73. For a thorough description of the politics behind the passage of the Equal Access Act, see Hertzke, *Representing God in Washington*, 161–98; see also, Moen, *The Christian Right and Congress*, 113–20.
74. *Board of Education of Westside Community Schools v. Mergens*, 110 S.Ct. 2356 (1990).
75. Hertzke, *Representing God in Washington*, 161–98.
76. See the brief for the National School Boards Association, *amicus curiae, Board of Westside Schools v. Mergens*, No. 88–1597.
77. Id.
78. Id.
79. Id.
80. Id.
81. See *Mergens*, 110 S.Ct. at 2393 (Justice Stevens, dissenting) ("The Court's construction of this Act, however, leads to a sweeping intrusion by the federal government into the operation of our public schools, and does so despite the absence of any indication that Congress intended to divest local school districts of their power to shape the educational environment.").
82. On this point, see especially Douglas Laycock, "Equal Access and Moments of Silence: The Equal Status of Religious Speech By Private Speakers," 81 *Northwestern University Law Review* 1, 52–53 (1986). Professor Laycock, whose article

strongly influenced the Court's opinion, confessed that abuse was possible from those political constituencies, especially on the religious right, "traditionally hostile both to the establishment clause and to the free exercise clause." Professor Laycock praised the determination on the part of the act's opponents to police implementation, but it is difficult to understand how such implementation does not raise entanglement problems, or provide insurance that school administrators supportive of state-sponsored religious exercises will constrain the potential excesses of the act. For additional comment since *Mergens*, see Frank R. Jimenez, "Beyond Mergens: Ensuring Equality of Student Religious Speech Under the Equal Access Act," 100 *Yale Law Review* 2149 (1990).

83. See *Mergens*, 110 S.Ct. at 2370-73. Justices O'Connor, White, Blackmun, and Chief Justice Rehnquist held the Equal Access Act not to violate the establishment clause under the *Lemon* test; Justices Kennedy and Scalia, concurring in part and concurring in the judgment, agreed that the Equal Access Act did not violate the establishment clause, but rejected *Lemon* as the analytical framework under which to review the constitutional issue. Instead, the Court need only determine whether the legislation directed benefits towards religion to such a degree that it establishes an official religion, or tends to do so, and whether the legislation coerces individuals into accepting religious beliefs against their will. Id. at 2376-78; Justices Marshall and Brennan, concurring in the judgment, concluded that, if properly implemented, the Equal Access Act could withstand establishment clause scrutiny, but wrote that, as construed, it raised more problems than the Court was willing to admit. Id. at 2378-83; dissenting, Justice Stevens, while not agreeing or disagreeing with the plurality's establishment clause analysis, concluded that the "question is much more difficult than the Court assumes." Id. at 2390.

84. Moen, *The Christian Right and Congress*, 113-19.

85. 130 *Congressional Record*, S8352, 8360, 27 June 1984.

86. See Laycock, "Equal Access and Moments of Silence," 55-57. Professor Laycock has called such a distinction "untenable."

87. Id., 9.

88. Id., 45-51.

89. 454 U.S. 263 (1981).

90. Id. at 265.

91. *Chess v. Widmar*, 635 F.2d 1310, 1314 (1980).

92. Id. at 1314-15.

93. *Chess v. Widmar*, 480 F. Supp. 907 (W.D. Mo. 1979).

94. *Chess v. Widmar*, 635 F.2d 1310 (1980).

95. Id. at 1315.

96. Id. at 1317.

97. *Widmar v. Vincent*, 454 U.S. 263 (1981).

98. Id. at 268.

99. Id. at 274.

100. Id. at 274-75.

101. Id. at 274, n. 14.

102. Id.

103. E.g., *Garnett v. Renton Area School District*, 865 F.2d 1121, *as modified*, 874 F.2d 608 (9th Cir. 1989); *Clark v. Dallas Independent School*, decided without opinion, 880 F.2d 411 (5th Cir. 1989); *Bell v. Little Axe Independent School District*, 766 F.2d 1391 (10th Cir. 1985); *Nartowicz v. Clayton County School District*, 736 F.2d 646 (11th Cir. 1984); *Lubbock Civil Liberties Union v. Lubbock Independent School*

District, 669 F.2d 1038 (5th Cir. 1982), cert. denied, 459 U.S. 1159 (1983); and *Brandon v. Board of Education*, 635 F.2d 971 (2nd Cir. 1980), *cert. denied*, 454 U.S. 1123 (1981).

104. E.g., *Mergens v. Westside Community School Board*, 867 F.2d 1076 (8th Cir. 1989); *Clergy and Laity Concerned v. Chicago Board of Education*, 586 F.Supp 1408 (N.D. Ill. 1984); and *Bender v. Williamsport*, 563 F.Supp 697 (3rd Cir. 1983), *vacated on other grounds*, 475 U.S. 534 (1984).

105. *Garnett v. Renton Area School District*, 865 F.2d 1121, *as modified*, 874 F.2d 608 (9th Cir. 1989); *Bender v. Williamsport Area School District*, 741 F.2d 538 (3rd Cir. 1984).

106. 110 S.Ct. 2356 (1990).

107. Id. at 2370-73.

108. Id. at 2378.

109. Id. at 2378-83 (Justice Marshall, concurring).

110. Id. at 2393 (Justice Stevens, dissenting).

111. 736 F.2d 646 (11th Cir. 1984).

112. 669 F.2d 1038 (5th Cir. 1982).

113. Id. at 1039.

114. Id. at 1041.

115. Id. at 1039-40.

116. Id.

117. *Lubbock*, 669 F.2d at 1045.

118. Id. at 1046.

119. 459 U.S. 1155 (1983).

120. *Nartowicz*, 736 F.2d at 647.

121. Id.

122. Id.

123. Id. at 649.

124. 865 F.2d 1121 (9th Cir. 1989).

125. 766 F.2d 1391 (10th Cir. 1985).

126. 787 F.2d 1105 (7th Cir. 1986).

127. 865 F.2d 1105 (10th Cir. 1985).

128. Okla.Stat., Title 70, Section 11-101.1 (1981).

129. *Little Axe*, 766 F.2d at 1399.

130. Id. at 1397.

131. Id. at 1411.

132. Id. at 1412-13.

133. Id.

134. Id. at 1407.

135. Compare Okla. Stat., Title 70, Section 11-101.1 (1981), with Alabama Code Section 16-1-20 (Supp. 1984).

136. 787 F.2d 1105 (1986).

137. *May v. Evansville-Vanderburgh School Corp.*, 615 F.Supp 761, 763-64 (S.D. Ill. 1985).

138. Id.

139. Id. at 765.

140. Id. at 766.

141. Id.

142. *May v. Evansville*, 787 F.2d 1105 (7th Cir. 1986).

143. Id. at 1113-14.

144. Id. at 1110–11.
145. 675 F. Supp. 1268 (W.D. Wash. 1987), *aff'd*, 865 F.2d 1121 (9th Cir. 1989), *as amended*, 874 F.2d 608 (9th Cir. 1989).
146. *Garnett*, 675 F. Supp. at 1270.
147. Id. at 1271.
148. Id. at 1270. The district court relied on the following provisions of the Washington constitution:

No public money or property shall be appropriated for or applied to any religious worship, exercise or instruction, or the support of any religious establishment. (Article I, Sec. 11)

All schools maintained or supported wholly or in part by the public funds shall be forever free from sectarian control or influence. (Article IX, Sec. 4)

149. Id. at 1274.
150. *Garnett*, 865 F.2d at 1124–26.
151. Id. at 1125–26.
152. Id. at 1128.
153. Id. at 1126.
154. Id.
155. Id. at 1127.
156. Briefs were filed in *Garnett* on behalf of Renton School District by the American Civil Liberties Union; the Anti-Defamation League of B'nai B'rith, the American Jewish Congress and Americans for Religious Liberty; and the American Jewish Committee and the Church Council of Greater Seattle.
   In addition to the United States, the Center for Law and Religious Freedom and Families for a Responsible Education Environment filed a brief in support of the equal access claim.
157. The relevant provision of the Equal Access Act, 20 U.S.C. 4071 (a) enjoins:

any public secondary school which receives Federal financial assistance and which has a limited open forum . . . equal access or a fair opportunity to, or discriminating against, any students who wish to conduct a meeting within that limited open forum on the basis of the religious, political, philosophical, or other content of the speech at such meetings.

158. *Garnett*, 865 F. 2d at 1126, citing Renton School District Policy No. 6470, which stated that "Renton School District does not offer a limited open forum."
159. Id. at 1128.
160. Id.
161. Numerous briefs were submitted, *amici curiae*, asking the Ninth Circuit to resolve the constitutional issue presented by the Equal Access Act in *Garnett*. Organizations filing briefs included: the Christian Legal Society and Families for a Responsible Educational Environment; the Anti-Defamation League, American Jewish Congress, and Americans for Religious Liberty; the American Jewish Committee and Church Council of Greater Seattle; the American Civil Liberties Union—Washington Foundation; and the United States.
162. 867 F.2d 1076 (1989).
163. *Mergens*, 110 S.Ct. at 2362.

164. Id. at 2362–63.
165. CV No. 85–0–426.
166. Id. at 13.
167. *Mergens*, 867 F.2d at 1078.
168. Id.
169. Id.
170. 454 U.S. 263 (1981).
171. *Mergens*, 867 F.2d at 1078.
172. Id.
173. Id.
174. *Mergens*, 110 S.Ct. at 2366.
175. Id. at 2366–67.
176. The major organizations involved in fighting the Equal Access Act in Congress, which included the American Civil Liberties Union, the American Jewish Congress, Americans United for the Separation of Church and State, and People for the American Way, submitted *amicus curiae* briefs in *Mergens*.
177. *Mergens*, 110 S.Ct. at 2370–73.
178. Id. at 2370–71.
179. *Widmar*, 454 U.S. at 274.
180. *Mergens*, 110 S.Ct. at 2071.
181. Id. at 2373.
182. Id. at 2371.
183. Id.
184. Id. at 2073.
185. 473 U.S. 373 (1985).
186. 473 U.S. 402 (1985).
187. *Lemon*, 403 U.S. at 619.
188. 413 U.S. 756 (1973).
189. Id. at 794.
190. E.g., *Sloan v. Lemon*, 413 U.S. 825 (1973); *Meek v. Pettinger*, 421 U.S. 349 (1975); *Wolman v. Walter*, 432 U.S. 229 (1977); *Aguilar v. Felton*, 473 U.S. 402 (1975); *Grand Rapids v. Ball*, 473 U.S. 373 (1985).
191. The Equal Access Act of 1984, 98 Stat. 1302, 20 U.S.C. 4071 (c)(2)(3)(5).
192. *Mergens*, 110 S.Ct. at 2373.
193. *Lemon*, 403 U.S. at 619.
194. *Aguilar v. Felton*, 473 U.S. 402 (1985).
195. *Lemon*, 413 U.S. at 617; see also, *Meek v. Pettinger*, 421 U.S. 349 (1975).
196. *Mergens*, 110 S.Ct. at 2373.
197. *Clark v. Dallas Independent School*, 880 F.2d 411 (5th Cir. 1989).
198. *May v. Evansville*, 787 F.2d 1105 (7th Cir. 1986).
199. *Garnett v. Renton Area School District*, 865 F.2d 1121 (9th Cir. 1989).
200. *Bell v. Little Axe Independent School District*, 736 F.2d 646 (10th Cir. 1985).
201. *Nartowicz v. Clayton County School District*, 736 F.2d 646 (11th Cir. 1984).
202. *Mergens*, 110 S.Ct. at 2366.
203. Id. at 2369.
204. Id. at 2383 (Justice Stevens, dissenting).
205. One example comes from the following exchange between the Equal Access Act's principal sponsor, Senator Mark Hatfield (R-Ore.) and one of its leading opponents, Senator Slade Gorton (R-Wash).

SENATOR GORTON: Would the school district have the full-authority to determine where the line is to be drawn between curriculum-related activities and noncurriculum activites?

SENATOR HATFIELD: We in no way seek to limit that discretion.

130 *Congressional Record* S8342-43 (daily ed. 27 June 1984).

206. See Laycock, "Equal Access and Moments of Silence," 16-19.

207. Id. at 16-17, 47-49.

208. 393 U.S. 503 (1969).

209. 319 U.S. 624 (1943).

210. On this point, see Geoffrey R. Stone, "The Equal Access Controversy: The Religion Clauses and the Meaning of Neutrality," 81 *Northwestern University Law Review* 168, 171-73 (1986). See also *Tinker*, 393 U.S., at 509 ("In order for the State in the person of school officials to justify prohibition of a particular expression of opinion, it must be able to show that action was caused by something more than a mere desire to avoid the discomfort and unpleasantness that always accompany an unpopular viewpoint").

211. Id., 72; see also, Steven K. Green, "The Misnomer of Equality Under the Equal Access Act," 14 *Vermont Law Review* 369 (1990); Ruti Teitel, "When Separate is Equal: Why Organized Religious Exercises, Unlike Chess, Do Not Belong in the Public Schools," 81 *Northwestern University Law Review* 175 (1986).

212. *New Jersey v. T.L.O.*, 469 U.S. 325 (1985).

213. *Hazelwood School District v. Kuhlmeier*, 484 U.S. 260 (1988).

214. *Bethel School District v. Fraser*, 478 U.S. 675 (1986).

215. See *Miller v. California*, 413 U.S. 15, 23-25 (1973).

216. E.g., *West Virginia v. Barnette*, 319 U.S. 624 (1943).

217. E.g., *Edwards v. Aguillard*, 482 U.S. 578 (1987); *Wallace v. Jaffree*, 472 U.S. 38 (1985); *Abington v. Schempp*, 374 U.S. 203 (1963).

218. *Edwards v. Aguillard*, 482 U.S. 578 (1987); *Wallace v. Jaffree*, 472 U.S. 38 (1985).

219. *Wallace*, 472 U.S. at 83 (Justice O'Connor, concurring).

220. Id. See also, *Thornton v. Caldor*, 472 U.S. 703 (1985).

221. Laycock, "Equal Access and Moments of Silence," 55-57.

222. See, for example, the brief of the Christian Legal Society, National Association of Evangelicals et al., *amicus curiae*, in *Lee v. Weisman, cert. granted*, 111 S. Ct. 1305 (1991) (No. 90-1014) (arguing, *inter alia*, that public school officials may allow guest speakers to engage in religious expression freely at a graduation ceremony and that prohibition of the religious component of a message delivered by an invited guest at a public event constitutes discriminatory content-based regulation of speech), 4-11; see also, the Brief of the United States Catholic Conference, id. (arguing that establishment clause does not prohibit the expression of religious beliefs in public places, even if forum is provided by government, because to do so violates the free speech clause), 16-28.

223. E.g., *Bowen v. Kendrick*, 108 S.Ct. 2562 (1988) (holding neutral public welfare legislation providing financial aid to religious institutions not to violate establishment clause, despite evidence of sectarian uses of these monies); *Wallace v. Jaffree*, 472 U.S. 38 (1985) (invalidating Alabama "voluntary prayer" statute for lack of secular purpose, but suggesting that moment-of-silence laws might be constitutional).

224. See *Mergens*, 110 U.S. at 2364-68; see also, Laycock, "Equal Access and Moments of Silence," 37-39.

225. *Scopes v. State*, 154 Tenn. 105, 289 S.W. 363 (1927).

226. 393 U.S. 97, 99 (1968).

227. Id. at 101–02.

228. Id. at 98.

229. Id. at 107–08.

230. Id.

231. For a description of the post-*Epperson* litigation strategies used by organized religious fundamentalists to attack the public school curriculum, see, generally, Wayne V. McIntosh, "Litigating Scientific Creationism, or 'Scopes' II, III . . .," 7 *Law and Policy* 375 (1985).

232. *West Virginia v. Barnette*, 319 U.S. 624 (1943); *Minersville School District v. Gobitis*, 310 U.S. 586 (1940).

233. 482 U.S. 578 (1987).

234. La Rev. Stat. Ann. Section 17:286.1 - 17:286.7 (West 1982).

235. *Keith v. Louisiana Department of Education*, 553 F. Supp. 295 (M.D. La. 1982).

236. *Aquillard v. Treen*, 634 F. Supp. 426 (E.D. La. 1985).

237. *Aguillard v. Edwards*, 765 F.2d 1251, 1257 (1985).

238. *Edwards v. Aguillard*, 482 U.S. 578, 592 (1987).

239. Id. at 587.

240. Id. at 603 (Justice Powell, concurring).

241. Id.

242. Id. at 604.

243. Id. at 639–40 (Justice Scalia, dissenting).

244. Id. at 627.

245. Id. at 636–40.

246. Id. at 636 ("I think the pessimistic evaluation that the Chief Justice made of the totality of *Lemon* is particularly applicable to the "purpose" prong: it is a 'constitutional theory (that) has no basis in the history of the amendment it seeks to interpret. . . .'").

247. Id. at 628.

248. *Board of Westside Community Schools v. Mergens*, 110 S.Ct. 2356 (1990) (concurring in part and concurring in the judgment); *Allgheny v. ACLU*, 109 S.Ct. 3086 (1989) (concurring in part and dissenting in part); *Bowen v. Kendrick*, 108 S.Ct. 2562 (1988).

249. See note 69, *supra*.

250. For a well-told account of the political maneuvering behind the Alabama textbook battles, see Peter Irons, *The Courage of Their Convictions* (New York: Free Press, 1988), 355–78.

251. 827 F.2d 684 (11th Cir. 1987).

252. See Karen O'Connor and Gregg Ivers, "Creationism, Evolution and the Courts," *PS* 21 (1988): 10–17, 14–15.

253. *Smith v. Board of School Commissioners of Mobile County*, 655 F. Supp. 939 (S.D. Ala. 1987), *rev'd and remanded*, 827 F.2d 684 (11th Cir. 1987).

254. *Smith*, 655 F. Supp. at 980–81.

255. Id.

256. Id. at 981.

257. Id. at 695 (emphasis in original).

258. *Smith*, 827 F.2d at 692.

259. 582 F.Supp 201 (1984), *rev'd and remanded*, 765 F.2d 75 (1985), *as modified*, 647 F.Supp. 1194 (1986), *rev'd*, 827 F.2d 1058 (1987).

260. *Mozert*, 827 F.2d at 1060–61.

261. Id. at 1061.

262. Id. at 1060.
263. O'Connor and Ivers, "Creationism, Evolution and the Courts," 15–16.
264. Id.
265. *Mozert*, 582 F.Supp. at 202.
266. *Mozert*, 765 F.2d at 79.
267. *Mozert*, 647 F.Supp. at 1200.
268. Id. at 1201.
269. 374 U.S. 398 (1963) (holding that a state cannot prohibit unemployment compensation to individuals who refuse work based on religious convictions if those persons are otherwise eligible to receive them. In order to bar individuals who cite religious objections from receiving public welfare benefits, the government must demonstrate that such action [1] advances a compelling state interest and [2] does so through the least restrictive means).
270. 450 U.S. 707 (1981) (ruling that the free exercise clause prohibits the denial of unemployment benefits to an individual who quits a job based on religious objections to the type of work required).
271. 480 U.S. 136 (1987) (holding that *Sherbert* standard applies to persons dismissed for religious objections to employment requirements, even if the religious claim was not asserted prior to beginning employment).
272. *Mozert*, 827 F.2d at 1065.
273. Id.
274. *West Virginia State Board of Education v. Barnette*, 319 U.S. 624 (1943); *Minersville School District v. Gobitis*, 310 U.S. 586 (1940).
275. 406 U.S. 205 (1972).
276. Id. at 1067.
277. Id. at 1066 ("In *Barnette* the unconstitutional burden consisted of compulsion either to do an act that violated the plaintiff's religious convictions or communicate an acceptance of a particular idea or affirm a belief. No similar compulsion exists in the present case"); Id. at 1067 ("*Yoder* was decided in large part on the impossibility of reconciling the goals of public education with the religious requirement of the Amish that their children be prepared for life in a separated community. No such threat exists in the present case . . .").
278. Id. at 1069.
279. See, for example, George W. Dent, Jr., "Religious Children, Secular Schools," 61 *Southern California Law Review* 863 (1988).
280. See, for example, Michael Farris, *Home Schooling* (1990).

2

Public Funds For Private Religion

When President Richard M. Nixon announced in June 1969 that Chief Justice Earl Warren would not return to the bench for the October term, more was at stake than the task of filling a single vacancy on the Supreme Court. Under the leadership of Chief Justice Warren, the Court had recast the institutional role of judicial review in the separation of powers and led a revolution in constitutional interpretation that shook the core of the extant relationship between individuals and their government. The Warren Court struck down legal barriers that once stood as obstacles for politically disenfranchised individuals and minorities to full and equal citizenship in the American constitutional scheme, and did so even in the face of what was often massive popular resistance.[1] While the Warren Court has been both praised[2] and attacked[3] for the legal revolution it created in the law of equal protection,[4] criminal procedure,[5] and legislative apportionment,[6] no less important in understanding the fundamental reordering in constitutional values taking place were its decisions banning state-sponsored religious devotionals in the public schools.

The Court's decisions in *Engel v. Vitale* (1962)[7] and *Abington v. Schempp* (1963)[8] were the most unpopular it made during the era of Chief Justice Earl Warren.[9] That is no small accomplishment, especially when considered against the backdrop of such decisions as *Brown v. Board of Education* (1954),[10] *Mapp v. Ohio* (1961)[11] and *Miranda v. Arizona* (1966),[12] none of which was well received by public opinion, but all of which convulsed settled constitutional law as much or more than *Engel* and *Schempp*. These decisions are the brush strokes most often used by religious conservatives to paint their picture of the Warren Court as one that ushered in a new era of judicial hostility to the traditional place of religion in American public life. But *Engel* and *Schempp* were hardly characteristic of the Warren Court's establishment clause jurisprudence. Even though both cases were decided by near-unanimous majorities,[13] *Engel* and *Schempp* are surprisingly self-conscious, bordering on apologetic, in their tone and prose. Absent are the bold, stark assertions of principle that characterized the Warren Court's decisions on racial segregation and criminal procedure. Even so, this hardly minimizes the liberating qualities that *Engel* and *Schempp* had for religious minorities long subjected to the indignities associated with coercive, state-sponsored religious exercises in the public schools, and the courage shown by the Warren Court in holding such practices unconstitutional.

But *Engel* and *Schempp* do not alone define the Warren Court's establishment clause jurisprudence. For example, just one term before *Engel* was decided, the Court ruled in four separate cases that state statutes requiring businesses to remain closed or refrain from selling certain products on Sunday did not violate the establishment or free exercise clauses.[14] Chief Justice Warren, writing for the Court in all four cases, seemed genuinely nonplussed that constitutional violations could be alleged under either the establishment or free exercise clauses against the Sunday closing laws, despite overwhelming evidence that such laws derived from a religious purpose and substantially burdened those religious minorities who closed their stores on Saturday to honor their Sabbath, but were unable to compensate for this loss by staying open on Sunday. For Chief Justice Warren, the Sunday closing laws were not about advancing religion, but about promoting the legitimate secular goal of setting aside a common day for rest and relaxation, about providing workers time off, and about encouraging family togetherness.[15] Even after the fallout from *Engel* and *Schempp* had settled, the Warren Court did not interpret the establishment clause to ban all government support for private religion. While in *Engel* and *Schempp* the Court could hold that government-sponsored religious exercises in the public schools amounted to an unconstitutional use of state power, in *Board of Education v. Allen* (1968),[16] it would rule that government financial subsidies to parochial schools, or parochaid, did not in all cases abridge the establishment clause. There, as in the *Sunday Closing Cases*, the Court ruled that the state's objective was to advance the welfare of individual children and not the parochial schools they attended.[17]

On balance, though, the Warren Court created innovative doctrine that substantially redefined the breadth of government power under the establishment clause to advance the interests of private religion in the public schools. Public schools no longer could serve as a state intermezzo for the dissemination of pan-Protestant religious values, regardless of the religious makeup of the student body or larger community these schools served. The Court also unanimously ruled that public schools no longer could shape their science and humanities curriculum to advance pedagogical doctrine rooted in the Christian fundamentalist tenets of biblical literalism.[18] But while the Warren Court took giant steps in redefining the constitutional relationship between public schools and private religion, it avoided almost entirely the other, equally divisive issue involving religion and education that had long simmered underneath this one— public aid for religious schools.

When Earl Warren assumed the position of Chief Justice just before the Court opened the 1953 term, less than a handful of cases had attempted to explicate the meaning of the establishment clause. In two of these cases, *McCollum v. Board of Education* (1948)[19] and *Zorach v. Clausen* (1952),[20] the Court handed down irreconcilable opinions on the issue of released time for religious education. In *McCollum*, the Court held that state-enacted programs permitting religious instruction to take place in public schools violated the establishment clause, while in *Zorach* the Court ruled that public schools were permitted to release students for off-campus religious instruction. While *McCollum* and *Zorach* generated much heated debate on and off the Court over the limits of state power to assist religious educators, released time never developed into the lasting, confrontational and divisive battle that stemmed from the issues first addressed and decided in *Everson v. Board of Education* (1947).[21]

In *Everson*, the Court held that a New Jersey law authorizing local school boards to reimburse parents for transportation costs associated with sending their children to parochial schools did not violate the establishment clause. The Court also, for the first time, gave judicial interpretation to the meaning of the establishment clause. In his historic opinion, Justice Hugo Black embraced Thomas Jefferson's "wall of separation" metaphor in comprehensive terms, holding that the establishment clause, at minimum, prohibited the passage of laws that "aid one religion, aid all religions, or prefer one religion over another," and that "no tax in any amount, large or small, can be levied to support any religious activities or institutions, whatever they may be called, or what form they may adopt to teach or practice religion."[22] But Justice Black, after concluding that the wall of separation must "remain high and impregnable,"[23] departed from his seminal interpretation of the establishment clause. Writing for a 5–4 Court, Justice Black held that New Jersey's reimbursement program was intended to promote the health and welfare of children, "regardless of their religion,"[24] not to channel institutional benefits to parochial schools.

Everson satisfied no one. Catholic organizations were pleased that the parents of parochial school children would receive state-subsidized assistance in defraying a portion of their educational costs, but disheartened over Justice Black's interpretation of the establishment clause for fear that it would impair future efforts to secure parochaid.[25] The coalition of secular, Jewish, and Protestant organizations that supported the lawsuit was pleased with the Court's endorsement of the first principles of strict separationism, but confused over its conclusion that public funds for parochial school students did not violate the establishment clause, while similar assistance that went to religious institutions did. Justice Robert H. Jackson, in a pungent dissent, found the Court's opinion inconsistent with both the text and intent of the establishment clause. Wrote Justice Jackson:

> This freedom was first in the Bill of Rights because it was first in the forefathers' minds; it was set forth in absolute terms, and its strength is its rigidity. It was intended not to keep the states' hands out of religion, but to keep religion's hands off the state, and, above all, to keep bitter religious controversy out of public life by denying to every denomination any advantage from getting control of public policy or the public purse.[26]

While *Everson* pulled the Court into the maelstrom of church-state politics once and for all, parochaid did not assume a dominant place in the Warren Court's pallete of constitutional concerns under the establishment clause. From 1953 to 1969, the Court's establishment clause jurisprudence reflected the fundamental-value approach of the new Chief Justice: religion could not be used as a condition to hold public office;[27] schools could not be used as instruments for religious instruction; and the rights of conscientious objectors to military service were expanded to include exemption on nonreligious grounds.[28] In each case, the Court ruled that the state could not use religion to elevate or diminish the status of individuals under the Constitution. But the Warren Court never decided how parochaid fit into its moral vision of the constitutional relationship between religion and the state. That was an issue that Earl Warren, when he retired from the Court in 1969, would leave for resolution to his successor, Warren Earl Burger.

Parochaid became the church-state issue that defined the establishment clause jurisprudence of the Burger Court. Having inherited just two parochaid cases, *Everson* and *Allen*, the Burger Court fashioned an establishment clause jurisprudence governing the relationship between the public purse and parochial schools that departed from those cases, and instead followed to a considerable degree the principles laid down in the Warren Court's school prayer opinions. From 1969, when Warren Burger became Chief Justice, through the 1986 term, the Court decided fourteen cases that involved challenges to federal and state statutes that provided funding for secondary and elementary parochial schools. In eleven cases, the Court held that such government aid packages for sectarian elementary and secondary schools violated the establishment clause.[29] But absent from the Burger Court's parochaid decisions was a consistent vision of what moral and constitutional commands the establishment clause heeded for those religious institutions that sought to claim their share of the public till.

For example, the Burger Court almost without exception[30] took a firm line against parochaid statutes that earmarked public monies for direct and indirect use by religious elementary and secondary schools for educational and support services.[31] But the Court developed far less stringent rules for governmental funds that flowed to sectarian colleges. Federal and state programs that provided aid to institutions of higher learning and students attending them was permissible under the establishment clause, provided that such funds were used for what the Court classified as nonsectarian purposes.[32] Over time, though, the Burger Court's parochaid decisions became more acrimonious, largely because it was never able to divorce principle from pragmatism, but also because between 1969 and 1986 the Court experienced dramatic personnel changes that made it difficult to lead. But there is no point in brooding over the intellectual and leadership difficulties of Chief Justice Warren Burger. Law scholars and political scientists have argued elsewhere that the Burger Court's atomistic approach to constitutional jurisprudence reflected the Chief Justice's poor leadership skills; Warren Burger never presided over a "Burger Court" because he was never able to inspire or lead it.[33] The Court under Chief Justice Burger was one whose institutional personality varied from opinion to opinion, from Justice to Justice, from year to year.

Even if one accepts this portrait of the Burger Court, one cannot dismiss the fact that it somehow managed to overcome internal incoherence long enough to severely limit government power to enact parochaid programs. Chief Justice Burger, though he later regretted it,[34] assumed a central role in shaping the analytical framework responsible for keeping the contents of the public coffers from parochial schools. So when Chief Justice Burger retired after the 1986 term, parochaid advocates viewed his departure with little remorse. This was, after all, the same Warren Burger who authored *Lemon v. Kurtzman* (1971),[35] in which the Court, in striking down a comprehensive state parochaid statute, first articulated in full form the purpose-effect-entanglement test that nonpreferentialists have since asked the Court to overturn.[36] While Chief Justice Burger eventually retreated from the separationist position he helped anchor in *Lemon*, parochaid advocates saved their optimism for his successor, William Rehnquist, who had consistently expressed his contempt for the Court's church-state jurisprudence since his appointment in 1971. Their faith proved to be well-placed when Chief Justice Rehnquist, in his second term at the Court's helm, assembled a 5–4 majority that upheld an establishment clause challenge to a federal statute providing block grants to religious organizations for adolescent sex education and restricted eligibility to those denominations whose programs included no discussion of abortion.[37] The Court's decision in *Bowen v. Kendrick* (1988) gave the first signal that the Rehnquist Court, which now included nonpreferentialists Antonin Scalia and Anthony Kennedy, would depart from its predecessor on the issue of public funds for parochial institutions.

Far less controversial and divisive was the Burger Court's initial venture into a related realm of the government aid issue: tax exemption for religion. In 1971, an 8–1 Court, in *Walz v. Tax Commission* (1970), ruled that exempting religious property used exclusively for worship or other religious purposes did not violate the establishment clause.[38] In his opinion for the Court, Chief Justice Burger held that exempting religion from taxation was intended to "guarantee the free exercise of all forms of religious beliefs."[39] This "unbroken practice" was consistent with establishment clause's command of "benevolent neutrality" in the relationship between religion and the state.[40] Organized American religion, whose differences abound on whether government should fund religious institutions, was unanimous in support of *Walz*[41] and has since remained unified on the tax exemption principle.[42]

But while *Walz* remains dispositive on the general principle that government cannot tax religious properties used for worship-related purposes, the Court has since ruled on several occasions that other religious activities are not exempt from general taxation.[43] In another case, the Court said that the government can refuse the participation of individuals in a general welfare program rather than grant them a religion-based exemption.[44] On two occasions, the Court held that such regulations do not violate the religion clauses, even if these levies place a substantial burden on religious free exercise, and even if the government cannot demonstrate how taxing faith-based religious conduct advances a compelling governmental interest.[45] To tax religious institutions for engaging in worship-related activities and to refuse government benefits otherwise available to religious individuals enervates the substantive meaning of religious free exercise.

The Court's decisions on parochaid and tax exemption, especially since the consolidation of the Rehnquist Court, have cut in two substantive directions. But a common methodological theme unites, rather than distinguishes, the Court's disparate outcomes. Here, as elsewhere in its religion clause jurisprudence, the Court has upheld the broad exercise of judicial and legislative power to advance temporal governmental objectives that support the mission of private religion. When those objectives include the disbursement of public funds to church-related institutions, religious bodies seeking such assistance now have a better chance than ever before of securing access to public funds. But while extending the power of the political process to legislate in the sphere of religion, the Court has also said that religious institutions are not exempt from state or federal tax policies. Such blind deference to government power exhibits almost no consideration of whether such action violates individual rights and liberties or breaches the constitutional limits of state power. How the Court evolved on these issues is the subject to which the remainder of this chapter now turns.

Parochial Institutions

The Warren Court's one major parochaid decision, *Board of Education v. Allen*, upheld a New York law that required the state to provide secular textbooks to students in private schools free of charge. In *Allen*, Justice White, writing for a 6–3 Court, ruled that the distribution of instructional textbooks to students in nonpublic schools, including those in sectarian schools, advanced the state's legitimate goal of furthering the "educational opportunities available to the young."[46] The Court relied on *Everson* and the principles established therein to uphold New York's textbook loan program. While the Court did not rule that the constitutional authority to initiate a textbook loan program was rooted in the state's police power function, which it held in *Everson* authorizing the state to provide transportation subsidies to parochial schools students, it did hold that such assistance was directed toward the child and not the church.[47] To assess the textbook statute, the Court applied the purpose-effect test outlined in *Schempp*.[48] The Court held that New York's purpose in enacting the statute was to make approved textbooks available to desirous students and that the loan program exhibited no unconstitutional effect.

Justice White, while not couching *Allen* in the police power rationale of *Everson*, did hold that New York's textbook program advanced the same objectives as New Jersey's transportation subsidies: to assist the child, not the church. Hence, Justice White simply applied Justice Black's "child benefit" theory to the facts in *Allen* and found no distinction. But Justice Black sure did. And unlike in *Everson*, Justice Black did not mince words. Dissenting, he wrote that "upholding a State's power to pay bus or streetcar fares for school children cannot provide support for the validity of a state law using tax-raised funds to buy school books for a religious school."[49] The two were wholly different. Wrote Justice Black:

> This . . . law, it may be said by some, makes but a small inroad and does not amount to complete state establishment of religion. But that is no excuse for upholding it. It requires no prophet to forsee that on the argument used to support this law others could be upheld providing for state or federal government funds to buy property on which to erect religious school buildings or to erect the buildings themselves, to pay the salaries of the religious school teachers, and finally to have the sectarian religious groups cease to rely on voluntary contributions of members of their sects while waiting for the Government to pick up all the bills for the religious schools.[50]

Justice Black's *Everson* opinion haunted him in *Allen*. His rationale in *Everson*, that assistance to individual students and not their churches was consistent with the establishment clause's ban on providing tax-raised funds for parochial institutions because such assistance promoted the general welfare of children "without regard to their religious belief,"[51] opened the door in *Allen* to the further abuse of this relationship. But Justice Black, whether recanting for *Everson* or because he viewed *Allen* as genuinely different, sounded a pessimistic warning that the Court had let the genie out of the bottle, and that once out it would be impossible to put back in. *Allen* launched a new chapter in the parochaid debate, one that fueled factional strife between and among religious denominations. If states could and would subsidize textbook costs, then why not teacher salaries, instructional materials, and administrative support? Would the Court treat parochaid statutes authorizing such assistance like books and buses? These were the questions that provided the first of several opportunities for the Burger Court to define the law on parochaid. But for those who believed that a new Court, under Warren Burger and minus the critical mass of Warren Court liberals, would regard *Allen* as the judicial benchmark from which to authorize the sweeping use of state power to assist parochial schools, disappointment lurked.

Lemon v. Kurtzman: *Establishing the Rules*

The Court's ruling in *Allen* provided encouragement to state legislatures, particularly those in the Northeast,[52] to enact even more ambitious parochaid statutes on the pretext that Justice White's opinion had paved the path for much more than just financial subsidies for textbooks and transportation. That two statutes, passed after *Allen* was decided, authorizing the use of public funds to supplement the salaries of parochial school teachers providing instruction in secular subjects would provide the Burger Court's initial confrontation with the issue came as no surprise. But the ease with which the Court struck down these statutes and the tough constitutional standards developed to curb the transfer of public funds to elementary and secondary parochial schools did. To the disappointment of those who wished otherwise, *Lemon*, and not *Allen*, became the foundation on which the Burger Court built its establishment clause jurisprudence to govern parochaid.

In *Lemon*, the Court considered two separate state statutes, one from Rhode Island and one from Pennsylvania, that provided financial support to elementary and secondary private schools, including church-related educational institutions. The Rhode Island statute authorized the use of public funds to supplement the salaries of teachers in private elementary schools that taught secular subjects. Rhode Island's private schools educated approximately 25 percent of the state's eligible school-age population; and 95 percent were Catholic parochial schools.[53] Pennsylvania's program authorized the state school superintendent to reimburse private schools for teacher salaries, textbooks, and instructional materials. The percentage of students enrolled in private schools was almost identical to Rhode Island; over 90 percent of these schools were affiliated with the Catholic church.[54]

The Court held that such direct assistance to parochial schools was not under the *Schempp* purpose and effect test violative of the establishment clause. In his opinion for the Court, Chief Justice Burger wrote that, "on the contrary, the statutes themselves clearly state that they are intended to enhance the quality of the secular education in all schools covered by the compulsory attendance laws."[55] The problem with the Rhode Island and Pennsylvania statutes was not their purpose and effect, but that each resulted in an "excessive entanglement between government and religion" that placed the institutional separation of church and state at risk.[56] The "entanglement" criterion was drawn from *Walz*,[57] decided the previous term. In *Walz*, the Court held that tax exemption for religious property was necessary to avoid such "excessive entanglement." In *Lemon*, the Court added the nonentanglement requirement articulated in *Walz* to the purpose-effect test developed in *Schempp*.

The *Lemon* test, as I argued in the previous chapter, now appears set for the judicial guillotine. But for well over the next decade, the *Lemon* test effectively stonewalled legislative efforts to funnel tax monies to parochial schools. State legislatures attempted subsequent to *Lemon* to escape the constitutional noose that the purpose-effect-entanglement test had placed around the neck of parochaid, but had little luck. Parochaid became the issue that dominated the Burger Court's church-state docket throughout the 1970s and into the early 1980s. Except on three occasions, the Court did not retreat from the stringent standards laid down in *Lemon* on parochaid challenges involving elementary and secondary schools.[58] And the Court, in all but one case,[59] applied the purpose-effect-entanglement test that the Chief Justice created in *Lemon* in every establishment clause case, including those outside the parochaid arena, it decided afterward.

What makes this line of decisions most remarkable is that, after *Lemon*, the Chief Justice departed from the Court's separationist wing on parochaid, as he also would later in cases involving state support for religious doctrine, while two of three other Nixon appointees, Justices Powell and Blackmun, joined the two Warren Court liberals, Justices Brennan and Marshall and either Justice Stewart or Stevens to produce the majorities needed to withstand such establishment clause challenges.[60] Following *Lemon*, Chief Justice Burger authored just one other majority opinion in this area, *Levitt v. PEARL* (1973),[61] which held unconstitutional a New York statute that authorized financial reimbursement for expenses incurred in the administration of state-mandated tests prepared by their teachers to students in parochial schools.[62] But *Lemon* and *Levitt* were anomalies in the Chief Justice's voting behavior. Chief Justice Burger found himself instead aligned with Justice Rehnquist, who became the most vociferous critic of the Court's church-state jurisprudence and in particular the *Lemon* test, and Justice White, who dissented in every single decision after *Allen* that struck down aid to church-related schools.[63] Victories for the pro-parochaid wing of the court, as in *PEARL v. Regan* (1980)[64] and *Mueller v. Allen* (1983)[65] came when Justice Powell, Justice Stewart, or, later, Justice O'Connor crossed over to support public power to aid private religion.[66] But Chief Justice Burger found himself most often in dissent, unable to undo what he had created in *Lemon*, while the Court he headed proceeded to disable, though not completely, the governmental financial pipeline to parochial schools.

Regan and Mueller: Lemon *in Retreat*

There were signals that, in *Regan* and *Mueller*, the Court was preparing to retreat from the separationist principles on which most post-*Lemon* cases had been decided. In *Regan*, a 5–4 Court, with Justices Powell and Stewart joining Chief Justice Burger and Justices White and Rehnquist, upheld a New York statute that reimbursed parochial schools for costs borne in administering state-prepared achievement tests. The Court held that no direct funds were paid to parochial schools to subsidize their own standardized student testing, but that whatever assistance such schools received was at most indirect, because they were complying with state regulations required of all schools.[67] This distinction between direct and indirect financial subsidies was enough for Justices Powell and Stewart to abandon their positions in *Levitt*; both had voted in *Levitt*, along with Chief Justice Burger, to strike down the contested subsidies. But none found similar fault with the statute at issue in *Regan*.

In *Mueller*, the Court upheld a challenge to a Minnesota law that allowed parents with children in public or private schools to deduct up to seven hundred dollars of their children's educational expenses from their taxable income. These tax-deductible expenses included tuition, textbooks, and transportation.[68] The Minnesota statute was neutral on its face—religious schools were not mentioned or excluded as beneficiaries—but it was no accident that, as Justice Marshall pointed out in his dissent, over 95 percent of private-school children attended church-related institutions; and that, of the 815,000 students in the Minnesota public school system, less than 100 paid any sort of tuition to attend a public institution.[69] This resulted in parents with children in parochial schools becoming the virtual sole beneficiaries of the Minnesota statute's tax-funded assistance.[70]

Here, as in *Regan*, the belief that a tax deduction was indirect assistance led Justice Powell to join Chief Justice Burger, Justice White, and Justice Rehnquist, who wrote his first establishment clause opinion for the Court since coming to the Court in 1971. But that made just four votes. The final vote came from Justice O'Connor, who took part in her first parochaid case since her appointment to the Court in 1981, replacing Justice Stewart. Justice O'Connor agreed with Justice Powell that tax deductions, even in cases such as these, were indirect subsidies with benign consequences for religion.[71] But for all practical purposes, the voting alignments in *Mueller* and *Regan* were the same.

Justice Rehnquist attempted in his opinion to distinguish the cash reimbursement and tax-credit plan struck down in *Nyquist* and the tax-deduction statute at issue in *Mueller*, but he was not persuasive. In *Nyquist*, the Court held that tuition reimbursements were unconstitutional because that state's objective was to relieve parents' "financial burden sufficiently to assure that they continue to have the option to send their children to religion-oriented schools."[72] Tax deductions were invalidated on a similar basis because there was "little difference [from cash reimbursement] for purposes of whether such aid has the effect of advancing religion, between the tax benefit allowed here and the tuition grant."[73] Justice Rehnquist denied the similarities between the New York and Minnesota policies, holding that the latter statute applied across the board to all parents with children in the state education system, and specified no special treatment for parochial schools.[74] But these "vital differences" between the two statutes, as Justice Rehnquist referred to them,[75] are contrived. *Mueller* cannot be defended on the principles articulated in *Nyquist.*

What had changed was not the law, but the Court's values. Having watched financial assistance programs wither in *Lemon's* shadow, the Court's outcasts on parochaid, Chief Justice Burger and Justices White and Rehnquist, now had the votes to move the Court in a new direction. From appearances, it looked as if Justice Powell was breaking ranks with the Court's separationists and that Justice O'Connor, President Reagan's first Court appointee, was more conservative than her predecessor, Potter Stewart.

Regan and *Mueller* appeared to signal a retrenchment in the Court's approach to parochaid. There were other signals that the Court's establishment clause jurisprudence was undergoing reexamination. Later that term, with Justice Blackmun joining the *Mueller* coalition to forge a 6–3 majority,[76] the Court ruled that state-funded and -supported legislative chaplaincies did not violate the establishment clause. Of equal if not more significance was the Court's rationale in *Marsh.* For the first time since 1971, the Court refused to subject the challenged practice under the establishment clause to the *Lemon* test. The evidence indicated that portentious shifts in the Court's establishment clause jurisprudence were in the offing. Thus separationists were braced for the Court's decisions in *Grand Rapids v. Ball* (1985)[77] and *Aguilar v. Felton* (1985),[78] which were expected to make the public coffers open wide to parochial schools.

But the Court did not take the path of least resistance predicted of it. Instead, the Court pulled back from *Regan* and *Mueller.* In *Grand Rapids,* a 7–2 Court, with Justices Powell and O'Connor in the majority, invalidated a Michigan statute that authorized local school districts to offer courses in parochial schools during and after regular class hours. *Aguilar* was much closer. There, a 5–4 Court, with Justice Powell providing the swing vote, ruled unconstitutional a federal program that subsidized educational programs for low-income children in private and parochial schools. *Grand Rapids* and *Aguilar* thus rendered *Mueller* and *Regan* to the constitutional margins, and instilled new life into *Lemon* and the principles for which it stood. But Justice Powell's retirement two terms later and his replacement by Justice Kennedy indicated just how fragile the *Grand Rapids* and *Aguilar* coalitions were. In his first term, Justice Kennedy provided the fifth vote in a crucial parochaid case, *Bowen v. Kendrick*, which upheld a federal funding scheme that provided block grants to secular and religious organizations for sex education counseling. These three cases are illustrative of the evolution taking place in the Court's parochaid jurisprudence, one that now approves where it once suspected the use of state power to advance sectarian religious objectives.

Aguilar *and* Grand Rapids: Lemon *Retained*

Aguilar involved another challenge brought by the Committee on Public Education and Religious Liberty (PEARL) against the use of public funds for parochial education. PEARL, the brainchild of the distinguished church-state scholar and lawyer Leo Pfeffer, had been responsible for the pivotal lawsuits initiated in the early 1970s against state and federal parochaid programs that had formed the core of the Court's precedents in this area. *Aguilar* centered not on a state parochaid statute, but on the municipal administration of a remedial education program authorized under Title I of the Elementary and Secondary Education Act, a federal statute enacted in 1965.[79] Under Title I, local educational agencies were eligible for reimbursement from the federal government for educational services and programs if students under their jurisdiction qualified under the statute's guidelines as either low-income or educationally deprived. Title I did not compel specific programming, but instead encouraged local school districts "to employ imaginative thinking and new approaches to meet the educational needs of poor children."[80] But Title I did provide that students in religious schools were eligible for Title I funds "on an equitable basis" with students in public schools if such funds were distributed across-the-board.[81]

Aguilar challenged New York City's administration of Title I programs. New York's programming consisted of instructional classes (remedial reading and mathematics, learning skills, and English as a second language) and clinical services (guidance counseling and speech therapy). These services were available to public and parochial students on the premises of their respective schools.[82] Title I regulations banned professional educators who work in parochial schools from teaching or encouraging religious doctrines or taking part in other sectarian activities.[83] The New York municipal school authorities also required that all classrooms in which such instruction took place in parochial schools have all religious symbols and references removed.[84]

The Title I litigation began in 1978, when PEARL filed a complaint in federal district court charging that the Title I program violated the establishment clause because it resulted in a joint operating agreement between the government and religious schools.[85] The lawsuit alleged that the Title I program violated the second and third prongs of the *Lemon* test because it assisted religious schools in their educational objectives and resulted in excessive entanglement between government and religion because of the pervasive, endemic nature of surveillance and supervision of Title I implementation. In October 1980 the district court rejected PEARL's constitutional challenge to New York's administration of Title I. PEARL appealed to the Supreme Court, which dismissed the case.[86] PEARL initiated a second challenge in federal court, but was again rebuffed.[87] On appeal, a unanimous panel for the Second Circuit Court reversed. The appellate court held that municipal supervision of the program resulted in excessive entanglement because of the permanent nature of the supervision and surveillance.[88]

The Court affirmed. Justice Brennan, who also wrote the Court's opinion in *Grand Rapids*, held that New York's administration of Title I violated the effect and entanglement prongs of *Lemon*. Justice Brennan ruled that *Aguilar* failed the effect test because the overwhelming recipients of Title I were schools affiliated with the Catholic church.[89] But Justice Brennan made not excessive entanglement effect the focal point of his opinion. Wrote Justice Brennan: "Even where state aid to parochial institutions does not have the primary effect of advancing religion, the provision of such aid may nonetheless violate the Establishment Clause owing to the nature of the interaction of church and state in the administration of that aid."[90] The Court also held that the scope and duration of the Title I program required a pervasive state presence in sectarian schools, noting that "agents of the State must visit and inspect the religious school regularly, alert for the subtle or overt presence of religious matter in Title I classes."[91] Justice Powell, while joining the Court's opinion, wrote separately to emphasize the importance of nonentanglement. "The constitutional defect in the Title I program . . . is that it provides a direct financial subsidy to be administrered in significant part by public school teachers within parochial schools—resulting in both the advancement of religion and forbidden entanglement."[92]

But Justice Powell was also sympathetic to governmental efforts to assist low-income or educationally disadvantaged students in church-related schools. Justice Powell used his concurrence, as on occasion he did,[93] to suggest correctives to a defective statute, writing in *Aguilar* that if "Congress could fashion a program of evenhanded financial assistance to both public and private schools that could be administered, without governmental supervision in the private schools, so as to prevent the diversion of the aid from secular purposes," the Court would face a different, and perhaps, less troubling question.[94] Chief Justice Burger and Justice O'Connor, both of whom joined the section of the Court's opinion in *Grand Rapids* that invalidated the Michigan parochaid program on entanglement grounds, dissented in *Aguilar*. But Justice Rehnquist entered the most acerbic dissent, accusing the Court of creating a "'Catch 22' paradox . . . whereby aid must be supervised to ensure no entanglement but the supervision itself is held to cause an entanglement."[95] Justice Rehnquist also renewed his call, announced earlier that term in *Wallace v. Jaffree*, for the Court to abandon *Lemon*, overrule *Everson* and adopt a nonpreferentialist framework for establishment clause interpretation.[96] Justice Rehnquist seemed to have Justice Powell's sympathies on nonpreferential financial assistance to religion, but not in *Aguilar* or in *Grand Rapids*. But Justice Powell's retirement made such anticipation moot, as his replacement, Justice Anthony Kennedy, left no doubt about whether *Aguilar* and *Grand Rapids* would chart the Court's future parochaid jurisprudence or whether these decisions were the final legacies of a passing era.

Bowen v. Kendrick: *The Rehnquist Court Opens the Public Purse*

In 1981, Congress passed the Adolescent Family Life Act (AFLA), which provided direct federal grants to public and nonprofit agencies, including religious institutions, to promote research and provide services related to adolescent sexual relations and pregnancy-related concerns.[97] The AFLA contained a provision that prohibited funding for eligible institutions that performed abortions, provided abortion counseling, or encouraged abortion as an alternative to childbirth. Congressional initiative on the AFLA came as a result of a vigorous lobbying campaign by pro-life religious and secular organizations, such as the United States Catholic Conference, Concerned Women for America, and the National Right to Life Committee. An energetic opposition was mounted by a coalition of prochoice religious and secular organizations, including the American Jewish Congress, the Baptist Joint Committee, the American Civil Liberties Union, and numerous other representatives of the prochoice Protestant, Catholic, and Jewish communities.

Opponents of the AFLA argued that the statute conditioned the distribution of funds on the recipient institution's position on abortion, which meant that religious organizations would receive federal funds to promote religion-based views on abortion and procreation. Such a relationship violated the establishment clause because it permitted Congress to provide direct grants to religious organizations to advance religious objectives. But Congress went ahead and passed the AFLA, which amended the Adolescent Health Services and Pregnancy Prevention Act of 1978 expressly to make religious organizations eligible for federal funds.[98] Given the campaign support that many lawmakers received in the 1980 election from conservative religious organizations,[99] it is not surprising that Congress was persuaded into providing federal support to such groups to advance their abortion policies. No Protestant, Catholic, or Jewish organization that failed to exclude abortion in its sex education and counseling programs received funding under the AFLA, which further attested to the suspect motives of this legislation.[100] That the AFLA later survived an establishment clause attack, despite a clear record of using public funds in so inappropriate a fashion, indicated that the Court's stance on parochaid is on the verge of dramatic change.

Bowen v. Kendrick originated as a facial challenge to the AFLA brought in federal district court by a coalition of individual taxpayers, the American Jewish Congress, and the American Civil Liberties Union. The lawsuit contested the direct financial grants to religious institutions for adolescent sex education services and the provision that prohibited funding to any institution that performed abortions; provided abortion counseling; or that advocated, promoted, or encouraged abortion. The district court did not find that statute to have the primary purpose of advancing religion, but it did hold that the AFLA failed the effect and entanglement prongs of the *Lemon* test.[101] Since religious institutions were the principal beneficiaries under the AFLA, it was impossible to conclude that the statute did not have the effect of advancing religion, since sectarian influence was incorporated in the sex education program provided by those institutions.[102] The court also held that the degree of government supervision to ensure that AFLA recipients would not use their funds to advance religion was not consistent with the nonentangle-ment requirement of *Lemon*.[103] The Department of Health and Human Services (HHS), which was defending its enforcement of the statute, appealed directly to the Supreme Court.

The Court reversed. Chief Justice Rehnquist, writing for a 5–4 major-ity, wrote that "it [was] clear from the face of the statute that the AFLA was motivated primarily, if not entirely, by a legitimate secular purpose—the elimination or reduction of social and economic problems caused by teenage sexuality, pregnancy and parenthood."[104] Whatever benefits possibly accorded to sectarian institutions were "at most incidental and remote."[105] The Chief Justice also rejected the district court's conclusion that the AFLA advanced religion because the religious institutions eligi-ble for federal funds provided educational and counseling services to adolescents who were highly impressionable and easily persuaded to choose options not in their best interests due to religious inculcation.[106]

The Court also regarded as "unwarranted" the presumption that sec-tarian grantees were incapable of performing their responsibilities under the AFLA in a lawful, secular manner.[107] Nor did the Court agree with the district court conclusion that the AFLA was invalid because it authorized "teaching by religious grant recipients on matters [that] are fundamental elements of religious doctrine, such as the harm of premar-ital sex and the reasons for choosing adoption over abortion."[108] The Court held that such educational alternatives "are not themselves specif-ically religious activities, and they are not converted into such activities by the fact that they are carried out by organizations with religious affiliations."[109]

Justice Blackmun, who was joined by Justices Brennan, Marshall, and Stevens, wrote a telling dissent. The establishment clause was not in-tended to permit the government to fund the social objectives of religious bodies, and here, wrote Justice Blackmun, "the record . . . is all too clear [that] federal tax dollars appropriated for AFLA purposes have been used, with Government approval, to support religious teaching."[110] Did the establishment clause permit the AFLA to authorize sex education instruc-tion, and counseling that included these approaches:

You want to know the church teachings on sexuality. . . . You are the church. You people sitting here are the body of Christ. The teachings of you and the things you value are, in fact, the values of the Catholic Church.[111]

Justice Blackmun also asked whether the First Amendment allowed Congress to enact legislation that "encouraged the use of public funds for such instruction, by giving religious groups a central pedagogical and counseling role without imposing any restraints on the sectarian quality of the participation,"[112] including curricula that stated:

The Church has always taught that the marriage act, or intercourse, seals the union of husband and wife, [and is a representation of their union on all levels]. Christ commits Himself to us when we come to ask for the sacrament of marriage. We ask Him to be active in our life. God is love. We ask Him to share His love in ours, and God procreates with us, He enters into our physical union with Him, and we begin new life.[113]

Justice Blackmun accused the Court of ignoring the lessons of past cases in assuming that administrators of sectarian institutions would not

breach statutory proscriptions and use government funds earmarked "for secular purposes only," to finance theological instruction or religious worship, in order to reject a challenge based on the risk of indoctrination inherent in "educational services relating to family life and problems associated with adolescent premarital sexual relations," or "outreach services to families of adolescents to discourage sexual relations among unemancipated minors."[114]

Justice Blackmun also pointed out that the AFLA departed from previous such statutes upheld by the Court because it authorized direct money transfers to teachers and counselors in related programs for the sole purpose of educating "impressionable young minds on issues of religious moment."[115] This relationship created "a symbolic and real partnership between the clergy and the fisc in addressing a problem with substantial religious overtones."[116] Justice Blackmun also communicated his desire that the lower court, on remand, not "after all its labors thus far . . . grow weary prematurely and read into the Court's decision a suggestion that the AFLA has been constitutionally implemented by the Government," especially since the Court's opinion "eschew[ed] any review of the facts."[117]

Kendrick sounded a transition in the Court's parochaid jurisprudence. Gone was Justice Powell and in his place was Justice Kennedy. That was the difference in *Kendrick*'s outcome.[118] Justice Powell had voted to invalidate several statutes that provided direct cash grants or reimburse-

ment to religion.[119] In *Grand Rapids* and *Aguilar*, Justice Powell voted
to strike down less blatant forms of governmental assistance, but offensive enough in their intrusion into the religious sphere that neither could
survive under the establishment clause. Compare Justice Powell's concurring opinion in *Aguilar*, "[t]he constitutional defect in the Title I
program . . . is that it provides a direct financial subsidy to be administered
in significant part by public school teachers within parochial schools—
resulting in both the advancement of religion and forbidden entanglement,"[120] with Justice Kennedy's concurrence in *Kendrick*:

> In sum, where, as in this case, a statute provides that the benefits of a program are to
> be distributed in a neutral fashion to religious and non-religious applicants alike, and
> the program withstands a facial challenge, it is not unconsitutional as applied solely
> by reason of the religious character of a specific recipient. The question in an
> as-applied challenge is not whether the entity is of a religious character, but how it
> spends its grant.[121]

Kendrick was limited to a facial challenge to the AFLA. But even so,
there is little reason to believe that the Court would have decided the case
differently had the AFLA been attacked on as-applied grounds. The
Rehnquist Court had begun to consolidate in the 1987–88 term, and one
of the more visible characteristics of its jurisprudence was it highly
deferential posture toward majoritarian decision making. This deferential
posture toward the political process, combined with no clear-cut philosophy on what values the establishment clause imparts and protects,
considerably informs the Rehnquist Court's approach to judicial review.[122] In *Kendrick*, the Court swept aside contentions that the AFLA
advanced religion because of the funds that went to sectarian institutions
for religion-based sex education and related programs. The Court held
that the AFLA was consistent with neutrality toward religion because it
did not require grantees to have religious affiliations, but only made such
organizations, along with all other nonreligious agencies, eligible for
federal funds.[123]

Thus the Court in *Kendrick* gave the constitutional go-ahead to Congress to make religious institutions eligible for public funds to use for
worthwhile social welfare goals, stipulating only that statutes offering
such assistance must not make religion a requirement for eligibility or
exclusion. If the government can distribute public funds to religious
institutions for sex education and counseling, can more traditional
parochaid measures have less claim to such aid? Will the Rehnquist

Court, highly deferential to the policy determinations of the political process, make *Kendrick*, not *Lemon*, the jurisprudential framework applicable in parochaid cases that involve elementary and secondary schools? Will the Rehnquist Court abandon the *Lemon* test in parochaid cases in favor of a rational-basis analysis, concerned simply with a statute's adherence to facial neutrality? If the Court continues to value deference to the political process more than intervention to constrain government power in defense of constitutional principles, then the answer, unlike the action, is affirmative.

Tax Exemption for Religion

In *Walz v. Tax Commission* (1970), the Court turned back a challenge to a New York statute that exempted religious property used for worship and related activities from general taxation regulations, holding that the primary purpose and effect of tax exemption for religious institutions and their related endeavors was not to promote or sponsor religion, but to ensure the independence of religion from the state.[124] For an 8–1 Court, Chief Justice Burger wrote that "[t]he exemption creates only a minimal and remote involvement between church and state and far less than taxation of churches. It restricts the fiscal relationship between church and state, and tends to complement and reinforce the desired separation insulating each from the other."[125] The Court had no constitutional foundation on which to base *Walz*; indeed, it even appeared, as Justice William O. Douglas pointed out in dissent, that tax exemption flouted *Everson* and the no-aid interpretation of the establishment clause.[126]

But the Court recognized that the Constitution alone did not inform the position taken in *Walz*. Chief Justice Burger, with the almost unanimous support of the Court, ruled that the historical record of tax exemption for religious institutions in the United States had been universal and uninterrupted.[127] That position was confirmed in the *amicus curiae* brief submitted by an ecumenical coalition of religious organizations supporting tax exemptions.[128] To buttress the Court's position that legislative tax exemptions advanced no religious purpose or effect, Chief Justice Burger added a third component to the *Schempp* test—entanglement:

> We must also be sure that the end result—the effect—is not an excessive government entanglement with religion. The test is inescapably one of degree. Either course, taxation or churches, occasions some involvement with religion. Elimination of

exemption would tend to expand the involvement of government by giving rise to tax valuation of church property, tax liens, tax foreclosures, and the direct confrontations and conflicts that follow in the train of those legal processes.[129]

The Court did not apply the newly constituted purpose-effect-entanglement test in full-force until the Court's next term in *Lemon v. Kurtzman*, which constituted a quite different context than *Walz*. The nonentanglement requirement developed in *Walz* became an inseparable component of the Court's establishment clause jurisprudence, especially in the parochaid sphere, where it often served as the fatal blow to government programs authorizing direct financial aid to religion.[130] Concern for nonentanglement was crucial in explaining the Court's posture toward tax exemption. Tax exemption neither harmed nor helped religion, and this benevolent position allowed religion to prosper free from the potentially corrupt and disruptive influence of the state. In this sense, the Court paid homage to Chief Justice John Marshall's admonition that the power to tax is the power to destroy.[131]

But tax exemption for religion is not absolute. Although federal and state tax codes recognize broad categorical exemption for religious institutions and their worship-related activities, governmental authorities have also classified certain religion-based conduct, whether exercised at the corporate or individual level, as not entitled to tax-exempt status. Governmental power to revoke the tax-exempt status of religious institutions or to deny individual religion-based claims is known as the "public policy doctrine."[132] Under this doctrine, governmental authorities possess the affirmative power to withold and revoke the tax exempt status of otherwise qualified institutions including religious institutions, whose policies and practices violate a compelling public policy interest. Since *Walz*, the Court has ruled on several occasions that conduct detrimental to broader societal interests is not entitled to tax-exempt status, even if such conduct is rooted in religious beliefs. The Court's rulings on religion-based tax exemption claims against the government have followed its overall trend to accord sweeping deference to the political process and to give little weight to individual claims against the government. The Court's decisions have had the most adverse effect, not surprisingly, on small or unpopular religions, those least likely to influence the outcome of the political process.

The most difficult case decided by the Court in the tax-exemption area and one that epitomizes the legal and moral complexities that make government regulation of religious institutions such a difficult and sensitive issue was *Bob Jones University v. U.S.* (1983).[133] Located in Greensville, South Carolina, Bob Jones University is a private, religious institution that places a special emphasis on the fundamental tenets of Christianity and the ethics revealed in the Holy Scriptures in its curriculum and code of students' conduct. Bob Jones believes that the Bible forbids interracial dating and marriage. Bob Jones refused to admit blacks until 1971, when the IRS announced that it could no longer find legal justification for allowing the university to retain tax-exempt status, ruling that admissions policies based on opposition to miscegnation violated a compelling public policy objective. In response to the determination of the IRS, Bob Jones modified its admissions policies to admit blacks who were married; in 1975, the university again changed its admissions policies, this time to admit single blacks, but continued to compel the segregation of students on campus, including their living arrangements, and to prohibit interracial dating and marriage.

That failed to satisfy the IRS. In 1976, the IRS revoked the tax-exempt status of Bob Jones University retroactive to 1970, and forced it to pay taxes accumulated during the intervening years. After a dispute over Bob Jones's tax obligation to the government ended in favor of the IRS, the university filed suit in federal district court, arguing that the free exercise clause prohibited the government from using tax power to force compliance with public policy inconsistent with their religious beliefs.[134] The court found in favor of Bob Jones, forcing the government to appeal. The Fourth Circuit reversed, interpreting the public policy doctrine to authorized wide latitude to the IRS in revoking the tax exempt status of institutions not in compliance with those goals, including religious organizations and worship bodies.[135]

The Supreme Court accepted *Bob Jones* for review during the 1981 term. But shortly after the Court announced its decision, President Reagan announced that the IRS was wrong in denying tax-exempt status to Bob Jones University. The president said that the provision in the IRS code permitting revocation of tax-exempt status for private institutions that practiced racial discrimination was excessive and an illegal arrogation of government power. The Department of Justice then filed an *amicus curiae* brief with the Court in support of Bob Jones. Since this action left the IRS without legal representation, the Court appointed William T. Coleman, President Ford's transportation secretary and one of the most prominent black Republicans at the national level. The Reagan administration's position in *Bob Jones* resulted in widespread and passionate criticism from career lawyers in the Department of Justice's civil rights division, Congress, and liberal civil rights groups, all of whom were astonished to find that President Reagan could lend the power and prestige of the federal government to behavior so wholly adverse to contemporary public policy as that of Bob Jones University. The Reagan administration, reacting to the nearly universal condemnation of its initial position in the case, reversed itself and defended the ruling of the IRS.[136]

In 1983, the Court, over the sole dissent of Chief Justice Rehnquist, held that the IRS had acted within its statutory authority when it revoked the tax exemption of Bob Jones University.[137] The Court did not address Bob Jones as a religious organization and the nature of the religious beliefs that formed the basis for its discriminatory policies, but as an educational institution. Thus, the Court ruled that the government's "fundamental, overriding interest in eradicating racial discrimination in education . . . substantially outweigh[ed] whatever burden denial of tax benefits places on its [free] exercise of religious beliefs."[138] The Court focused not on the religion-based claim of Bob Jones, but on its role as an institution of higher education. Discrimination in education, at whatever level, was not consistent with established public policy on issues of racial equality:

> [t]he governmental interest at stake here is compelling.. . . [T]he Government has a fundamental, overriding interest in eradicating racial discrimination in education— discrimination that prevailed, with official approval, for the first 165 years of this Nation's history. That governmental interest substantially outweighs whatever burden denial of tax benefits places on petitioners' exercise of their religious beliefs. The interests asserted by petitioners cannot be accommodated with that compelling governmental interest, . . . and no "less restrictive means," are available to achieve the governmental interest.[139]

The Court had never held that government lacked the power to order compliance with government regulations simply on the grounds that the request for exemptions to such regulations are religion-based. Just the previous term, the Court ruled that the government's public policy interest in uniform compliance with federal tax regulations enabled it to deny religion-based exemption from federal tax regulations on the public policy doctrine,[140] even if such a decision burdened religious free exercise. In *Bob Jones*, the Court acknowledged that the IRS ruling burdened the operating practices of the university, and would burden the operation of private religious schools in general. But the Court held that the distinction between the constitutional protection afforded to religious belief and that given to religious conduct had always differed.[141] The government's interest in nondiscrimination in higher education was compelling, said the Court; and that determination did not come at the expense of religious belief, but conduct. Upon the demonstration of a compelling state interest, the latter was within the scope of governmental power to regulate.

The facts in *Bob Jones* torment even-handed analysis of the constitutional issues. The government has an undeniable compelling interest in enforcing nondiscrimination in education, and revocation of the tax-exempt status of educational institutions that engage in racial discrimination is a perfectly legitimate governmental response to such behavior. But another, troubling question lurked not too far in the background. If the government can revoke the tax-exempt status of sectarian universities that discriminate, then can it also force churches to comply with federal antidiscrimination law in their employment and hiring decisions; or compel churches or synagogues to admit women into ministerial or rabbinical training; or hold clergy accountable to secular courts for malpractice; or make religious bodies subject to federal tax regulation?

In *Bob Jones*, the Court did not address these possibilities. The Court confined *Bob Jones* to the facts, and treated the case as one involving discrimination in higher education, not one that questioned the scope of government intervention in religious affairs. Still, the case is not as simple as holding educational institutions accountable in their treatment of racial minorities. *Bob Jones* was, after all, also about the right to autonomy of religious institutions. And autonomy for church-related institutions is at the heart of religious liberty.[142] *Bob Jones* may, over time, turn out to be a special case, one whose fusion of highly charged religious and secular values forced an outcome that avoided making new constitutional law and instead required a narrow resolution to a politically uncomfortable situation.

The Court also has ruled that individual requests for religion-based exemptions to federal tax rules are not required under the free exercise clause because compliance with such regulations is related to the compelling governmental interest of enforcing uniform compliance with this basic responsibility of citizenship. In *U.S. v. Lee* (1982)[143] and *Bowen v.*

Roy (1986),[144] the Court refused to grant such a religion-based exemption to individual members of the Old Order Amish and Native American church, respectively, on the grounds that the government has a compelling interest in enforcing compliance with federal tax regulations, which are generally applicable, even if such compliance results in the supression of a faith-compelled practice. In each case, the Court invoked the belief-action distinction long used to explain that, while powerless to control or criminalize held or professed religious beliefs, the government possessed the legitimate power to regulate religious practices when a compelling governmental interest required such intervention. In each case, the Court ruled that enforcing citizen compliance with the tax system was a governmental interest of the highest order, and that to recognize a religion-based exemption under the free exercise clause would undermine "this most basic purpose of government"[145] and require "the government to conduct its own internal affairs in ways that comport with the religious beliefs of particular citizens."[146] *Lee* was unanimous; *Roy* was decided 8–1.

Lee and *Roy* were discomforting on another level. In *Lee*, the Court applied the compelling state interest/least restrictive means test in holding that members of the Old Order Amish were not entitled to a religion-based exemption from social security taxes. The unanimous decision in *Lee* indicated little disagreement within the Court on the compelling interest of the government to enforce uniform provisions of the tax code as one that outweighed whatever burden it placed on religious free exercise.[147] But Justice Stevens entered an ominous concurrence expressing his discomfort with the Court's continued practice of subjecting free exercise claims made against generally applicable statutes to the compelling state interest test. Justice Stevens wrote that "the objector . . . must shoulder the burden of demonstrating" the reason for a religion-based exemption from a facially neutral law having application to the general population, not the government.[148] Justice Stevens's concurrence did not appear to signal that changes were on the horizon in the Court's free exercise jurisprudence. But four years later, the Court indicated that a less formidable burden on the government was appropriate in cases when an alleged infringement on religious free exercise resulted from enforcement of a generally applicable law.

In *Roy*, the Court rejected a free exercise challenge brought by Native American parents requesting a religion-based exemption for their daughter from a federal regulation requiring participants in AFDC and food stamp programs to hold a social security number. Chief Justice Burger, in his plurality opinion, wrote that "[a]bsent proof of an intent to discriminate . . . , the government meets its burden when it demonstrates that a challenged requirement for government benefits, neutral and uniform in its application, is a *reasonable means of promoting a legitimate interest*."[149] The Chief Justice was unable to command a majority on this point, but the Court's increasing tendency to view free exercise claims brought against generally applicable laws as subject to review under a rational basis test was discouraging. Concurring, Justice O'Connor wrote that judicial guidelines in free exercise cases should not vary according to whether the issue involved government penalties for religious conduct or denial of government benefits under generally applicable laws.[150] Justice O'Connor, joined by Justices Brennan and Marshall, was troubled by the plurality's casual use of the reasonableness standard to review free exercise claims:

> Even if the Founding Fathers did not live in a society with the broad range of benefits [and] complex programs that the Federal Government administers today, they constructed a society in which the Constitution placed express limits upon governmental actions limiting the freedoms of that society's members. The rise of the welfare state was not the fall of the Free Exercise Clause.[151]

Justice O'Connor further criticized the Chief Justice's approach to such cases, writing that the reasonableness standard had "no basis in precedent and relegates a serious First Amendment value to the barest level of minimal scrutiny."[152] The Chief Justice did not muster the votes in *Roy* to make the reasonableness standard binding in future cases. But the Court's pattern of calling for a reconsideration of the compelling state interest test to analyze free exercise cases involving challenges to neutral statutes was an obvious signal that a major departure from the Court's settled jurisprudence in this area was on the horizon. Four years after *Roy*, the Court held in *Employment Division of Oregon v. Smith* (1990) that claims brought under the free exercise clause alleging that a generally applicable law placed a burden on religion-based conduct were not entitled to strict scrutiny.[153] I discuss the disastrous consequences of this decision in much more detail in chapter 5. But *Lee* and *Roy* sent signals long before *Smith* that the Court was becoming much more deferential to stated governmental objectives in free exercise cases involving tax exemption.

The Court decided two more important cases involving governmental power to tax religious institutions and their faith-compelled activities, *Texas Monthly v. Bullock* (1989)[154] and *Swaggart v. Board of Equalization* (1990).[155] Unlike *Lee* and *Roy*, *Texas Monthly* did not involve a request for a religion-based exemption to a neutral state statute that burdened religious free exercise, but an establishment clause challenge to the constitutionality of such an exemption. In *Texas Monthly*, the plaintiff argued that a provision in the Texas tax code that exempted religious publications from state sales tax amounted to an unconstitutional preference for religion because religious publications were entitled to a special benefit through statute not available to the general population. A state district court agreed that a tax exemption for religious publications violated the establishment clause, but the Texas Court of Appeals reversed.[156]

The Supreme Court, 6–3, ruled that the Texas statute violated the establishment clause because it advanced religion. While the Court acknowledged that it had long upheld the power of the political process to permit religion-based exemptions to laws having general application, the Texas statute set aside special benefits for religion not available to the general population. The Court acknowledged as well that neutral statutes having a secular purpose which nonetheless resulted in incidental benefits to religion were constitutional, but under the Texas statute religious institutions were the sole beneficiaries of the tax exemption. Because the tax exemption was religion-specific, the Court held that it was "difficult to view Texas' narrow exemption as anything but State sponsorship of religious belief."[157] The Court rejected the free exercise arguments of the plaintiffs, holding that tax exemption for religion was required when the government could demonstrate a compelling interest.[158]

Justice Scalia, joined by Chief Justice Rehnquist and Justice Kennedy, entered a blistering dissent. Justice Scalia called the Court's opinion a "judicial demolition project" that had "no basis in the text of the Constitution, the decisions of this Court or the traditions of our people for disapproving th[e] longstanding and widespread practice" of granting religion-based exemptions to generally applicable laws.[159] Justice Scalia said that *Walz* controlled the establishment clause issues presented in *Texas Monthly*.[160] In *Walz*, the Court held that tax exemptions did not subsidize religion, but left it free to flourish independent of corrosive state regulation. The Court, said Justice Scalia, had taken the view that what is not required under the religion clauses is not permitted, a rule that would make it almost impossible for religious exemptions to survive constitutional review.[161]

Whatever the merits of Justice Scalia's arguments in *Texas Monthly*, it is impossible to reconcile them with his opinion the following Term in *Smith*. In *Smith*, Justice Scalia held that the free exercise clause did not require the Court to review religion-based claims to generally applicable laws under the compelling interest test. Such exemptions, said Justice Scalia, were "constitutional anomal[ies]" with no claim to compelled constitutional protection. In fact, Justice Scalia said that the Court had never recognized the right to such exemptions.[162] But in *Texas Monthly*, Justice Scalia criticized the Court's refusal to grant an exemption to religious publications under the Texas law, and pointed out that it had, in similar cases, "*required* religious beliefs to be accommodated by granting religion-specific exemptions from otherwise applicable laws."[163]

In *Swaggart*, decided just four months before *Smith*, a unanimous Court held that a generally applicable state statute that did not exempt from sales and use taxes religious materials and literature sold within the state and through mail-order nationwide did not violate the religion clauses. The Court held that the California law at issue in *Swaggart* did not amount to a flat tax or prior restraint on the dissemination of religious speech.[164] Because the statute was facially neutral, did not interfere with religious worship, and did not discriminate against religious institutions, the Court held that the California law did not violate the religion clauses.[165] In *Swaggart*, Justice Scalia joined a unanimous Court. When one considers the Court's posture in *Texas Monthly* and *Swaggart*, the crucial lesson that emerges is the further concentration of power in the political process to legislate in the arena of religion.

Conclusion

Debate over the power of government to aid parochial institutions has been controversial since the First Amendment first formally disestablished religion from the state. James Madison's admonition in the *Memorial and Remonstrance Against Religious Assessments* that "the same authority which can force a citizen to contribute three pence only of his property for the support of any one establishment, may force him to conform to any other establishment in all cases" provides the philosophical foundation for absolute position under the establishment clause against government aid to religion. For government to provide public funds to religious institutions breaches the establishment clause because it compels the general population to support private religion. The principle is simple, but its enforcement is clouded with political turbulence. In the modern administrative welfare state, interest groups clamor for public funds to subsidize every imaginable endeavor and then some. Religious organizations are not immune from the pull of the Madisonian model of factional pluralism; they, too, are powerful representatives of important constituencies; and they, too, are entitled to express their views on public affairs.

But religious institutions are not entitled to public funds, no matter how righteous their cause, how good their works and how noble their faith-compelled mission. Religious institutions an perform indispensable service as mediating institutions in caring for the sick, educating the poor, feeding the hungry, and sheltering the homeless. But the government cannot support the callings of faith any more than it can prohibit them. The separation of religion from the state is the predicate of religious freedom; if government is prohibited from exercising jurisdiction over religious conscience; if government is prohibited from intervening in the internal affairs of religion; and if government is prohibited from supporting or disturbing religion, the religion cannot, consistent with the Madisonian vision, extract from government what government cannot extract from religion. Independence from government financial coercion or comfort is the price of religious freedom.

In *Everson*, the Court articulated a "no aid" interpretation of the establishment clause, but it never made that position the law. Still, the Court, after *Everson* and through the early 1980s, interpreted the wall of separation with resonance. The Court ruled unconstitutional most direct governmental aid to religious institutions, and did so in the face of substantial political pressure. The Court struck down scores of state parochaid programs and invalidated key provisions of federal education statutes whose passage had come after pressure from politically powerful segments of organized religion. The Court did waver on occasion from the separation principle, motivated by pragmatism over principle, but it managed to remain true to the text and intent of the establishment clause, even if it was a *de facto* Brennan Court, and not the Burger Court, that led the charge.

But the salad era of private religion's severence from the public purse is over. While the Rehnquist Court has decided just one case involving public aid to religious institutions, it has demonstrated in several others that deference to the political process, whether at the national or state level, operates at the center of its religion clause jurisprudence. In *Kendrick* and in the tax exemption cases it decided, the Court found in favor of the government. Yet, this deferential posture yielded disparate substantive outcomes: politically powerful religious groups have been successful in seeking public funds from government to support their private education and social welfare work, all of which promotes majoritarian religious values. But smaller religions and unpopular faiths, unable to persuade majoritarian bodies, lose in the Rehnquist Court. The triumph of deference means the triumph of political will, a value foreign to the intent of the establishment clause, but nevertheless one that stands poised to radically restructure the financial relationship between government and religion.

Notes

1. For a discussion of the Warren Court and the backlash it produced, see, for example, Archibald Cox, *The Court and the Constitution* (New York: Houghton Mifflin, 1986); Bernard Schwartz, *Super Chief: Earl Warren and the Supreme Court* (New York: New York University Press, 1983); Cox, *The Warren Court* (Cambridge, Mass.: Harvard University Press, 1968).
2. See, for example, Schwartz, *Super Chief*; John Hart Ely, *Democracy and Distrust* (Cambridge, Mass.: Harvard University Press, 1978).
3. See, for example, Robert Bork, *The Tempting of America* (New York: The Free Press, 1990).
4. E.g., *Katzenbach v. Morgan*, 384 U.S. 641 (1965); *Katzenbach v. McClung*, 379 U.S. 294 (1964); *Brown v. Board of Education*, 347 U.S. 483 (1954).
5. E.g., *Miranda v. Arizona*, 384 U.S. 436 (1966); *Escobedo v. Illinois*, 378 U.S. 478 (1965); *Mapp v. Ohio*, 367 U.S. 643 (1961).
6. E.g., *Reynolds v. Sims*, 377 U.S. 533 (1964); *Baker v. Carr*, 369 U.S. 186 (1962).
7. 370 U.S. 421 (1962).
8. 374 U.S. 203 (1963).
9. Bernard Schwartz, *The Ascent of Pragmatism: The Burger Court in Action* (Reading, Mass.: Addison-Wesley, 1990), 187.
10. 347 U.S. 483 (1954).
11. 367 U.S. 643 (1961).
12. 384 U.S. 436 (1966).
13. *Engel* and *Schempp* were each decided over one dissent; each dissent was filed by Justice Potter Stewart.

14. *Gallagher v. Crown Kosher Market*, 366 U.S. 617 (1961); *Braunfeld v. Brown*, 366 U.S. 599 (1961); *Two Guys v. McGinley*, 366 U.S. 582 (1961); *McGowan v. Maryland*, 366 U.S. 420 (1961).
15. *McGowan*, 366 U.S. at 444–45 (1961).
16. 392 U.S. 236 (1968).
17. Id. at 244–47.
18. *Epperson v. Arkansas*, 393 U.S. 97 (1968) (holding Arkansas statute making criminal the teaching of evolution in state schools, including colleges and universites to violate establishment clause).
19. 333 U.S. 203 (1948).
20. 343 U.S. 306 (1952).
21. 330 U.S. 1 (1947).
22. Id. at 15.
23. Id. at 18.
24. Id.
25. See, for example, Robert F. Drinan, *Religion, the Courts and Public Policy* (New York: McGraw-Hill, 1963).
26. Id. at 26–27 (Justice Jackson, dissenting).
27. *Torcaso v. Watkins*, 367 U.S. 488 (1961).
28. *U.S. v. Seeger*, 380 U.S. 163 (1965).
29. The Court struck down parochaid statutes in whole or in substantial part in *Aguilar v. Felton*, 473 U.S. 402 (1985); *Grand Rapids v. Ball*, 473 U.S. 373 (1985); *New York v. Cathedral Academy*, 434 U.S. 125 (1977); *Wolman v. Walter*, 432 U.S. 229 (1977) (striking down, in part, provisions of an Ohio statute that permitted state reimbursement to parochial schools for special educational services); *Meek v. Pettinger*, 421 U.S. 349 (1975); *Wheeler v. Barrera*, 417 U.S. 402 (1974); *Sloan v. Lemon*, 413 U.S. 825 (1973); *PEARL v. Nyquist*, 413 U.S. 756 (1973); *Levitt v. PEARL*, 413 U.S. 472 (1973); *Norwood v. Hardison*, 413 U.S. 455 (1973); and *Lemon v. Kurtzman*, 403 U.S. 602 (1971).
    The Court upheld parochaid programs in whole or in part in *Mueller v. Allen*, 463 U.S. 388 (1983); *PEARL v. Regan*, 444 U.S. 646 (1980); *Wolman v. Walter*, 432 U.S. 229 (1977) (upholding section of Ohio parochaid scheme that allowed public school employees to provide diagnostic services and remedial services to religious schools); *Lemon v. Kurtzman II*, 411 U.S. 192 (1973).
30. E.g., *Mueller v. Allen*, 463 U.S. 388 (1983); *Wollman v. Walter*, 433 U.S. 229 (1977) (upholding provisions of an Ohio statute permitting public school employees to provide in-house diagnostic services to religious schools and remedial services to parochial students off campus, but striking down provision authorizing state reimbursement for other educational services).
31. E.g., *Aguilar v. Felton*, 473 U.S. 402 (1985) (ruling the municipal administration of Title I of the federal Elementary and Secondary Education Act of 1965 in New York City parochial schools to violate the entanglement prong of the *Lemon* test); *Grand Rapids v. Ball*, 473 U.S. 373 (1985) (holding a state program that permitted public school teachers to offer general curriculum courses in parochial schools during regular and after-school hours violative of the establishment clause); *Meek v. Pettinger*, 421 U.S. 349 (1975) (striking down a Pennsylvania law allowing the state to furnish auxiliary support services to parochial schools); *PEARL v. Nyquist*, 413 U.S. 756 (1973) (ruling that a New York state funding scheme designed to relieve parents of parochial school students of tax and tuition burdens violated the establishment clause); *Lemon v. Kurtzman*, 403 U.S. 602 (1971) (declaring govern-

ment block grants and financial subsidies for parochial schools to pay salaries and other costs associated with instruction unconstitutional).

32. E.g., *Witters v. Washington*, 474 U.S. 481 (1986) (holding extension of aid under state vocational rehabilitation program to finance ministerial student at sectarian college not to violate establishment clause); *Hunt v. McNair*, 413 U.S. 734 (1982) (upholding state bond issue for construction of academic buildings for nonreligious purposes by sectarian schools); *Tilton v. Richardson*, 403 U.S. 672 (1971) (upholding federal program providing public funds for construction of academic buildings at sectarian colleges).

33. For effective criticism of the leadership skills of Warren Burger as Chief Justice, see, for example, Schwartz *The Ascent of Pragmatism*; Joseph F. Kobylka, "Leadership on the Supreme Court of the United States: Chief Justice Burger and the Establishment Clause," 42 *Western Political Quarterly* 545 (1989); Vincent Blasi, "The Rootless Activism of the Burger Court," in *The Burger Court: The Counterrevolution That Wasn't*, ed., Vincent Blasi, (New Haven, Conn.: Yale University Press, 1983), 198–217.

34. Kobylka, "Leadership on the Supreme Court."

35. 403 U.S. 602 (1971).

36. Id. at 612–15.

37. *Bowen v. Kendrick*, 108 S.Ct. 2562 (1988).

38. 397 U.S. 664 (1971).

39. Id. at 672–74.

40. Id. at 669.

41. Ecumenical support for tax exemption was unanimous in *Walz*. Religious organizations filing *amicus curiae* briefs in *Walz* included the National Council of Churches; the Synagogue Council of America (representing the American Jewish Committee, American Jewish Congress, Anti-Defamation League of B'nai B'rith and numerous Orthodox, Conservative and Reform congregations); the United States Catholic Conference; the Baptist Joint Committee on Public Affairs; and the National Jewish Commission on Law and Public Affairs.

42. For a discussion of religious organizations' positions in subsequent tax exemption cases, see Gregg Ivers, "Organized Religion and the Supreme Court," 32 *Journal of Church and State* 775–930 (1990); Leo Pfeffer, "Amici in Church-State Litigation," 44 *Law and Contemporary Problems*, 83–110 (1981). The one exception to this pattern came in *Bob Jones University v. U.S.*, 461 U.S. 574 (1983). In *Bob Jones*, the Anti-Defamation League of B'nai B'rith and the American Jewish Committee filed separate *amicus* briefs on behalf of the IRS's position refusing to grant tax exemption to educational institutions that discriminated on the basis of race.

43. *Swaggart Ministeries v. Board of Equalization*, 110 S.Ct. 688 (1990); *U.S. v. Lee*, 455 U.S. 252 (1981).

44. *Bowen v. Roy*, 476 U.S. 693 (1986).

45. *Swaggart Ministeries v. Board of Equalization*, 110 S.Ct. 688 (1990); *Bowen v. Roy*, 476 U.S. 693 (1986).

46. 392 U.S. 236, 243 (1968).

47. Id. at 244.

48. See *Schempp*, 374 U.S. at 222 (1963) ("The test may be stated as follows: what are the purpose and the primary effect of the enactment? If either is the advancement or inhibition of religion then the enactment exceeds the scope of legislative power as circumscribed by the Constitution").

49. *Allen*, 368 U.S. at 252 (Justice Black, dissenting).

50. Id. at 253.
51. *Everson*, 330 U.S. at 16.
52. See, for example, Richard E. Morgan, *The Supreme Court and Religion* (New York: The Free Press, 1972).
53. *Lemon*, 403 U.S. at 608.
54. Id. at 609–11.
55. Id. at 613.
56. Id. at 614.
57. *Walz*, 397 U.S. at 674.
58. See note 29, *supra*.
59. *Marsh v. Chambers*, 463 U.S. 783 (1983).
60. E.g., *Aguilar v. Felton*, 473 U.S. 402 (1985) (Justices Brennan, Marshall, Blackmun, Powell, and Stevens forming majority to strike down federal parochaid plan); *Grand Rapids v. Ball*, 473 U.S. 373 (1985) (Justices Brennan, Marshall, Blackmun, Powell, and Stevens forming majority striking down state parochaid program permitting secular teachers in religious schools); *New York v. Cathedral Academy*, 434 U.S. 125 (1977) (Justices Brennan, Marshall, Blackmun, Powell, and Stewart forming majority to strike down statute authorizing reimbursement to sectarian schools for expenses related to performing state testing and administrative services); *Meek v. Pettinger*, 421 U.S. 349 (1975) (Justices Brennan, Marshall, Blackmun, Powell, and Stewart forming majority to strike down in part state statute that provided auxiliary services to parochial schools); *Sloan v. Lemon*, 413 U.S. 825 (1973) (Justices Brennan, Marshall, Blackmun, Powell, and Stewart forming majority to strike down state reimbursement plan for parochial schools).
61. The Chief Justice wrote for the Court in *Tilton v. Richardson*, 403 U.S. 672 (1971), decided on the same day as *Lemon*. In *Tilton*, the Court, 5–4, upheld Title I of the Higher Education Facilities Act of 1963, which provided construction grants for buildings and facilities used exclusively for secular educational purposes.
62. 413 U.S. 472 (1973).
63. This data is collected is Leo Pfeffer, *Religion, State and the Burger Court* (Buffalo, N.Y.: Prometheus Books, 1984).
64. 444 U.S. 646 (1980).
65. 463 U.S. 388 (1983).
66. In *Regan*, Justices Powell and Stewart joined Chief Justice Burger and Justices White and Rehnquist to form the 5–4 majority. In *Mueller*, Justice O'Connor, who replaced Justice Stewart in 1981, joined this alignment to form the 5–4 majority.
67. *Regan*, 444 U.S. at 657–59.
68. Minn.Stat. Sec. 290.09, subd. 22 (1982).
69. *Mueller*, 463 U.S. at 405 (Justice Marshall, dissenting).
70. Id. at 401.
71. For a discussion of the Justices' rationale, see Schwartz, *The Ascent of Pragmatism*, 190–99, 194.
72. *Nyquist*, 413 U.S. at 783.
73. Id. at 790–91.
74. *Mueller*, 463 U.S. at 397.
75. Id. at 398.
76. *Marsh v. Chambers*, 463 U.S. 783 (1983).
77. 473 U.S. 373 (1985).
78. 473 U.S. 402 (1985).

79. The Elementary and Secondary Education Act of 1965, Pub.L. 89–10, 92 Stat. 2153, 20 U.S.C. 2740 *et. seq.*

80. The Elementary and Secondary Education Act of 1965, 20 U.S.C, at 2701.

81. Id.

82. *Aguilar*, 473 U.S. at 404–07.

83. Id.

84. *Aguilar*, 473 U.S. at 407.

85. *PEARL v. Harris*, 489 F.Supp. 1248 (S.D. N.Y. 1980).

86. *PEARL v. Harris, appeal dismissed on jurisdictional grounds*, 449 U.S. 808 (1980).

87. 489 F.Supp. 1248 (1980).

88. *Felton v. Secretary, U.S. Department of Education*, 739 F.2d 48 (1984).

89. *Aguilar*, 473 U.S. at 412–14.

90. Id. at 409.

91. Id. at 413.

92. Id. at 418 (Justice Powell, concurring).

93. E.g., *Wallace v. Jaffree*, 472 U.S. 38, 62–67 (1985) (Justice Powell concurring).

94. *Aguilar*, 473 U.S. at 420 (Justice Powell, concurring).

95. Id. at 420–21 (Justice Rehnquist, dissenting).

96. Id.

97. The Adolescent Family Life Act, Pub.L. 97–35, Stat. 578, 42 U.S.C. Sec. 300z *et. seq.*

98. The Adolescent Health Services and Pregnancy Prevention Act of 1978, 92 Stat. 3595–3601.

99. For an excellent description of this phenomenon, see, for example, Matthew C. Moen, *The Christian Right and Congress* (Tuscaloosa, Ala.: University of Alabama Press, 1989); A. James Reichley, *Religion and American Public Life* (Washington, D.C.: The Brookings Institution, 1985), 311–39.

100. See *Bowen v. Kendrick*, 108 S.Ct. 2562, 2582 (1988) (Justice Blackmun, dissenting).

101. *Kendrick v. Bowen*, 657 F.Supp 1547 (D.C. 1987).

102. Id. at 1554.

103. Id. at 1568.

104. *Bowen v. Kendrick*, 108 S.Ct. 2562, 2571 (1988).

105. Id. at 2573.

106. Id. at 2572.

107. Id. at 2575–76.

108. Id. at 2576.

109. Id.

110. Id. at 2583 (Justice Blackmun, dissenting).

111. Id.

112. Id.

113. Id.

114. Id. at 2589.

115. Id. at 2589.

116. Id. at 2596.

117. Id. at 2596–97.

118. Justice Scalia, still in his second term, voted to uphold the AFLA. But there is little doubt that Chief Justice Burger, whom he replaced, would also have voted to uphold the statute.

119. See note 60, *supra*.

120. See *Aguilar*, 473 U.S. at 413 (Justice Powell, concurring).

121. Id. at 2582 (Justice Kennedy, concurring).

123. *Kendrick*, 108 S.Ct. at 2570-71.

124. *Walz v. Tax Commission*, 397 U.S. 664, 674-675 (1970).

125. Id. at 676.

126. Id. at 703 (Justice Douglas, dissenting).

127. Id.

128. See Note 41, *supra*.

129. *Walz*, 397 U.S. at 674.

130. E.g., *Aguilar v. Felton*, 373 U.S. 402 (1985); *Grand Rapids v. Ball*, 473 U.S. 373 (1985); *New York v. Cathedral Academy*, 434 U.S. 125 (1977); *PEARL v. Nyquist*, 413 U.S. 756 (1973); *Lemon v. Kurtzman*, 403 U.S. 602 (1971).

131. *McCulloch v. Maryland*, 17 U.S. 316 (1819).

132. E.g., *Tank Truck Rentals v. Commissioner*, 356 U.S. 30 (1958) (holding that "public policy doctrine" authorized IRS to rule that business expenses could not be deducted for tax purposes where the allowance of such deductions would frustrate sharply defined national or state policies proscribing particular types of conduct); *Green v. Connally*, 330 F. Supp. 1150 (D.D.C. 1971), *aff'd per curiam sub nom, Coit v. Green*, 404 U.S. 997 (1971) (upholding court order compelling the IRS to deny tax-exempt status to racially discriminatory private schools on grounds that federal public policy prohibited racial discrimination in education).

133. *Bob Jones University v. U.S.*, together with *Goldsboro Christian Schools v. U.S.*, 461 U.S. 574 (1983).

134. *Bob Jones University v. U.S.*, 468 F. Supp. 890 (1983).

135. *Bob Jones University v. U.S.*, 639 F.2d 147, 150 (1980).

136. For a critical discussion of the Reagan adminstration's conduct in the *Bob Jones* case, see Lincoln Caplan, *The Tenth Justice* (New York: Vintage Books, 1987), 51-64.

137. *Bob Jones University v. U.S.*, 461 U.S. 574 (1983).

138. Id. at 604.

139. Id. at 595.

140. *U.S. v. Lee*, 455 U.S. 252 (1982).

141. *Bob Jones*, 461 U.S. at 602-3.

142. On this point, see Douglas Laycock, "Towards a General Theory of the Religion Clauses: The Case of Church Labor Relations and the Right to Church Autonomy," 81 *Columbia Law Review* 1373 (1981).

143. 455 U.S. 252 (1982).

144. 476 U.S. 693 (1986).

145. *Lee*, 455 U.S. at 260.

146. *Roy*, 476 U.S. at 699.

147. *Lee*, 455 U.S. at 260-61.

148. Id. at 262 (Justice Stevens, concurring).

149. *Roy*, 476 U.S. at 707-8 (emphasis added).

150. Id. at 724-33 (Justice O'Connor, concurring).

151. Id. at 732.

152. Id. at 727.

153. 110 S.Ct. 1595 (1990).

154. 109 S.Ct. 890 (1989).

155. 110 S.Ct. 688 (1990).

156. *Bullock v. Texas Monthly*, 731 S.W.2d 160 (1987).

157. *Texas Monthly*, 109 S.Ct. at 900.
158. Id.
159. Id. at 907, 909 (Justice Scalia, dissenting).
160. Id. at 911 ("It should be apparent from this discussion that *Walz* . . . is utterly dispositive of the Establishment Clause claim before us here").
161. Id. at 914.
162. *Smith*, 110 S.Ct. at 1602.
163. *Texas Monthly*, 109 S.Ct. at 912 (emphasis in original).
164. *Swaggart*, 110 S.Ct. at 688-97.
165. Id. at 699.

3

Religion in Public Places

In the three decades after the landmark Supreme Court decision of *Everson v. Board of Education* (1947),[1] controversies involving state-sponsored religious practices in and government financial aid to the public school system for the most part defined establishment clause law. Numerous other issues touching upon the guarantee of church-state separation, such as the display of religious symbols on public land, tax-supported legislative chaplaincies and state-endorsed celebrations of religious holidays, were considered problems for community relations specialists, civil rights agencies, and public school administrators. During the tumultuous, redefining era of church-state relations that commenced after *Everson* and continued through the reign of Chief Justice Earl Warren, the Court did not issue a full opinion in one of these areas. Instead, the Court directed its energies toward the more controversial issues that comprised the heart of the church-state debate: released-time,[2] religious devotionals in public schools[3] and government funds for parochial institutions.[4]

Disputes concerning government sponsorship of Christmas-time religious displays, or the appropriateness of religious holiday celebrations in public schools, were considered more benign when compared to other church-state issues. Since these were rituals more rooted in community tradition than in promoting religious values through coercive indoctrination in the public schools, conflicts that arose over them were more often settled through negotiation and compromise among local political, church and school leaders. Settling these disagreements without resorting to a court-ordered solution was considered a preferable alternative to the political divisiveness that often accompanies much church-state litigation. More recently, though, the trend in resolving these often emotional issues has turned toward litigation, not negotiation. The Supreme Court entered these conflicts with full throttle on the pretext of resolving them; instead, the Court made things far worse than one could have imagined. Several of its decisions wove major changes into the law of church and state. As a closer look at their language and logic will show, their impact has been genuine and, in some cases, far-reaching.

Religious Symbols and the Public Forum

Perhaps no other area of recent church-state conflict generated as much political divisiveness and bruised feelings over such a short period of time as did the several visible and controversial cases involving challenges to state-sponsored displays of religious symbols in public places. In numerous communities across the nation, these practices are time-honored custom and tradition. Elaborate recreations of the Nativity Scene, as much as the public lighting of Christmas trees or a visit to Santa Claus and his reindeer at the local department store, are regular Christmas-season events. More often than not, these religious celebrations are confined to the lawns of churches, synagogues, and other private forums.

Several of the disputes that materialized over the constitutionality of these seasonal religious celebrations originated with complaints brought by religious and civil libertarian groups against religious celebrations conducted in the public domain, either with public funds or on public land. For the religious and secular organizations active in this litigation as either sponsoring parties or *amicus curiae*, including the American Jewish Congress, the National Council of Churches, the Anti-Defamation League, the Baptist Joint Committee, the American Civil Liberties Union, and Americans United for the Separation of Church and State, all of whom share a deep and lasting commitment to the preservation of religious freedom and tolerance, challenging the constitutional authority of government to lend its prestige and support to sectarian religious celebrations in public or private forums has always involved hard choices. The political component of these cases never makes it as simple as finding a constitutional violation and attacking it through court action. No one wants to play the role of Scrooge during the Christmas season.

   Perception problems historically have been of even more concern to the separationist Jewish organizations involved in these cases. On several occasions, their involvement has been construed in some communities as an attempt to thwart the celebration of Christmas. However, that concern soon became forgotten when a bizarre turn of events placed all the major separationist Jewish civil rights agencies, including the American Jewish Committee, the American Jewish Congress, and the Anti-Defamation League, and numerous Reform and Conservative Jewish congregational groups, against segments of the Orthodox Jewish Lubavitch movement. That inversion of roles, with Jews suing Jews over establishment clause violations began in earnest around 1984, when the Lubavitch embarked on a national campaign to persuade municipal governments to include menorahs in their annual displays of Christmas trees and Nativity Scenes in the public square.

   This often acrimonious litigation has bequeathed a confusing and inconsistent body of case law that clarifies few of the genuine establishment clause problems associated with this genre of government preference for sectarian religion. Beginning in the early 1980s, the Supreme Court issued several flawed decisions in this area, none of which outlined the proper constitutional limitations for the lower courts to follow. This has left the lower courts without a consistent set of judicial rules for application in their own cases, resulting in frequent conflict among the federal circuits and state courts of last resort.[5]

   The Court has failed to resolve its own internal inconsistencies on this question. It has abstained from drawing "bright lines" to sharpen the definition of the law for implementing institutions and populations. Rather than recognize government-sponsored religious displays for what they are—an unconstitutional use of state power to promote private religious beliefs—the Court has created an indefensible and unprincipled set of guidelines to determine if religious displays are, in fact, really religious. The absurdities in these decisions abound. For example, the Court has said that a "free-standing" creche displayed on public land is unconstitutional,[6] but a creche situated among "secular" symbols, such as a plastic Santa Claus and colored Christmas tree lights, is not.[7] In similar fashion, the Court has insisted that a Hanukkah menorah, used to celebrate the Jewish holiday commemorating the redication of the Temple of Jersualem upon winning it back from the Greeks, while having religious origins, is now a secular reminder of a "contemporaneous alternative" religious tradition.[8] Likewise, Christmas trees communicate no religious message, except if placed in proximity to a creche.[9]

The Court first opened the door to this constitutional puzzle house in the landmark *Lynch v. Donnelly* (1984)[10] and further exacerbated the problem in *County of Allegheny v. American Civil Liberties Union* (1989).[11] In these two tortuous decisions, the Court further submerged the resilience of the establishment clause as a prohibition on unconstitutional acts of political majorities.

In *Lynch*, the Supreme Court upheld the constitutionality of a life-size Nativity Scene owned and erected by the City of Pawtucket, Rhode Island. The creche was displayed in a private park as part of Pawtucket's annual Christmas celebration. These facts did not impair the Court's analysis. Writing for a 5–4 Court, Chief Justice Burger wrote that:

> notwithstanding the religious significance of the creche . . . [w]hen viewed in the proper context of the Christmas Holiday season, it is apparent that, on this record, there is insufficient evidence to establish that the inclusion of the creche is a purposeful or surreptitious effort to express some kind of subtle governmental advocacy of a particular religious message. . . . The creche in the display depicts the historical origins of this traditional event long recognized as a National Holiday.[12]

The Court's decision overturned the ruling of the First Circuit Court of Appeals, which had earlier sustained the decision of the district court. Both lower courts had held the Nativity Scene display to violate the establishment clause.[13] In order to satisfy the purpose and effect prongs of the *Lemon* test, Chief Justice Burger redefined the sacred qualities associated with the creche in the Christian religions. The purpose was to achieve the dubious goal of allowing the Nativity Scene to survive constitutional review. Theological significance became expendable, a consequence that the National Council of Churches, in an *amicus* brief co-filed with the American Jewish Committee, informed the Court was an expense not worth incurring.[14] The Chief Justice did not let that minor caveat deter his reasoning. Because the creche did not stand on its own, but next to a facade of reindeer pulling the sleigh of Santa Claus, a Christmas tree, and other secular ornaments, including multicolored lights, candy canes, and animals traditionally associated with the "winter holiday season," the Nativity Scene did not convey a religious message.[15] The Court ruled that the "secular context" of the display made irrelevant the religious significance that the creche might have if it stood alone.[16]

That the *Lynch* majority found a government-sponsored display depicting the birth of Jesus Christ, whose life and teachings comprise the foundation upon which most Christian religions have developed their theologies, to have a "legitimate secular purpose"[17] simply because it stood next to candy canes, colored lights, and reindeer is illogical. To reach this conclusion requires both an ignorance of religion and settled establishment clause law. Moreover, the Court showed no remorse for its failure to use the traditional tripartite *Lemon* test to analyze the facts in *Lynch*, such was its enthusiasm to uphold the Pawtucket display. The Chief Justice did not explain what led him to ignore *Lemon* in this particular setting, despite the fact that the Court had used it, with just one exception,[18] in each establishment clause case decided since its formulation in 1971. Instead, the Court opted for a "historical analysis" similar to the one it utilized the term before *Marsh v. Chambers* (1983).[19]

In a manner analogous to its treatment of legislative chaplaincies in *Marsh*, the Court found that religious displays in public places had been a well-established practice in the traditional American celebration of Christmas. Throughout his opinion, Chief Justice Burger likened the tolerance of public Nativity Scenes to other "official references to the value and invocation of Divine guidance" in American public life, including Thanksgiving, which was "celebrated as a religious holiday to give thanks for the bounties of Nature as gifts from God,"[20] the "statutorily prescribed national motto 'In God We Trust,'"[21] and the Pledge of Allegiance, which includes the phrase, "One Nation under God."[22] The Chief Justice wrote that it was clear that "[G]overnment has long recognized—indeed it has subsidized—holidays with religious significance."[23] The Chief Justice concluded that these examples of government efforts to accommodate religious traditions and celebrate their rituals were part of the American heritage. As such, held the Chief Justice, the Framers never intended for the First Amendment to banish religious celebrations from public life, but rather insisted that their place in the civic culture mandated constitutional accommodation.[24] Placing the prohibitive language of the establishment clause aside, the Chief Justice ruled that such benign accommodation of religion did not contravene the constitutional text because the Framers themselves had recognized the value of integrating religion into our civic culture. To insist on such a stringent application of the establishment clause would eventually read religion out of public life. That, wrote the Chief Justice has never been thought either possible or desirable . . . nor required [because the Constitution] affirmatively mandates accommodation, not merely tolerance, of all religions, and forbids hostility toward any. Anything less would require the "callous indifference" we have said was never intended by the Establishment Clause. Indeed, we have observed, such hostility would bring us into "war with our national tradition as embodied in the First Amendment's guarantee of the free exercise of religion."[25]

In a vigorous and forceful dissent, Justice Brennan, joined by Justices Blackmun, Marshall, and Stevens, reacted to the Chief Justice's opinion with bewilderment for its casual dismissal of the religiosity of the creche and conclusion that municipal sponsorship of a sectarian religious celebration furthered Pawtucket's stated secular goal of promoting commerce in its downtown shopping distict during the Christmas season.[26] Justice Brennan found the Chief Justice's reasoning, which asserted that because the creche comprised a minor portion of a more inclusive secular celebration of a national holiday it lacked religious significance, analytically bogus. Justice Brennan also argued that the designation of Christmas as a public holiday did not mean that all forms of government association with Christmas are constitutionally permitted. Furthermore, Justice Brennan argued that "[p]lainly, the city and its leaders understood that the inclusion of the creche in its display would serve the wholly religious purpose of 'keeping Christ in Christmas.'"[27] Justice Brennan concluded his dissent, using even more powerful language, with an eloquent and sensitive interpretation of the message sent by the Pawtucket display:

[The Nativity Scene] is the chief symbol of the characteristically Christian belief that a divine Savior was brought into the world and that the purpose of this miraculous birth was to illuminate a path toward salvation and redemption. For Christians, that path is exclusive, precious, and holy.[28]

But for those who do not share these beliefs, the symbolic reenactment of the birth of a divine being who has been miraculously incarnated as a man stands as a a dramatic reminder of their differences with the Christian faith. . . . To be so excluded on religious grounds by one's elected government is an insult and an injury that, until today, could not be countenanced by the Establishment Clause.[29]

[T]he city's action should be recognized for what it is: a coercive, though perhaps small, step toward establishing the sectarian preferences of the majority at the expense of the minority, accomplished by placing public facilities and funds in support of the religious symbolism and theological tidings that the creche conveys.[30]

Despite the sweeping language of the Court's opinion, which turned out to be a transitional signal of a more relaxed attitude toward accommodating preference for religion in public places, the *Lynch* holding was itself narrow. Justice Brennan, in his dissent, read *Lynch* in quite restrictive terms. The Court's opinion sounded approval for similar displays, but did not indicate whether similar displays on government land would be constitutional.[31] The litigation that followed in the wake of *Lynch* raised these variations of the constitutional questions presented in *Lynch*. The results have somehow managed to add to the confusion that *Lynch* generated. The outcomes that followed *Lynch*, which are even more nonsensical than the originator, did nothing but muddle the constitutional waters over the constitutional limitations against religious displays in public places and government property.

For example, the Court could have clarified the breadth of its holding in *Lynch* the following term in *Scarsdale v. McCreary* (1985),[32] which involved the display of a privately owned creche in a public park in Scarsdale, New York. The Court split 4–4 in its opinion,[33] thus leaving intact the decision of the Second Circuit Court of Appeals, which had upheld Scarsdale's Nativity Scene on free speech grounds.[34] Perhaps unclear as to *Lynch*'s application, the Second Circuit instead subjected the creche to the analytical framework commonly used in deciding cases involving free speech rights in public forums.[35] The Second Circuit concluded that the public park in which the creche was displayed qualified as a traditional public forum under free speech analysis. Therefore, the park must be open to all substantive expression—religious and nonreligious—so long as it did not contravene the time, place, and manner interests of the government. This reasoning was crucial to the court's analysis:

> the Village's actions in permitting access to Boniface Circle for display of a creche— the same actions that would be necessary in pemitting access for any display —"do not lead it into such an intimate relationship with religious authority that it appears . . . to be sponsoring that authority."[36]

The Second Circuit flatly rejected the argument that the Scarsdale creche, which stood alone on public land and was devoid of secular trappings was distinguishable from the *Lynch* display, which was augmented by less religiously obstrusive symbols.[37] The court also found the Christmas celebration in Scarsdale did not differ significantly from the celebration described in *Lynch*. For years the public park hosting the Nativity Scene had also accommodated annual Christmas celebrations, some of which had private sponsors, while others were supported by government. In addition to involving the decoration of Scarsdale's Christmas tree and the singing of Christmas carols, the festivities had included a creche.[38]

The appellate court's effort to distinguish the Scarsdale display from the one found constitutional in *Lynch* did not really matter, since it ruled that the district court had erred in treating the case as an establishment clause issue.[39] The Second Circuit said that the Scarsdale authorities wanted nothing more than to allow individuals or groups sponsoring religious celebrations to have the same access to a traditional public forum for the public expression of personal beliefs as nonreligious speakers. The Second Circuit remanded the case for rehearing under the speech clause.[40] But *Scarsdale*, which had never carried the force of precedent because of the tie vote on the Supreme Court, now lacks even symbolic importance in the law governing religion in public places. That irrelevance comes as a result of the Court's most recent and even more analytically tortuous pronouncement in this area, *County of Allegheny v. ACLU.*[41]

Allegheny involved a consolidated challenge brought by the Greater Pittsburgh chapter of the American Civil Liberties Union against two religious displays sponsored by the Allegheny County government during the 1986 Christmas season. One featured an unadorned Nativity Scene displayed inside the Allegheny County courthouse, accompanied by a banner that proclaimed "Gloria in Excelsis Deo!" ("Glory to God the Highest"). Since 1981, the Holy Name Society, a Roman Catholic group, had provided the creche to the Allegheny government. The other was located one block down the street in front of the City-County Building, which was jointly owned by the City of Pittsburgh and Allegheny County. In a novel factual twist, this display did not include a Nativity Scene, but a forty-five-foot Christmas tree and eighteen-foot menorah standing side by side.

For several years, Pittsburgh had placed the Christmas tree outside the City-County building at its own expense and allowed city employees to decorate it with city-provided ornaments and lights. Beginning in 1982, the city expanded its holiday display to include the menorah as a symbolic representation of Hanukkah, a minor Jewish holiday that traditionally falls closest but bears no relationship to, Christmas. The menorah featured in the display was owned by Chabad, an Orthodox Jewish group formed by the Lubavitch movement. The menorah was stored, maintained, and erected by Pittsburgh.[42]

In December 1986, the Pittsburgh chapter of the American Civil Liberties Union filed suit against the county and the city, asking a federal district court for a permanent injunction enjoining the government from allowing either display. Chabad asked for and received permission to intervene so it could defend the menorah display. In May 1987, the district court issued an opinion refusing to grant the injunction against either the Nativity Scene or the display featuring the menorah and Christmas tree, holding that each was constitutional under *Lynch*.[43] Following *Lynch* to the letter, the district court also ruled that "the creche was but a part of the holiday decoration of the stairwell and a foreground for the high school choirs which entertained each day at noon."[44] Furthermore, the court concluded that the menorah "was but an insignificant part of another holiday display," that both "displays had a secular purpose" and neither one created "an excessive entanglement of government with religion."[45]

On appeal, a divided Third Circuit Court of Appeals reversed, holding that the display of the unadorned Nativity Scene in the courthouse and, separately, the menorah featured in town square had the impermissible result of endorsing the Christian and Jewish religions. The Third Circuit noted that each display "was located at or in a public building devoted to core functions of government."[46] Distinguishing the facts in *Allegheny* from those in *Lynch*, the court stated that, "while the menorah was placed near a Christmas tree, neither the creche nor the menorah can reasonably be deemed to have been subsumed by a larger display on non-religious items."[47] The Third Circuit concluded that both the Nativity Scene and menorah displays violated the establishment clause under the purpose prong of the *Lemon* test.[48] The Third Circuit refused to rehear the case *en banc*, but the Supreme Court granted certiorari for the following term.

Writing for a Court splintered along sharp lines, Justice Blackmun upheld the Third Circuit's decision that held the Nativity Scene to violate the establishment clause, but reversed the lower court judgment that struck down the joint display of the Christmas tree and menorah. Justices Brennan, Marshall, O'Connor and Stevens joined the sections of Justice Blackmun's opinion striking down the Nativity Scene, with Justices Kennedy, O'Connor, Scalia, White and Chief Justice Rehnquist forming the majority to uphold the Christmas tree-menorah display. Only Justice O'Connor joined Justice Blackmun's entire opinion.

Turning first to the Nativity Scene, Justice Blackmun wrote that

> the creche in this lawsuit uses the words, as well as the picture of the nativity scene, to make its religious meaning unmistakably clear. "Glory to God the Highest!" says the angel in the creche—Glory to God because of the birth of Jesus. This praise to God in Christian terms is indisputably religious—indeed sectarian—just as it is when said in the Gospel or in a church service.[49]

Returning to the contextual analysis set forth in *Lynch*, the *Allegheny* Court found that, in contrast to the Pawtucket case, nothing in the creche's setting detracted from the sectarian message sent by the unadorned Nativity Scene. That message was crystal clear. Justice Blackmun stated that, while "the government may acknowledge Christmas as a cultural phenomenon . . . it may not observe it as a Christian holy day by suggesting that people praise God for the birth of Jesus."[50]

But Justice Blackmun, in an analytical leap of faith, found no establishment clause barrier to the erection of the Christmas tree and menorah in front of the City-County Building. Retaining only Justice O'Connor from his ruling striking down the Nativity Scene, Justice Blackmun held that the joint display of the Christmas tree and menorah did not have the effect of endorsing Christianity or Judaism, but simply recognized that both Christmas and Hanukkah are part of the same "winter holiday season."[51] Justice Blackmun maintained that each holiday had attained a secular status in our society.[52] Placing the Christmas tree-menorah display in the analytical framework established in *Lynch*, Justice Blackmun concluded that it could not be "interpreted as a simultaneous endorsement of Christian and Jewish faiths," but as a conveyence of the "city's secular recognition of different traditions for celebrating the winter-holiday season."[53]

Rather than clarifying the issues raised in *Lynch*, the five opinions issued in *Allegheny* made things worse. Without question, *Allegheny* is a resolute failure. Justice Blackmun had the chance to refine and further narrow *Lynch*, where he had joined Justice Brennan's dissent, and to piece together the loose threads that characterized the Court's analysis in *Lynch* and in *Scarsdale*. Given his erudite and welcome endorsement of separationist establishment clause principles that stand behind his decision to strike down the creche display, there is no evident explanation of why Justice Blackmun chose to embrace in Allegheny the principles from which he dissented in *Lynch*. Justice Brennan's dissent in *Lynch* expressly rejected Chief Justice Burger's euphemistic "winter holiday season" as a permissible metaphor for Christmas, a point he repeated in *Allegheny*.[54] Unconvinced and untroubled by the overlapping issues, Justice Blackmun accepted precisely that metaphor in *Allegheny* one that he had joined Justice Brennan in *Lynch* to reject to allow the government to sponsor the display of the Christmas tree and menorah on public land. Here is Justice Blackmun, dissenting, in *Lynch*:

> *Lemon . . . compels* an affirmance here. Not only does the Court's resolution of this controversy make light of our precedents, but also, ironically, the majority does an injustice to the creche and the message it manifests. The import of the Court's decision is to encourage use of the creche in a municipally sponsored display, a setting where Christians feel constrained in acknowledging its symbolic meaning and non-Christians feel alienated by its presence. Surely, this is a misuse of a sacred symbol. I cannot join the Court in denying either the force of our precedents or the sacred message that is at the core of the creche.[55]

Five years later, here is Justice Blackmun, for the Court, in *Allegheny*:

> The Christmas tree alone in the Pittsburgh location does not endorse Christian belief; and, on the facts before us, the addition of the menorah 'cannot fairly be understood to' result in the simultaneous endorsement of Christian and Jewish faiths. On the contrary, for purposes of the Establishment Clause, the city's overall display must be understood as conveying the city's secular recognition of different traditions for celebrating the winter-holiday season.[56]

Concluding, Justice Blackmun wrote:

> *Lynch v. Donnelly* confirms, and in no way repudiates, the long-standing constitutional principle that government may not engage in a practice that has the effect of promoting or endorsing religious beliefs. The display of the creche . . . has this unconstitutional effect. The display of the menorah . . . does not have this effect, given its "particular physical setting."[57]

Justice Blackmun's about-face, and his reasoning behind it, made little sense to the Court's then most junior member, Justice Anthony Kennedy. But Justice Kennedy viewed things from a different angle. In a blistering dissent in which he presented his first published views on an establishment clause issue, Justice Kennedy criticized Justice Blackmun for an analysis that reflected "an unjustified hostility toward religion."[58] Justice Kennedy would have upheld the creche and the menorah displays, arguing that the establishment clause permits government some latitude in recognizing and accommodating the central role religion plays in our society. Any approach less sensitive to our heritage would border on latent hostility toward religion, as it would require government in all its multifaceted roles to acknowledge only the secular, to the exclusion and so to the detriment of religious.[59]

Justice Kennedy also sounded his first clarion against the *Lemon* test, writing that he was "not content" to continue with it as an analytical device in establishment clause cases.[60] Justice Kennedy then criticized Justice O'Connor's endorsement test as an equally unsatisfactory alternative to *Lemon*, calling it "flawed in its fundamentals and unworkable in practice."[61]

In place of *Lemon*, Justice Kennedy would have the courts analyze establishment clause cases under a "noncoercion" test. This framework would allow that "non-coercive government action within the realm of flexible accommodation or passive acknowledgment of existing symbols does not violate the Establishment Clause unless it benefits religion in a way more direct and more substantial than practices that are accepted in our national heritage."[62] Justice Kennedy did not indicate just what common religious practices are acceptable in our multireligious, multi-denominational national character. Nor did he indicate when government coercion trespassed the "border between accommodation and establishment," a line which he acknowledged required "diligent observance" to guard against unconstitutional encroachment.[63] Still, Justice Kennedy did make clear that government could—and should—promote religious values through civic means.[64] Justice Blackmun did not find much of value in his junior colleague's denunciation of the Court's establishment clause jurisprudence, responding that adoption of Justice Kennedy's "noncoercion" test would "gut the core of the Establishment Clause as this Court understands it."[65] But that assessment might evolve into cries in the wind because as I discussed in chapter 2, it appears now that Justice Kennedy's *dicta* in *Allgheny* might well form the basis for the Court's future establishment clause jurisprudence.

This constitutional hairsplitting appeared to perplex Justices Stevens and Brennan. Each dissented from Justice Blackmun's decision to uphold the Christmas tree-menorah display. Justice Stevens wrote that,

a lighted, 45-foot tree might convey holiday greetings linked too tenuously to Christianity to have constitutional moment. Juxtaposition of this tree with an 18-foot menorah does not make the latter secular, as Justice Blackmun contends. Rather, the presence of the Hanukkah menorah, unquestionably a religious symbol, gives religious significance to the Christmas tree.[66]

Justice Brennan, in a separate opinion, was even more direct:

The government-sponsored display of the menorah along side a Christmas tree also works a distortion of the Jewish religious calendar. . . . It is the proximity of Christmas that undoubtedly accounts for the city's decision to participate in the celebration of Hanukkah, rather than the far more significant Jewish holidays of Rosh Hashanah and Yom Kippur.[67]

Contrary to the impression the city and Justices Blackmun and O'Connor seem to create, with their emphasis of the "winter-holiday season," December is not the holiday season for Judaism. Thus, the city's erection alongside the Christmas tree of the symbol of a relatively minor Jewish religious holiday, far from conveying "the city's secular recognition of different traditions for celebrating the winter-holiday season," or "a message of pluralism and freedom of belief," has the effect of promoting a Christianized version of Judaism. . . .And those religions that have no holiday at all during the period between Thanksgiving and New Year's Day will not benefit, even in a second-class manner, from the city's once-a-year tribute to "liberty" and "freedom of belief." This is not "pluralism" as I understand it.[68]

In *Allegheny*, the Court cast into stone a jurisprudential course that eliminates whatever slim hope existed for serious analytical treatment of future cases challenging the constitutionality of state-sponsored religious displays. One tragic consequence of these cases has been the degrading treatment accorded to the theological qualities of religious rituals and symbols in order for religion to assume a contrived ecumenism sufficiently neutral to survive constitutional review under the establishment clause. Another consequence has been to manufacture an artificial consolidation of divergent religious faiths under the rubric of a Judeo-Christian tradition more embedded in American popular culture than to recognize the real plural, multidenominational nature of American religious life.

The myopic lens through which the Court views the range of religious life in America now threatens to permeate further its establishment clause jurisprudence. The Court either cannot or will not recognize the growth of religious movements outside the Protestant, Catholic, and Jewish mainstream. While still the dominant religions in America, none has title to constitutional privilege. Moreover, the Court has shown that, even within the Protestant, Catholic, and Jewish mainstream, some religious denominations receive preferential treatment over others, with political influence in the legislature usually accounting for the disadvantageous position of religious minorities. The increasing statist tendencies that the Court has demonstrated in both its establishment and free exercise decisions since the mid-1980s have resulted in adverse consequences for smaller religions, such as Judaism and the Native American church, and less influential Protestant denominations, such as Seventh-day Adventists and other religious traditions observing the Saturday Sabbath.

Justice O'Connor's endorsement standard, though not an optimal framework under which to analyze establishment clause cases, remains sensitive to the status of religious minorities in a civic and religious culture still dominated by the more populous and politically powerful religions. Justice Kennedy's *dicta* in *Allegheny* fails miserably on this count. In fact, Justice Kennedy in *Allegheny* criticized Justice O'Connor's endorsement rule in harsh terms. Justice O'Connor's endorsement rule asks whether, to "a reasonable observer, government action sen[ds] a message to nonadherents that they are outsiders, not full members of the political community."[69] If the answer is affirmative, then government has crossed over the constitutionally permissible line of influence in religious affairs. The endorsement test does not subject the alleged state sponsorship of religious influences to the same tough standard as *Lemon*, but a less rigorous, albeit principled, establishment clause jurisprudence was the basis for which Justice O'Connor developed it. Most importantly, the endorsement test still requires courts to *judge* the competing claims in establishment clause cases before them, not blindly defer to the stated majoritarian preferences of legislative bodies. At bottom, Justice O'Connor's endorsement test is but another contribution to the core method of modern constitutional interpretation—balancing.

The noncoercive rationale that Justice Kennedy has argued for eliminates a fundamental role distinction between jurists and legislators—the constitutional obligation to judge the relative importance of the competing interests at work in a particular case. Justice Kennedy's approach is a transparently statist one because it eliminates any requirement for judges to characterize, weigh, and balance the competing interests before them. *Allegheny* is illustrative of the crossroads position in which the Court has placed itself. It has forced upon itself the obligation to choose between one of two quite different methods of constitutional interpretation in establishment clause cases. If Justice Kennedy does not believe that government sponsorship of sectarian religious symbols on public land, whether a creche or a menorah, sends a message to nonrepresented adherents in that particular locale that their beliefs are preferred or discounted because of the government's choice to support one religious tradition over another, then one wonders what does. There was little informed discussion of these problems in *Allegheny*. Instead, the Justices have been more content to spend their time accusing each other of not knowing what constitutes an establishment of religion.[70] Fratricidal relationships on a Court that continues to grow more and more intellectually galvanized is not good for the Court or for the law, especially when there is a guarded interest in keeping establishment clause law from spinning out of control.

Critics of *Lemon* have indicated that the "noncoercion" framework is an acceptable compromise replacement for the *Lemon* test, falling somewhere between Justice O'Connor's more moderate endorsement standard and Chief Justice Rehnquist's reactionary nonpreferentialism, which he spelled out in his articulate and frank *Wallace v. Jaffree* dissent.[71] The Department of Justice has asked the Court, in a case argued during the 1991-92 term,[72] to abandon the use of the *Lemon* test, at the very least, in establishment clause cases not involving parochaid and replace it with the "noncoercion" test first suggested by Justice Kennedy in *Allegheny*.[73] Several other *amici* followed suit.[74] There is little doubt that these briefs are intended to persuade the Court to adopt Justice Kennedy's test. Indeed, several of the briefs submitted in support of the appellant Rhode Island school board specifically asked the Court to replace *Lemon* with Justice Kennedy's noncoercion test.[75]

With Chief Justice Rehnquist and Justices Kennedy, Scalia, and White on record as wanting to abandon *Lemon*, the pivotal vote could well be Justice David Souter. During his first term, Justice Souter voted with Justice O'Connor 90 percent of the time, more than he did with any other Justice.[76] They voted together more often than any other combination of Justices.[77] But Justice Souter has not yet cast a vote in an establishment clause case. Moreoever, Justice Souter split with Justice O'Connor in an important case decided during the 1990 term involving a First Amendment free speech challenge to federal regulations regulating how private clinics offering family planning services could spend congressionally authorized funds. In *Rust v. Sullivan* (1991),[78] the Court, dividing 5-4, ruled that Title X of the Public Health Service Act prohibits clinics receiving federal funds not only from providing abortions, but also from providing abortion counseling. Justice Souter sided with Chief Justice Rehnquist's majority opinion, while Justice O'Connor dissented.[79] Thus, while his decision as to whether to side with Justice O'Connor's endorsement test or to join the other four to overturn *Lemon* will draw much attention for those groups and individuals interested in the outcome, predicting Justice Souter's vote is a more risky outcome. Or the Court's newest Justice, former D.C. Court of Appeals judge Clarence Thomas, who replaces the staunch separationist Thurgood Marshall, might vote in such a manner as to make speculation over Justice Souter's vote irrelevant. But since Judge Thomas has never written or voted on an establishment or free exercise clause issue in his short judicial career, attempts to decipher his leanings are equally, if not more, difficult.

Conflict in the Lower Federal Courts

Lynch and *Allegheny* accomplished a rare judicial feat: together, the two decisions turned the establishment clause into a constitutional pretzel. So it should come as no surprise that the lower courts are not in harmony in their own opinions on the subject.[80] Cases that have involved often identical fact patterns have resulted in disparate decisions, even within the same federal judicial circuit! For example, the Seventh Circuit Court of Appeals, which, in *American Jewish Congress v. City of Chicago* (1987),[81] had affirmed a district court decision enjoining the display of a Chicago-owned Nativity Scene in the central lobby of its city hall, later reversed a separate federal district court decision that barred a Chicago suburb from maintaining a creche on the lawn of its town hall.

In *Mather v. Village of Mundelein* (1989),[82] a federal district court, distinguishing *Lynch v. Donnelly* and relying instead on *American Jewish Congress*, held a religious display in violation of the establishment clause and permanently enjoined the village from displaying the creche. Two years after the district court ruling, the Seventh Circuit issued a *per curiam* order holding that *Lynch*, not *American Jewish Congress*, controlled *Mundelin*, and ruled that the village was free to display the creche during the Christmas season. Also noteworthy about the Seventh Circuit's decision is the fact that it did not hear arguments nor accept briefs on the merits, but instead chose to grant summary disposition. But the most startling aspect of this litigation is that the two decisions, handed down soon after *Lynch* and decided in the same circuit only two years apart, had diametric outcomes.

Mundelein stands in contrast not only to *American Jewish Congress*, but also the case upon which the latter rests for authority. In 1986, the Sixth Circuit Court of Appeals, in a 7–1 decision, ruled that a free-standing Nativity Scene displayed on the lawn of the Birmingham, Michigan, City Hall violated the establishment clause. In deciding, the Sixth Circuit also distinguished *Lynch* from the Nativity Scene at issue in the Birmingham case *ACLU v. City of Birmingham* (1986).[83] The Sixth Circuit upheld the federal trial court decision, which ruled that neither *Lynch* nor *Scarsdale* controlled the issues present in *City of Birmingham*. Unlike the Nativity Scene the Supreme Court found constitutional in *Lynch*, the district court said that Birmingham had requested it to

> discover an implied presumption in favor of the "secularization" of the nativity scene, such that the religious symbolism apparent . . . should be somehow overshadowed, balanced or neutralized by the aura of Christmas shopping and holiday cheer. This court cannot so find. . . . The display conveys the restrictive message that Christianity is the chosen religion of the City of Birmingham.[84]

In affirming, the Sixth Circuit agreed with the lower court that *Lynch* and *Scarsdale* failed to control the display of the Birmingham creche, but scrutinized the facts under a different rationale. In holding the creche unconstitutional, the Sixth Circuit ruled that Birmingham had not violated the purpose or entanglement prongs of the *Lemon* test. The appellate court held instead that the municipal creche had the primary effect of advancing religion, thus failing the second prong of *Lemon*. It applied a hybrid analysis drawn from *Lynch* to determine the constitutionality of the creche, relying on both Chief Justice Burger's requirement of proximate secular symbols and Justice O'Connor's endorsement test. Thus, it found the creche to have the "direct and immediate effect" of showing support for the Christian religion because Birmingham had failed to place identifiable secular symbols next to it.[85] The Sixth Circuit also concluded that "[i]t is difficult to believe that the city's practice of displaying an unadorned creche on the city hall lawn would not convey to a non-Christian a message that the city endorses Christianity, thus 'send[ing] a message to nonadherents that they are outsiders, not full members of the political community.'"[86]

The Sixth Circuit opinion was consistent with the line of decisions issued by other lower federal courts that had dealt with similar cases before and after the *Lynch* decision. Soon after *City of Birmingham* was decided, the Seventh Circuit Court of Appeals decided *ACLU v. City of St. Charles* (1986).[87] There, the court granted an injunction prohibiting the display of a cross on public property because it clearly symbolized the Easter holiday, even when placed in a Christmas context. In similar fashion, the Fifth Circuit Court of Appeals, in *ACLU v. Eckels* (1984),[88] refused to hear the appeal from a Texas district court, that held a display consisting of three Latin crosses and a Star of David, constructed and maintained in a public park, to violate the establishment clause. In *Eckels*, the district court distinguished *Lynch*, ruling that the display of religious symbols by Harris County, Texas, failed the purpose and effect prongs of the *Lemon* test.[89] The district court dismissed the claim of the county that removal of the religious symbols would result in the establishment of the nontheistic religion of secular humanism. The court said that the removal of the religious symbols did not result in hostility toward religion, but constitutional neutrality, and "safeguard[ed] the rights of minorities—in this case the rights of those who are not Christians and Jews."[90]

The irretractable divisiveness of the constitutional debate over the appropriateness of state-sponsored displays of religious symbols in public places perhaps is best symbolized by the more recent campaign launched by the Orthodox Jewish Lubavitch movement to persuade local governments to permit the placement of menorahs in public parks and in front of public buildings. The basis for the Lubavitch's case rests upon the argument that the menorah, which most Jews believe is a religious symbol, is, in fact, devoid of religious significance. The Lubavitch argue that the Talmud, which forms the basis of Jewish law, does not define the menorah as a religious symbol.[91] This argument has found no audience among Conservative and Reform Jews. which constitute about 90 percent of American Jews having religious beliefs.[92] Nor have the major national Jewish civil rights groups been keen on the Lubavitch's Talmudic interpretation. These disagreements have resulted in Reform and Conservative Jewish congregational groups and American Jewish civil rights organizations supporting lawsuits to enjoin the Lubavitch from placing menorahs on public land.[93]

For much of the litigation involving religious displays, Jewish civil rights organizations having strict separationist orientations on church-state matters, such as the American Jewish Congress, the American

Jewish Committee, and the Anti-Defamation League, and other secular groups, such as the ACLU and People for the American Way, and separationist Protestant organizations, such as the National Council of Churches, took the lead in legal efforts to prohibit the display of religious, primarily Christian, symbols in public places. That battle eventually came full circle, with organizational representatives of the different branches of American Judaism arguing in the federal courts not only the risks to church-state separation posed by government endorsement of public religious displays, but also the Talmudic and constitutional definition of the religious significance of the menorah.[94] The basis for Jewish opposition to the placement of the menorah on public land was, on the one hand, rooted in the establishment clause. On the other hand, the separationist Jewish coalition shared a concern previously voiced by their Christian allies in the earlier cases. For the menorah to gain constitutional acceptance, a case would have to be made that it lacked religious significance; and that, like chicken soup, it was associated with secular, not religious, Jewish life.

The Lubavitch were unsuccessful in the early going in having Hanukkah menorahs displayed on public land.[95] Down but not out, the Lubavitch lobbied the local governments of two Florida cities, Tampa and Sarasota, the following year to allow their menorahs to be placed on public property. In each case, with the strong support and encouragement of local and national Jewish groups, the courts denied the request of the Lubavitch movement. The Lubavitch organizations then brought suit, in separate actions, in federal district court asking for injunctive relief permitting it to display their menorahs in these two cities, both of which have sizable and well-represented Jewish communities.

The lower court consolidated the two cases, *Chabad Lubavitch v. Sarasota* (1988)[96] and *Chabad Lubavitch v. Tampa* (1988),[97] and then refused to issue the injunctions. It then ordered a trial. But Chabad Lubavitch was not able to secure counsel, forcing it to withdraw from the litigation. The cases were dismissed in Fall 1988, shortly before the beginning of the "winter holiday season." However, Lubavitch's failure to compel Tampa and Sarasota to display Hanukkah menorahs proved to be just a temporary setback. Less than a year later, the Supreme Court decided *Allegheny*. Ironically, the Court rejected the arguments of the Lubavitch that the menorah lacked religious significance, and instead upheld its constitutionality based on the "secular" context in which it was presented.[98]

The Court's ruling in *Allegheny* provided even more incentive for the Lubavitch movement to continue its nationwide effort to display menorahs in public places, despite the fact that it is the proximity of Hanukkah to Christmas, not the lack of religious aura around the menorah, that will account for the decisions of other municipalities to celebrate Hanukkah in a similar fashion. Several federal appellate decisions reported since *Allegheny* affirm this new direction.[99] One is inclined to doubt that the same muncipalities that permit the placement of menorahs during the Christmas season would be as forthcoming if the Lubavitch, or any other Jewish organization, requested a public lighting of weekly Sabbath candles, or a publicly financed and supported Sukkah in a traditional public forum, such as a town square, to celebrate the Jewish holiday of Sukkot. Perhaps that will be next.

Religious Preferences in the Public Domain

Government sponsorship of religious displays, whether on public or private land, is perhaps the most conspicuous example of government support for religion in the public realm. It is not, however, the sole constitutional issue concerning government support for religion in public places. The Supreme Court decided two other constitutional cases involving the extent to which government can incorporate sectarian religious objectives into the core functions of government. One case involved the power of churches to exercise veto power over the government's issuance of liquor licenses. The other challenged a long-standing American tradition: the opening of legislative sessions with prayers given by state-funded chaplains. Moreover, in an important lower court decision, the Ninth Circuit Court of Appeals decided that a Hawaii statute making Good Friday a paid government holiday did not violate the establishment clause. All three cases are important in understanding the leverage that government now has to grant public recognition for the wishes of religious majorities well-situated in the elected branches of government.

In *Marsh v. Chambers* (1983),[100] the Court ruled that the Nebraska legislature's sixteen year-old practice of opening each legislative session with prayer said by a state-employed chaplain did not violate the establishment clause of the First Amendment. Beginning in 1965, Nebraska had paid the same chaplain for sixteen consecutive years to provide invocational prayers before the commencement of legislative business. Chaplain Robert E. Palmer, a Presbyterian minister, began each morning with the following prayer:

> Father in heaven, the suffering and death of your son brought life to the whole world moving our hearts to praise your glory. The power of the cross reveals your concern for the world and the wonder of Christ crucified. The days of his life-giving death and glorious resurrection are approaching. This is the hour when he triumphed over Satan's pride; the time when we celebrate the great event of our redemption.[101]

After a Nebraska state legislator complained about the practice, Reverend Palmer removed all "explicitly sectarian" references to Christianity. He changed his morning prayer to include new, more ecumenical language couched in the "Judeo-Christian" tradition. That did not relieve the complaints. Another member of the Nebraska legislature, Ernest Chambers, filed a lawsuit in federal district court arguing that state-funded chaplaincies per se violated the establishment clause. The district court ruled that the use of public monies to compensate legislative chaplains violated the establishment clause, but it declined to enjoin the recitation of prayers.[102] On appeal, the Eighth Circuit Court of Appeals held the Nebraska practice to violate all three prongs of the *Lemon* test.[103]

Writing for a 6–3 majority, Chief Justice Burger ruled that "the practice of opening legislative sessions with prayer has become part of the fabric of our society. To invoke Divine guidance on a public body entrusted with making the laws is not, in these circumstances, an 'establishment of religion or a step toward establishment; it is simply a *tolerable acknowledgement of beliefs widely held among the people of this country.*"[104] The Chief Justice found no proof in the historical record or in the facts of the case that the continous service of the same legislative chaplain stemmed from an impermissible motive. Thus, the Court did not find the Nebraska practice to conflict with the establishment clause.

The Court's reversal of the Eighth Circuit on the merits was discouraging enough, but its refusal to scrutinize the Nebraska practice under the *Lemon* test in reaching its decision made matters worse. The Eighth Circuit had relied on *Lemon* to reach its decision, but that did not hinder the Court from departing wholesale from the purpose-effect-entanglement test. After a *pro forma* acknowledgement of the Eighth Circuit's use of the *Lemon* rationale, the Court then inexplicably shelved it in favor

of an historical analysis. The Chief Justice wrote that legislative chaplaincies were a "traditional and time-honored" American practice whose
legacy extended back to the First Congress, which granted statutory
authorization for legislative chaplains. Said the Chief Justice:

> Clearly the men who wrote the First Amendment Religion Clauses did not view paid
> legislative chaplains and opening prayers as a violation of that Amendment, for the
> practice of opening sessions with prayer has continued without interruption ever since
> that early session of Congress.[105]

The Court provided no basis for its failure to scrutinize the Nebraska
practice under the *Lemon* test, except for perhaps the unstated assumption
that it could not have survived analysis under such strict review.

The Court's aberrant departure from traditional establishment clause
jurisprudence in *Marsh* remains befuddling when one considers that,
during the same term, it used the *Lemon* test to strike down a Massachusetts statute authorizing a "church or school" to veto liquor licenses if the
grantee was located within 500 feet of either building. What makes the
8-1 opinion in *Larkin v. Grendel's Den* (1982)[106] of such interest is not
that it disposes of an especially difficult question, but that it was written
by an unusually forceful Chief Justice Burger just six months before
Marsh came down. The Chief Justice, affirming the First Circuit Court
of Appeals, ruled that "this statute enmeshes churches in the exercise of
substantial governmental powers contrary to our consistent interpretation
of the Establishment Clause [by granting them veto power over public
policy]. . . . Ordinary human experience and a long line of cases teach
that few entanglements could be more offensive to the spirit of the
Constitution."[107] Compare that to *Marsh*, where the Chief Justice found
no such "offensive entanglements" when state treasuries fund legislative
chaplaincies of sectarian cast.

A more recent and perhaps more troubling case involving government
preference for religion in the public milieu concerns a constitutional
challenge to a state legislative act granting official recognition of a
religious holiday. In *Cammack v. Waihee* (1987),[108] the Hawaii affiliate
of the ACLU, representing a group of local taxpayers, brought suit
against a Hawaii statute designating Good Friday, the Christian holiday
commemorating the crucifixion of Jesus Christ, as a state holiday. Unlike
Christmas and Thanksgiving, which federal courts have found to have
de minimus religious significance,[109] Good Friday bears no place in the
American civic culture. Distinguishing *Lynch* and *Marsh*, the plaintiffs

argued that the Hawaii statute respects not a long-held and universally recognized American practice, but a governmental endorsement of a sectarian religious observance at state expense, a purpose incompatible with the establishment clause.

The U.S. District Court of Hawaii rejected the plaintiffs' arguments that the statute violated the establishment clause, both on its face and as applied, under the *Lemon* test. The trial court instead held that the Hawaii legislature, even assuming that it "enact[ed] the Good Friday statute with sectarian purposes in mind [and] to allow the religious to worship on Good Friday and to allow [the] churches to call the faithful to prayer,"[110] intended to create a "needed day off from work." This time did not have to be earmarked for religious observance. It could be used to "emphasize those aspects of the holiday, the secular or the sectarian, which he or she chooses to emphasize."[111]

In April 1991, the Ninth Circuit Court of Appeals, dividing 2–1, affirmed that ruling. It held that "[t]here is nothing impermissible about considering for holiday status days on which many people choose to be absent from work for religious reasons."[112] The Ninth Circuit opinion relied heavily on *McGowan v. Maryland*[113] and *Lynch*[114] to reach its conclusion that establishing a state holiday to coincide with the Christian religious calendar accomplishes the constitutional goal of furthering a secular objective while, "at the same time, accommodat[ing] the widespread religious practices of its citizenry."[115] The court held that the Hawaii legislature furthered a valid secular purpose in creating a paid, state holiday on Good Friday, stating that "nothing more is 'established' ... than an extra day of rest for a weary public labor-force."[116] Commenting that the Supreme Court, in *Lynch*, had interpreted the establishment clause to bar those practices having the purpose and effect of "endorsing" but not "accommodating" religion, the Ninth Circuit found that "[i]t is of no constitutional moment that Hawaii selected a day of traditional Christian worship rather than a neutral date, for its spring holiday once it identified the need."[117]

There is a pattern in these decisions, and it is not an encouraging one. First, the Supreme Court took the Christ out of Christmas in order to uphold the placement of religious symbols in public places, including public land, lacking in religious significance metamorphosed to secular objects. Second, it reinvented Christmas as the "winter holiday season" to rationalize the inclusion of Hanukkah menorahs in public religious displays. The Court also ignored the theological significance of the menorah, viewing it instead as a cultural, but not religious, reminder of the Jewish holiday of Hanukkah. Now, one of the most influential federal appelate courts has decided that Good Friday is so sufficiently lacking in religious meaning that a state statute granting it official status does not violate the establishment clause because this holiest of Christian holidays is but a part of the "spring holiday season." As if this rationale did not stretch even the outer boundaries of nonpreferentialist establishment clause jurisprudence, much less merit a flunking in a course on comparative religion, the Ninth Circuit also relied on *Oregon v. Smith*, brought and decided on free exercise grounds, to support government accommodation of majoritarian religion in an *establishment clause case!*

Nodding approval at *Smith*, the Ninth Circuit concluded that "the Supreme Court has recently identified as an 'unavoidable consequence of democratic government' the majority's political accommodation of its own religious practices and corresponding 'relative disadvantage to those religious practices that are not widely engaged in.'"[118] The Ninth Circuit's decision lacks plausible reasoning, since *Smith* did not involve government action taken on behalf of religion, but rather a challenge to a state statute that burdened individual religious rights.

Conclusion

Government endorsement of religion in the public sphere presents a quandry that goes directly to the heart of what the establishment clause was designed to prevent—government preference for religious values over nonreligious values and privileges accorded to one religion over others. The cases discussed in this chapter raise different moral and legal establishment clause problems than those discussed earlier. Government endorsement of religion in public places, unlike government sponsorship of religious practices in the public schools, does not involve the coercion of innocent third parties. Citizens are not compelled to view a religious display in front of City Hall; nor are most citizen-legislators in state legislatures required to acknowledge a legislative prayer prior to the opening of a session.

The case is fundamentally different for schoolchildren refusing to take part in "moments-of-silence" or to join student religious clubs. In those cases, the government, via its most potent and omnipresent symbol, the public schoolhouse, directly shapes the values transmitted to elementary and secondary school students. The potential isolation felt by students who do not subscribe to the majoritarian religious beliefs of a school district is real and constant for nine months of the year. Government financial aid to religious institutions is even more constitutionally problematic. Beyond the obvious establishment clause problems raised by the extraction of, to paraphrase Madison, "three pence" for the support of the religious missions of sectarian institutions, government aid to religion requires dissidents to submit to the taxing authority of government without consent, posing a fundamental threat to the moral basis upon which representative government is based.

Still, government preference accorded to religion in the public sphere is, in many ways, even more offensive. Government-sponsored religious displays, although displayed seasonally, nonetheless put forth a clear message—that some religions are officially recognized and preferred above all others. Religious accommodationists argue that the solution is for the offended citizen to turn the other way, but that does not eliminate the feeling that persons of different religious beliefs or no religious beliefs at all are guests in their own country. Government support for Nativity Scenes and menorahs signals to citizens identifying with neither that certain beliefs deserve official recognition, endorsement, and celebration, and that others do not. So, too, does government support for legislative chaplaincies. The legislator whose religious views are neglected or offended through government-sponsored invocation can only step away. Legislative chaplaincies do not involve the same coercive measures that, at least before the Court's decision to revisit the issue in *Lee v. Weisman*,[119] have doomed attempts at restoring religious exercises in the public schools. But the preferred status that the Supreme Court has conferred upon sectarian religion in the civic culture communicates an equally disturbing message about the place of religious minorities in American public life. Even worse, this support for religious preference comes at government expense.

The Court might view legislative chaplaincies, such as the one at issue in *Marsh*, as an acceptable establishment of religion because of their long-standing place in the American tradition. The Court's opinions in *Lynch* and *Allegheny* make clear that it views government support for seasonal religious displays as an acceptable form of religious establishment, so long as a creche is not displayed in an overtly religious manner, or the Christmas tree and menorah are presented tastefully. But neither the text nor the intent of the establishment clause permits government to place its approval behind religious practices it finds benign or acceptable. The establishment clause means that government cannot assist in or declare the establishment of religion in the public or private sphere. The size and scope of such establishments should be irrelevant considerations in constitutional decision making, but the logic evident in the cases discussed here indicate that such factors have become of central, but mistaken, importance in the Court's establishment clause jurisprudence.

Notes

1. 330 U.S. 1 (1947).
2. *McCollum v. Board of Education*, 333 U.S. 203 (1948); *Zorach v. Clauson*, 343 U.S. 306 (1952).
3. *Abington v. Schempp*, 374 U.S. 203 (1963); *Engel v. Vitale*, 370 U.S. 421 (1962).
4. *Board of Education v. Allen*, 392 U.S. 236 (1968).
5. Compare, for example, *Doe v. Ferguson*, 934 F.2d 743 (7th Cir. 1991) (holding Jaycee-sponsored display of sixteen larger-than-life pictures of Jesus Christ in public park unconstitutional) and *Kaplan v. City of Burlington*, 891 F.2d 1024 (1st Cir. 1989) (prohibiting Lubavitch from displaying Hanukkah menorah in public park) with *Congregation Lubavitch v. City of Cincinnati*, 923 F.2d 458 (6th Cir. 1991) (requiring city to accommodate a menorah display on public land despite opposition) and *Doe v. City of Warren*, 889 F.2d 1087 (6th Cir. 1989) (permitting municipal sponsorship of display including creche, menorah, Santa Claus, and colored lights); also, compare *Mather v. Village of Mundelein*, 864 F.2d 1291 (7th Cir. 1989) (holding display of creche on municipal building lawn not to violate establishment clause) with *American Jewish Congress v. City of Chicago*, 827 F.2d 120 (7th Cir. 1987) (striking down creche displayed in City Hall building).
6. *County of Allegheny v. American Civil Liberties Union*, 109 S.Ct. 3086 (1989).
7. *Lynch v. Donnelly*, 465 U.S. 668 (1984).
8. *Allegheny*, 109 S.Ct. at 3111.
9. Id. at 3110–12.
10. 465 U.S. 668 (1984).
11. 109 S.Ct. 3086 (1989).
12. *Lynch*, 465 U.S. at 680.
13. *Donnelly v. Lynch*, 691 F.2d 1029 (1st Cir. 1982), *Donnelly v. Lynch*, 525 F.Supp. 1150 (D.C. R.I. 1981).
14. Brief of the American Jewish Committee and the National Council of Churches, *amicus curiae*, *Lynch v. Donnelly*, No. 82-1256, at 13–16.
15. *Lynch*, 465 U.S. at 676.
16. Id.
17. *Lynch*, 465 U.S. at 681.
18. *Marsh v. Chambers*, 463 U.S. 783 (1983).
19. Id.
20. *Lynch*, 465 U.S. at 675.

21. Id. at 676.
22. Id.
23. Id.
24. Id. at 672–73.
25. Id. at 673.
26. Id. at 695–97 (Justice Brennan, dissenting).
27. Id. at 700–1.
28. Id. at 708.
29. Id. at 708–9.
30. Id. at 725–26.
31. Id. at 695.
32. 471 U.S. 83 (1985).
33. Justice Powell, due to illness, did not hear the case and recused from the vote.
34. *McCreary v. Stone*, 739 F.2d 716 (2nd Cir. 1984).
35. Id. at 727–29.
36. Id. at 727.
37. Id. at 729.
38. Id. at 724–25.
39. Id. at 729.
40. Id.
41. 109 S.Ct. 3086 (1989).
42. Id. at 3097.
43. Cited in *ACLU v. County of Allegheny*, 842 F.2d 655, 660 (3rd Cir. 1988).
44. Id.
45. Id.
46. Id. at 662.
47. Id.
48. Id. at 662–63.
49. *Allegheny*, 109 S.Ct. at 3103.
50. Id. at 3105.
51. Id. at 3115.
52. Id.
53. Id.
54. Id. at 3128–29, *infra*, (Justice Brennan, dissenting).
55. *Lynch*, 465 U.S. at 726–27 (Justice Blackmun, dissenting) (emphasis in original).
56. *Allegheny*, 109 S.Ct. at 3114.
57. Id. at 3115.
58. Id. at 3134 (Justice Kennedy, concurring in part and dissenting in part).
59. Id. at 3135.
60. Id. at 3134.
61. Id. at 3141.
62. Id. at 3138.
63. Id. at 3136.
64. Id. at 3146 ("In my view, the principles of the Establishment Clause and our Nation's historic traditions of diversity and pluralism allow communities to make reasonable judgments respecting the accommodation or acknowledgement of holidays with both cultural and religious aspects. No constitutional violation occurs when they do so by displaying a symbol of the holiday's religious origins").
65. Id. at 3106.

66. *Allegheny*, 109 S.Ct. at 3133 (Justice Stevens, concurring in part and dissenting in part).

67. Id. at 3128 (Justice Brennan, concurring in part and dissenting in part).

68. Id. at 3128–29.

69. See *Allegheny*, 109 S.Ct. at 3141, citing *Lynch*, 465 U.S. at 688 (Justice Kennedy, concurring in part and dissenting in part).

70. See the exchange between Justice Blackmun and Justice Kennedy, concurring in part and dissenting in part, in *Allegheny*, 109 S.Ct., at 3106, 3110 ("Justice Kennedy's reading of *Marsh v. Chambers* [citations omitted] would gut the core of the Establishment Clause, as this Court understands it. . . . Although Justice Kennedy repeatedly accuses the Court of harboring a 'latent hostility' or 'callous indifference' towards religion, nothing could be further from the truth, and the accusations could be said to be as offensive as they are absurd. Justice Kennedy apparently has misperceived a respect for religious pluralism, a respect commanded by the Constitution, as hostility or indifference to religion. No misperception could be more antithetical to the values embodied in the Establishment Clause"), Justice Kennedy, id. at 3146 ("The approach adopted by the majority contradicts important values embodied in the Clause. Obsessive, implacable resistance to all but the most carefully scripted and secularized forms of accommodation requires this Court to act as censor, issuing national decrees as to what is orthodox and what is not. What is orthodox, in this context, means what is secular; the only Christmas the State can acknowledge is one in which references to religion have been held to a minimum. The Court thus lends its assistance to an Orwellian rewriting of history as many understand it. I can conceive of no judicial function more antithetical to the First Amendment").

71. See *Wallace v. Jaffree*, 472 U.S. 38, 91–114 (1985) (Justice Rehnquist dissenting).

72. *Lee v. Weisman, cert. granted*, 111 S.Ct. 1305 (1991) (No. 90–1014).

73. Brief of the United States Department of Justice, *amicus curiae, Lee v. Weisman*, 111 S. Ct. 1305 (1991), No. 90–1014 at 8–9.

74. Briefs, *amicus curiae*, were filed in support of the appellant Rhode Island school board by the Liberty Counsel; the National School Boards Association; the Christian Legal Society, the National Association of Evangelicals, and the Fellowship of Legislative Chaplains; the National Legal Foundation; the National Jewish Commission on Law and Public Affairs; the Southern Baptist Convention Christian Life Commission; the Institute in Basic Life Principles; the Clarendon Foundation; Concerned Women for America and Free Speech Advocates; the United States Catholic Conference; and the State of Delaware.

Briefs, *amicus curiae*, were submitted on behalf of appellee Daniel Weisman by the Americans for Religious Liberty; the American Civil Liberties Union Foundation of Utah; the Council on Religious Freedom and Americans United for the Separation of Church and State; and the American Jewish Congress, the Anti-Defamation League of B'nai B'rith, the Baptist Joint Committee, and the National Council of Churches.

75. See chapter 1, *supra*, note 222.

76. "Souter Becomes a Consistent, Though Independent Vote for Conservative Bloc," *Wall Street Journal*, 28 June 1991.

77. Id.

78. 111 S.Ct. 1759 (1991).

79. Id. at 1788–89 (Justice O'Connor, dissenting).

80. See note 2, *supra*.

81. 827 F.2d 120 (7th Cir. 1987).

82. 869 F.2d 356 (7th Cir. 1989).

83. 791 F.2d 1561 (6th Cir. 1986).

84. 588 F. Supp. 1337, 1339-40 (E.D. Mich. 1984).

85. *ACLU v. City of Birmingham*, 791 F.2d 1561, 1564 (6th Cir. 1986).

86. Id. at 1566, quoting *Lynch*, 465 U.S. at 688 (Justice O'Connor, concurring).

87. 794 F.2d 265 (7th Cir. 1986), *cert. denied*, 107 S.Ct. 458 (1987).

88. 589 F.Supp. 222 (S.D. Tex. 1984).

89. Id. at 234-35.

90. Id. at 240.

91. Brief of Petitioner-Intervenor Chabad, *County of Allegheny v. American Civil Liberties Union*, No. 88-2050, 88-96, 88-90, at 30 ("[The menorah] has no particular religious significance when placed in a public location beyond signifying a 'Light to the World' somewhat like the Christmas message 'Peace of Earth, Goodwill to Men'").

92. Brief of the American Jewish Committee, the National Council of Churches, the Union of American Hebrew Congregations and Americans United for the Separation of Church and State, *amicus curiae, County of Allegheny v. American Civil Liberties Union*, No. 88-2050, 88-96, 88-90, at 13-17.

93. E.g., *Kaplan v. City of Burlington*, 891 F.2d 1024 (1st Cir. 1989) (coalition of Jewish religious leaders successfully sued Burlington, Vt. to prevent it from allowing Lubavitch to display a menorah in town square).

94. E.g., *Allegheny*, 109 S.Ct. at 3094-97 (comparing positions of Jewish organizations filing *amicus curiae* briefs in support of and opposition to the menorah display, as well as Petitioner-Intervenor Chabad).

95. E.g., *Lubavitch of Iowa, Inc. v. Walters*, 684 F. Supp. 610 (S.D. Iowa 1988), *aff'd*, 808 F.2d 656 (8th Cir. 1988)

96. No. 87-1808 (M.D. Fla. 1988).

97. No. 87-1809 (M.D. Fla. 1988).

98. See *Allegheny*, 109 S.Ct. at 3113-15.

99. See note 2, *supra*.

100. 463 U.S. 783 (1983).

101. Id. at 823, n.2 (Justice Stevens, dissenting).

102. *Chambers v. Marsh*, 504 F.Supp 585 (D. Neb. 1980).

103. *Chambers v. Marsh*, 675 F.2d 228 (8th Cir. 1982).

104. 463 U.S. at 792 (emphasis added).

105. Id., at 788.

106. 459 U.S. 116 (1982).

107. Id. at 126-27.

108. 673 F.Supp. 1524 (D. Hawaii 1987).

109. See e.g., *Lynch v. Donnelly*, 465 U.S. 668 (1984); *McGowan v. Maryland*, 366 U.S. 420 (1961).

110. *Waihee*, 673 F. Supp. at 1535.

111. Id. at 1537.

112. *Cammack v. Waihee*, 932 F.2d 765, 777 (9th Cir. 1991).

113. 366 U.S. 420 (1961).

114. 465 U.S. 668 (1984).

115. *Cammack*, 932 F.2d at 777.

116. Id. at 782.

117. Id. at 776.

118. Id. at 776, citing *Smith*, 110 S.Ct. 1595, 1606 (1990).
119. 908 F.2d 1090 (1st Cir. 1990), *cert. granted*, 111 S.Ct. 1305 (1991) (No. 90–1014).

4

Religious Free Exercise

The free exercise clause of the First Amendment places an absolute bar on government action criminalizing held or professed religious beliefs, or compelling the affirmation or existence of repugnant religious beliefs or making religious faith a criterion upon which to base citizenship or to receive government benefits. The establishment and free exercise clauses were created not to inform or encourage conflicts between religious rights and government interests, but to ensure robust protection for religious freedom. Public institutions are insulated from governmental efforts to advance religious interests through the separation of organized religion from the state. Government also is prohibited from supporting, encouraging, and endorsing a single religious denomination at the expense of others, or religion over the interests of nonreligion. The separation of church and state is a necessary predicate for religious free exercise; and free exercise is the touchstone of individual and denominational religious freedom.

The language of the free exercise clause is direct in the prohibition it places on government power to criminalize held religious faith or to coerce individuals into accepting religious beliefs against their will. But that same text is not as clear in exposing the protection accorded to religious *conduct* linked to those beliefs. The Supreme Court has said that religious conduct is indeed the "exercise of religion [that] often involves not only belief and profession but the performance of (or abstention from) physical acts."[1] The Court has also said that state or federal statutes banning religious acts or abstentions from them would be "prohibiting the free exercise of religion" if such conduct were proscribed only for religious reasons.[2] But the Court, while recognizing that the free exercise clause includes protection for religious conduct, has also said that religious acts are less protected than religious beliefs,[3] more protected if exercised in conjunction with other constitutionally protected rights,[4] and in some cases not protected at all.[5]

In contrast to the most recent free exercise rulings of the Supreme Court, I assume here that the free exercise clause does create a substantive constitutional right rather than just a procedural safeguard against government sanction;[6] and that it does protect the right to engage in religious conduct associated with religious faith, even if such behavior, in certain cases, necessitates an exemption from civil and criminal laws otherwise applicable to the general population.[7] But to discern the point at which the constitutional rights of religious free exercise yield to constitutional obligation to carry out its functions is a much more difficult assignment.

I will argue in this chapter that the Court, particularly in light of the coalescence of the Rehnquist Court over the last two terms, has gotten this relationship all wrong. I also will argue that, while the Rehnquist Court has certainly expedited the judicial demolition of religious rights, the Court's retreat from vigorous enforcement of the free exercise clause began long before its much-criticized decision in *Employment Division of Oregon v. Smith* (1990). I also will argue that the Rehnquist Court's crabbed and misconceived interpretation of the free exercise clause will have disastrous consequences for religious freedom.

The Evolution of Free Exercise Doctrine

Writing just over fifty years ago, Supreme Court Justice Owen J. Roberts captured this dilemma well. In his opinion for the Court in *Cantwell v. Connecticut* (1940),[8] a landmark decision striking down a Connecticut statute that banned religious proselyting in public places, Justice Roberts wrote that

[t]he constitutional inhibition of legislation on the subject of religion has a double aspect. On the one hand, it forestalls compulsion by law of the acceptance of any creed or the practice of any form of worship. Freedom of conscience and freedom to adhere to such religious organizations or form of worship as the individual may choose cannot be restricted by law. On the other hand, it safeguards the free exercise of the chosen form of religion. Thus the Amendment embraces two concepts—freedom to believe and freedom to act.[9]

Justice Roberts also was careful to note that, although the free exercise of religion included the right to believe and to act on those beliefs, their level of constitutional protection differed. The textual absolutism of the free exercise clause applied in full to protect those religious beliefs held and professed, but not to conduct compelled by adherence to those beliefs.[10] Such conduct "remains subject to regulation for the protection of society. The freedom to act must have appropriate definition to preserve the enforcement of that protection."[11] But Justice Roberts also commented that "[i]n every case the power to regulate must be so exercised as not, in attaining a permissible end, unduly to infringe the protected freedom."[12] From 1940 onward, the Supreme Court followed the direction it charted in *Cantwell*. The Court built a line of formidable precedent that placed most minoritarian religious practices out of the reach of government sanction. The central, controlling principle of the Court's free exercise clause jurisprudence became the compelling interest test. Government could not unduly burden or prohibit religious practices unless it could demonstrate a compelling state interest, or an objective of the "highest order."[13] The compelling interest requirement meant that government had to scrutinize federal or state statutes burdening the rights of religious minorities under the same standard as those which implicated other constitutional rights, such as freedom of speech or equal protection guarantees.

Cantwell marked a first, crucial step toward a more inclusive free exercise jurisprudence. It elevated the right to religious free exercise to preferred constitutional status. Of equal significance was the incorporation of the free exercise clause into the due process provision of the Fourteenth Amendment; the guarantee against governmental encroachment, which expressly forbade Congress from making laws prohibiting the "free exercise of religion," now applied to state governments as well. *Cantwell* was ratified and later expanded in subsequent decisions to include broad constitutional protection for religious minorities whose beliefs, rituals, and conduct would otherwise fall subject to the potentially harsh consequences of majoritarian rule.[14] *Cantwell* also indicated that the Court understood the importance of meaningful judicial safeguards for religious denominations whose numbers limited their political influence in the elected branches, and refused to equate their size with their constitutional status. Indeed, as Justice Robert H. Jackson wrote with characteristic literary grace in *West Virginia v. Barnette* (1943),[15]

[t]he very purpose of the Bill of Rights was to withdraw certain subjects from the vicissitudes of political controversy, to place them beyond the reach of majorities and officials and to establish them as legal principles to be applied by the courts. One's right to life, liberty . . . freedom of worship and assembly, and other fundamental rights may not be submitted to vote; they depend on the outcome of no elections.[16]

The highwater mark for the protection of individual religious rights came in 1981. Then, the Supreme Court, in *Thomas v. Review Board of Indiana*,[17] articulated its most imposing standard required of the government to date in order to justify an infringement on religious practices. In *Thomas*, the Court upheld the right of a Jehovah's Witness to unemployment compensation after he was dismissed from his job for refusing to work on an armaments project. The plaintiff claimed that his new job responsibility forced him to violate his religious beliefs. Chief Justice Warren Burger, writing for an 8–1 Court, held that

[t]he state may justify an inroad on religious liberty by showing that it is the least restrictive means of achieving some compelling interest. However, it is still true that "the essence of all that has been said and written on the subject is that only those interests of the highest order, and those not otherwise served can overbalance legitimate claims to the free exercise of religion."[18]

If *Thomas* meant to signal a sustained new direction in the Court's free exercise jurisprudence, as one might assume from the sweeping language of Chief Justice Burger's opinion, then it sent a false message. Soon after *Thomas*, the Court, in *United States v. Lee* (1982),[19] ruled that the Amish possessed no right under the free exercise clause to a constitutional religious exemption from their civic requirement to pay social security taxes. Writing for a unanimous Court, Chief Justice Burger found the government's interest in ensuring citizen compliance with the tax code an "overriding governmental interest" sufficient to overcome the religious objections of the Amish. *Lee* marked Chief Justice Burger's second encounter with the religious customs of the Old Order Amish. In *Wisconsin v. Yoder* (1972),[20] the Chief Justice wrote the Court's 6–1 opinion[21] affirming the right of Amish parents under the First and Fourteenth Amendment to exempt their children from Wisconsin's compulsory education laws. There, the Court relied on the unenumerated Fourteenth Amendment "right of parents to control the education of their children," established in *Pierce v. Society of Sisters* (1925),[22] and the free exercise rights of the Amish to direct the religious development of their children, who would be irreparably damaged if exposed to the wordly influences of secular education.[23]

The *Lee* Court did not find that refusing an exemption for the Amish from social security taxes presented an equivalent dilemma. The Court did not distinguish why the public interest in maintaining a competent system of tax collection was more substantial than requiring compliance with state compulsory education laws. The Chief Justice did seem to find important the fact that the Amish had entered into a commercial farming enterprise. The decision of the Amish to cross the line from their self-contained religious world to the secular, commercial domain was one made on their own volition. In cases such as these, the Chief Justice ruled, religious observers could not remain automatically exempt from government regulation, even if that meant compliance with such regulations resulted in a substantial burden on religious conduct.[24]

Yoder and *Lee* each raised the question of whether religious exemptions from statutes otherwise applicable to the general population were constitutionally required. In each case, the Court applied the compelling state interest test, but reached different results. Whether these disparate outcomes were due simply to the Court's loss of Justices Douglas and Stewart and their replacement with Justices Stevens and O'Connor is doubtful. Justice Douglas dissented in *Yoder*[25] and Justice Stewart interpreted the Court's opinion quite narrowly.[26] Thus, it appeared as if the Court, although willing to defer to government the authority necessary to advance those interests of the "highest order," still respected principled religious objections enough to give them strict scrutiny under the free exercise clause. But a closer reading of Justice Stevens' concurring opinion in *Lee* suggests that a subtle reconsideration of *Sherbert* might have been circulating among the Justices long before *Smith* was decided.

In *Lee*, Justice Stevens, concurring in the judgment, wrote that religious exemptions to facially neutral laws having application to the general population were almost never constitutionally required. His views on the matter were roughly parallel to those of Justice John Harlan, who, dissenting in *Sherbert*, argued that "situations in which the Constitution may require special treatment are . . . few and far between.[27] But Justice Stevens extended that argument. A constitutional requirement that states "carve out an exception"[28] for individuals whose religious faith makes civic obedience impossible in certain instances is compatible with the free exercise clause only in the narrowest of circumstances. Even then, wrote Justice Stevens, no "compelling interest test" is required, for "it is the objector who must shoulder the burden of demonstrating that there is a unique reason for allowing him a special exemption from a valid law of general applicability."[29]

One term before, Justice Rehnquist had said in *Thomas* that *Sherbert* should be overruled. *Lee* did not inspire him to repeat his call, but it becomes clear over time that the votes to revisit *Sherbert* were slowly falling into place. In *Smith*, four Justices signed Justice Scalia's opinion: Justice Rehnquist, Justice Stevens, Justice White, who dissented in *Sherbert*,[30] and Justice Kennedy, who, as did the other four Justices, voted with the Court in *Lyng v. Northwest Cemetery Protective Association* (1988), which upheld the decision of the federal government to build a road through and around an Indian burial ground, and did so without subjecting the claim to the compelling state interest test.[31] That the Court decided to discard *Sherbert*'s application in free exercise cases involving challenges to neutral laws having general application is less surprising than the manner in which it chose to do so.

In *Smith*,[32] the Court eviscerated *Sherbert, Thomas,* and their progeny in language so clear that it left no doubt about its purpose in hearing the case. Prior to *Smith*, the Court had been moving in an unsettling direction in its treatment of free exercise claims, having failed to apply the Sherbert rule in several cases since *Thomas*.[33] But the Court had left undisturbed the viability of the compelling state interest test.[34] On several occasions, the Court has ruled that the free exercise clause, in certain circumstances, requires that religious conduct remain exempt from criminal and civil laws otherwise applicable to the general population.[35] In other cases, the Court has indicated that religious exemptions, while not required, are nonetheless permissible.[36] But if the Court meant what it said in *Smith*, and there is no reason to think otherwise, then all these distinctions become irrelevant. Legislatures will not have to explain the burden or restrictions that formally neutral state statutes have on religious conduct. Political bodies will be able to do what they please, whether out of negligence, through evil designs, or for no reason at all, so long as the statute does not single out religion for discriminatory treatment.

In *Smith*, the Court upheld an Oregon statute that criminalized the sacramental use of peyote, a hallucinogenic drug, by adherents of the Native American church, even though the use of peyote as part of established Indian religious ritual is a central tenet of the faith. But the

Court did not just stop there. Without requesting briefs or arguments on the question, the Court held that laws that burden religious conduct but are otherwise applicable to the general population "need not be justified by a compelling governmental interest" standard of review.[37] Customarily, the Court asks for briefs on the merits of the issue when it announces that it wants to revisit a previous holding or jurisprudential method.[38] In an abrupt departure from settled practice, the Court in *Smith* gave no signal that its free exercise jurisprudence was under direct reconsideration. This left the nation's religious denominations and their organizational representatives helpless to submit *amicus* briefs informing the Court of the implications of such a rule change.

The Native American church, the American Jewish Congress and Synagogue Council of America, and the American Civil Liberties Union and its Oregon affiliate each filed *amicus* briefs asking the Court to find in favor of Alfred Smith and Galen Black, the dismissed Native American drug counselors, on the grounds that Oregon had shown no compelling interest to ban the ritual use of peyote. None of these *amici* addressed the consequences of overruling *Sherbert* because none knew, or even suspected, that the Court had the intention of emsaculating the law of free exercise. Other religious organizations strongly supportive of expansive religious free exercise rights, such as the Baptist Joint Committee, the National Council of Churches, and the National Association of Evangelicals, did not even file *amicus* briefs in *Smith*, because none had any idea that the Court was going to sound *Sherbert*'s death knell. These groups, with the Baptist Joint Committee serving as the chair for the Coalition for the Free Exercise of Religion, an ad hoc group consisting of some 45 religious and secular organizations, have since been out front in encouraging Congress to repeal the *Smith* decision through federal statute.[39] Had the Court informed the parties of the stakes in *Smith*, the reaction would have been much, much different, as it has been since, to have the compelling state interest/least restrictive means test restored.

Perhaps the Court had no invidious motives in mind when it decided *Smith*, but simply viewed it as another corrective to what it believes was the misguided constitutional jurisprudence of the Warren and early Burger Courts. Indeed, the two self-identified apostles of judicial conservatism, Justice Scalia and Chief Justice Rehnquist, have not been bashful about using judicial activism to overturn undesirable precedent. Both are on record as having no qualms about revisiting established decisions that they consider "wrong" or "unworkable."[40] Both would like to see the Court's role reduced to one that merely ratifies political judgments. Neither believes the Court should use legislative history as a guide to deciphering legislative intent or give exacting scrutiny to majority acts that implicate constitutional rights.[41] If *Smith* is a harbinger of this Court's path toward a greater constitutional vision, then a radical demolition of current law and the redefinition of the judicial and legislative functions in the separation of powers, signs of which are now unmistakably in place, promises to proceed apace.

Smith contains staggering implications for what religious minorities can expect in the future. The message cannot be clearer: protecting the free exercise rights of religious minorities is no longer the presumptive obligation of the courts, but of the political process. The Court reached this conclusion even while acknowledging that "it may be fairly said that leaving accommodation to the political process will place *at a relative disadvantage those religious practices that are not widely engaged in,*" a result which the Court merely deemed "an unavoidable consequence of democratic government."[42] In other words, the Court does not view statutes, regardless of their oppressive cast, that burden religious conduct, no matter how central such behavior is to the tenets of one's faith, as deserving more than deferential review. Such is the place of religious rights in the Rehnquist Court's scheme of preferred constitutional values.

How the Court arrived at its decision in *Smith* can be better understood through a review of its free exercise jurisprudence over the last decade, the subject to which the remainder of this chapter now turns.

The Protection of Unorthodox Religious Conduct

The struggle of religious minorities to remove the legal shackles that are often imposed on their right to conduct their lives according to the requirements of their religious conscience is still an incomplete process. There is no question that the power of legislative majorities to transfer their held prejudices and suspicions of religious minorites into oppressive law has been muted in the modern constitutional era. Such diverse religious denominations as the Jehovah's Witnesses, the Seventh-day Adventists, the Amish, and the Quakers have overcome hostile and often prejudicial government action reflective of popular opinion, which has often viewed the practices of smaller and less well-known religions as foreign, obnoxious, and illegitimate.[43]

For these small but well-organized religious communities, litigation has served as the most effective tool of collective action through which to vindicate their constitutional right to full and equal status in the American religious milieu.[44] It is no exaggeration to state that, for religious minorities, the constitutional rights secured as a result of the Jehovah's Witnesses' decision to challenge laws ranging from state antiproselytizing measures[45] to federal regulations governing conscientious objection status under the selective service laws,[46] of Seventh-day Adventist Adell Sherbert to challenge South Carolina's refusal to provide her unemployment compensation because she refused jobs that required her to work on her Saturday Sabbath,[47] and of the Amish to insist that religious belief and tradition prevented them from sending their children to public schools,[48] are equal in importance to the great victories that the National Association for the Advancement of Colored People (NAACP) achieved for black Americans and other ethnic minorities in their meticulous campaign to have racially discriminatory practices declared unconstitutional.[49]

The Supreme Court used *Cantwell* as the foundation on which to construct its free exercise jurisprudence. The Court never ruled that constitutional protection for religiously motivated conduct was absolute, but then that had never been the goal of religious minorities seeking judicial redress. For religious minorities whose practices are considered outside the dominant mainstream of organized American religion, their principal objective was to force the language of the First Amendment to be true to its promise. In the forty years after *Cantwell*, religious minorities were able to secure their constitutional rights with a level of success equal to other social movements that had used planned, test-case litigation to achieve similar goals. Political jurisprudence had the effect of revolutionizing both the meaning of the First Amendment and the rights of those dependent upon its guarantees for their religious freedom.

In *Cantwell*, the Court created and adhered to a free exercise jurisprudence that granted substantial protection against government abridgement of religious conduct. In a line of cases representing an amalgam of religious freedom claims, the Court had interpreted the provisions of the free exercise clause to include the practices of religious nonconformists as part of the diverse mosaic of American spiritual life. *Smith* changes all that. But prior to *Smith*, the Court had been slowly, but surely, moving away from this vigilant posture.

The first clear signal that the Court might be backing away from its established free exercise jurisprudence came in *Goldman v. Weinberger* (1986).[50] Simcha Goldman, an Orthodox Jew, was a clinical psychologist and captain in the United States Air Force. Goldman, an ordained rabbi, served as an air force chaplain between 1970 and 1972. He then took leave from those responsibilities to enter an armed forces program in the health professions and sciences. In 1977, after completing his Ph.D. in psychology, he received an assignment to an air force base in Riverside, California. From 1977 to 1981, Goldman wore his yarmulke while on official duty. He had never been told that wearing a yarmulke while in uniform was problematic; indeed, the subject had not even been brought up. In fact, the air force recognized Captain Goldman for distinguished service on several occasions. It had never given him reason to believe that his religious beliefs posed a problem in carrying out his professional responsibilities.

In April 1981, Goldman, while testifying as a defense witness in a court-martial trial, was told, for the first time, that wearing his yarmulke while on duty violated an air force uniform dress regulation. The regulation, AFR 35–10, states, in relevant part, that "headgear will not be worn . . . [w]hile indoors except by armed security police in the performance of their duties."[51] Goldman was told by his superior officers to cease wearing his yarmulke while on duty. He refused to comply with the order. Goldman was then issued a formal letter of reprimand and threatened with court-martial proceedings. In addition, a positive recommendation that had been submitted on behalf of Goldman for a one-year extension of service in the air force was withdrawn and a negative evaluation submitted in its place.

Goldman, seeking to enjoin the enforcement of AFR 35–10, initiated a lawsuit in federal district court against the secretary of defense. He claimed that application of the air force regulation violated his rights under the free exercise clause. Granting the injunction, the U.S. District Court for the District of Columbia ruled that the air force had failed to demonstrate a compelling state interest that justified violating the legitimate free exercise rights of Goldman. The court ordered the air force to withdraw the letter of reprimand and the negative evaluation.[52]

On appeal, the D.C. Circuit Court of Appeals reversed. The divided panel, 2-1, held that the air force regulation was narrowly drawn and linked to the legitimate military goal of enforcing a uniform standard of dress.[53] The appeals court acknowledged that the regulation was "arbitrary." Nonetheless, the court ruled that the air force's interest in enforcing uniform codes of conduct and the traditional deference shown to the interests of the military did not require accommodation of what the court acknowledged was a legitimate First Amendment claim.

The Supreme Court, 5-4, affirmed. Writing for the Court, Justice Rehnquist ruled that the traditional deference shown to the "professional judgment of the air force" in matters concerning military regulation included the enforcement of a uniform standard of military dress.[54] In affirming the appeals court, the Court admitted that, "to the extent the regulations do not permit the wearing of religious apparel such as a yarmulke, a practice described by [Goldman] as silent devotion akin to prayer, military life may be more objectionable for [Goldman] and probably others."[55] Still, the Court concluded that the armed forces were under "no constitutional mandate to abandon their considered professional judgment."[56]

In his concurring opinion, Justice Stevens noted that "Captain Goldman presents an especially attractive case for an exception" to military dress regulations because of his sincere religious faith, the familiarity of a yarmulke and its symbolism, and because it serves as an "eloquent rebuke to the ugliness of anti-Semitism."[57] Furthermore, Justice Stevens wrote that a constitutionally required exemption for Goldman would not disrupt the military. He also expressed distaste for the retributional tactics that the air force used to intimidate Goldman. But Justice Stevens' greater concern was directed toward the consequences of creating a constitutional exemption to AFR 35-10. Raising possibilities of future litigation contesting the demands of Sikhs or Rastafarians for turbans and dreadlocks, Justice Stevens concluded that AFR 35-10 was written and enforced in a "neutral, completely objective" manner.[58] Since it drew no distinctions based upon religious affiliation, the air force had not crossed over the forbidden line of discriminatory intent. Creating a constitutional exemption for yarmulkes would subvert the traditional control of the armed forces over such matters. It was not discrimination, but the "true principle of uniformity that supports that rule."[59]

Dissenting, Justice Brennan observed that the air force was asking Goldman "to violate the tenets of his faith virtually every minute of every workday."[60] He also criticized the Court for reviewing Goldman's case under a rational basis standard, arguing that all free exercise claims, regardless of their context, should be subject to the same rigorous standard of exacting judicial scrutiny normally applied in such cases. In an even more pungent tone, Justice Brennan wrote that "[the Court had] abdicate[d] its role as principal expositor of the Constitution and protector of individual liberties in favor of credulous deference to unsupported assertions of military necessity."[61]

Justice Brennan did not stop there. He charged the Court with simply restating the assertions of the military "without offering any explanation how the exception Dr. Goldman requests reasonably could interfere with the air force's interests,"[62] arguing that had the Court "given actual consideration to Goldman's claim, it would have been compelled to decide in his favor."[63] Finally, Justice Brennan rejected the Court's reasoning that because AFR 35-10 was facially neutral and lacked an invidious motive, it did not burden religious rights in a constitutionally obnoxious manner. In his view, this rationale allowed the government to repress religious rights, so long as it did so in a fair fashion, with the result being "that under the guise of neutrality and evenhandedness, majority religions are favored over distinctive minority faiths."[64]

The following term, the Court again relied on the deference doctrine, which states that courts should defer to the authority of administrative agencies to implement statutes as it suits their needs,[65] to uphold the power of governmental authorities to suppress free exercise rights when it decided *O'Lone v. Shabazz* (1987).[66] In *Shabazz*, two Islamic inmates in a New Jersey state prison requested an exemption from prison policies that burdened their ability to attend Jumu'ah, a weekly Muslim congregational service. Until April 1983, the Islamic prisoners were able to attend Jumu'ah services. Then, new regulations were instituted governing the free movement of inmates throughout different sections of the prison. Ironically, the inmates classified under less stringent security regulations were the ones who were no longer able to attend Jumu'ah services. After negotiations between the Islamic prisoners and prison officials failed to produce an agreement that would permit the inmates to attend religious services, the inmates instituted a federal lawsuit alleging that the prison policies constituted a violation of their religious rights.

Upon review, a federal district court ruled that the new prison policies regulating prisoner movement were reasonable and did not unconstitutionally infringe upon the free exercise rights of the prisoners.[67] The district court rejected the prisoners' arguments that equal and alternative arrangements were mandated under the free exercise clause. It held that the post-April 1983 prison regulations on inmate movement advanced the plausible institutional goals of security, order, and rehabilitation.[68] The district court concluded that the prison had enacted reasonable regulations that bore a rational relationship to legitimate penological interests, and that the prison had adopted the least restrictive means available without "compromising a legitimate institutional objective."[69]

The Third Circuit Court of Appeals, hearing the case *en banc*, reversed the lower court judgment. It ruled that the district court had not examined the prisoners' free exercise claim under the proper jurisprudential standard of strict scrutiny.[70] The circuit court held that, when asked to justify institutional regulations that encroached upon the religious rights of inmates, the prison was required to demonstrate the compelling interest advanced through such policies. The prison could not escape under the rational basis test. The Third Circuit concluded that the prison had violated the free exercise rights of its Muslim prisoners because it had not demonstrated a compelling state interest, had attempted to accommodate the needs of the inmates through alternative or less restrictive means.[71] The prison appealed.

The Supreme Court, 5–4, reversed. In his opinion for the Court, Chief Justice Rehnquist held that the prison regulations, even though they had the effect of compromising the free exercise rights of the inmates, were linked to the important penological interest of maintaining control over inmate movement. The Court also ruled that the Third Circuit had erred in requiring the prison to show that more reasonable methods were available to accommodate the prisoners' religious conduct than the policies challenged. In contravening this assertion, and in the process continuing the Court's disturbing trend of deferring to "rationally-based" governmental objectives instead of using the *Sherbert* compelling interest test to analyze free exercise claims outside the unemployment compensation or education arenas, Chief Justice Rehnquist wrote that "[w]e take this opportunity to reaffirm our refusal, even where claims are made under the First Amendment, to 'substitute our judgment on difficult matters of institutional administration,' for the determinations of those charged with the formidable task of running a prison."[72] The Court ruled that prisons had no obligation to meet the compelling interest/least restrictive means test otherwise applicable in free exercise cases because of their special relationship to noncivilian individuals.[73]

Dissenting, Justice Brennan argued that prisoners, even though they were no longer citizens with full political and civil rights, are still entitled to have their constitutional claims alleging an abridgement of a fundamental freedom reviewed under the Court's strict scrutiny standard. Justice Brennan argued that the Court's reliance on the "reasonableness standard" in such cases, which it endorsed as a jurisprudential vehicle to "review *all* constitutional challenges by inmates," is not an adequate standard of review to analyze alleged infringements of fundamental rights.[74] Lamenting the wide latitude that the Court had granted to the prison authorities, Justice Brennan concluded that "[t]o deny the opportunity to affirm membership in a spiritual community, however, may extinguish an inmate's last source of hope for dignity and redemption. Such a denial requires more justification than mere assertion that any other course of action is infeasible."[75]

The following term, the Court answered doubts about whether *Goldman* and *Shabazz* were aberrant jurisprudential exceptions granted to military and prison authorities so that they enforce policies that advanced special interests not applicable to general civilian conduct. To skeptical observers, these decisions were part of a more unpleasant pattern of growing judicial unwillingness to uphold exemptions for unorthodox religious behavior. The Court's decision in *Lyng v. Northwest Indian Cemetery Protective Association* (1988)[76] confirmed the latter view.

The issue in *Lyng* centered on whether the free exercise clause prevented the United States Forest Service from building roads that would go through and around the Chimney Rock section of the Six Rivers National Forest, a national park historically used by Native American tribes for cultural and religious purposes. Studies commissioned by the Forest Service on the history of Native American cultural and religious sites in the area found that the entire Chimney Rock area was "significant as an integral and indispensable part of Indian religious conceptualization and practice."[77] The study concluded that building a road along any of the proposed routes "would cause serious and irreparable damage to the sacred areas which are an integral and necessary part of the belief systems and lifeway of Northwest California Indian peoples."[78]

The Forest Service rejected the report's recommendation that road construction cease. It selected another proposed route for the road that would have much less impact on the identified burial grounds, but that would still disturb the ritual and religious ceremonies of the Native American tribes. After exhausting all their administrative remedies, a coalition of Native American organizations sued the Forest Service in federal district court to enjoin the completion of the proposed road's construction. The district court ruled in favor of the Northwest Indian Cemetary Protective Association. It issued a permanent injunction that prohibited the Forest Service from building in the Chimney Rock section of the park or putting a timber-harvesting management plan into effect.[79] The Ninth Circuit Court of Appeals affirmed.[80]

The Supreme Court, 5-3, reversed.[81] Justice O'Connor, in her opinion for the Court, held that the government's actions did not coerce the Native American tribes into violating their religious beliefs through compulsion or threat.[82] Interpreting the free exercise clause in the narrowest possible terms, Justice O'Connor ruled that the free exercise clause prohibits government from compelling individuals into accepting religious beliefs or acting against those beliefs, but it does not prohibit state action that has an "incidental effect on certain religious practices."[83] Justice O'Connor did not contest the evidence that showed the devastating impact that the logging and road-construction projects would have on traditional Native American religious practices. Nonetheless, she concluded that the free exercise clause did not require the Court to "satisfy every citizen's religious needs and desires."[84] Government must retain the authority to advance important and legitimate government objectives, even if those goals burden individual religious rights.[85]

Justice O'Connor's crabbed reading of the free exercise clause in *Lyng* continued the Court's gradual and consistent movement away from *Sherbert* and its progeny. *Lyng* left proponents of broad free exercise rights pessimistic over the Court's approach to future claims involving unorthodox religious conduct. *Lyng* indicated that the Court was willing to analyze free exercise claims under the rational basis standard in cases involving other than noncivilian needs, or in other cases that it claimed involved special circumstances. The Court's analysis of the claims brought forth in *Goldman*, *Shabazz*, and *Lyng* begin to reveal quite openly its reluctance to read the free exercise clause in substantive terms.

The pattern of reasoning in these cases revealed the return of the belief-action distinction as the preferred analytical device for reviewing free exercise claims. Under this framework, the free exercise clause prohibits government from criminalizing religious beliefs, whether held or professed, but does not impose on the government the same restriction to limit or prohibit religious conduct.[86] The Court, in *Goldman*, *Shabazz*, *Lyng*, and *Smith*, still required the government to show some justification for restricting sincere religious conduct, but also said that the reason only needs to be a reasonable or legitimate one. Simcha Goldman can remain an Orthodox Jew; and Ahmad Uthman Shabazz can continue to ascribe to the Islamic faith. The Court reaffirmed that the government cannot criminalize religious beliefs of individuals for holding them. But neither is the government obligated to exempt religious individuals from civil laws that force them to choose between their faith and citizenship. What they can believe, and what they can do, are separate constitutional problems. Thus, while the Court's action in *Smith* remains surprising for its unannounced departure from procedural norms and,[87] its even more scandalous holding, when placed in context, was the next logical step after *Lyng*.

Seen in this light, Justice O'Connor's sharply worded concurring opinion in *Smith*, in which she dissented from the Court's decision to shelve the compelling interest test once and for all in free exercise cases involving neutral and generally applicable statutes, is bitterly ironic.[88] In *Smith*, Justice O'Connor, in no uncertain terms, criticized Justice Scalia's opinion for misreading "settled First Amendment precedent"[89] to reach the decision, one that she argued could have been reached by applying "our established free exercise jurisprudence."[90] But it is important to point out that, while Justice O'Connor professes a sincere concern for the protection of religious minorities as expressed in her written opinions, her voting behavior in free exercise cases does not demonstrate an attempt through searching examination to recognize the importance of meaningful statutory and constitutional exemptions from government policies that cripple practice of religious beliefs.

Examine the record: In *Goldman*,[91] Justice O'Connor dissented from both the Court's opinion and judgment. In her *Goldman* dissent, Justice O'Connor criticized the majority for reviewing the asserted free exercise claim under the "reasonableness standard,"[92] as well as for failing to accommodate Captain Goldman's request, which she maintained had far more proportionate weight when balancing the military's interest in uniformity against the "sincere religious beliefs of the individual."[93] Leaving *Goldman* aside, Justice O'Connor, voted with the Court, in addition to *Shabazz* and *Lyng*, in *Kendrick*,[94] *Lee*,[95] *Smith I*,[96] *Heffron v. ISKCON*,[97] *Ansonia v. Philbrook*,[98] and wrote the Court's opinion Swaggert.[99] In *Shabazz*, Justice O'Connor saw no need to distance herself from Chief Justice Rehnquist's opinion for the Court, which held that free exercise claims asserted in a penological context did not merit strict scrutiny because of the special need of prisons to maintain inmate discipline.[100] In her *Lyng* opinion, Justice O'Connor did not find *Sherbert* relevant, even though the factual record before the Court indicated that the planned road, if completed, "could have devastating effects on traditional Indian religious practices."[101]

Justice O'Connor voted with the Court to uphold free exercise claims in three routine unemployment compensation cases, *Thomas v. Review Board of Indiana*,[102] *Hobbie v. Unemployment Appeals Commission*,[103] and *Frazee v. Illinois Department of Employment Security*.[104] Each case followed *Sherbert*. *Thomas* and *Hobbie* were decided by 8–1 votes; *Frazee* was unanimous. What is perhaps more telling is that Justice O'Connor and Justice Scalia have voted together in each of these cases since the latter joined the Court for the 1986 term. If Justice O'Connor possesses a firm conviction of the constitutional protection required for religious rights under the free exercise clause that is somehow more enlightened than her conservative colleagues, then it remains a held belief. While her rhetoric is less strident than, for example, Justices Scalia or Rehnquist, Justice O'Connor has voted to strike down free exercise claims as consistently as other members of the Court's conservative wing.

In dissent, Justice Brennan, joined by Justices Blackmun and Marshall, wrote that the Court had reached an "astonishing" conclusion.[105] Continuing the line of criticism formulated in his *Goldman* and *Shabazz* dissents, Justice Brennan again chastised the Court for failing to employ a strict scrutiny analysis to actions of government "that frustrate or inhibit religious practice."[106] Justice Brennan also criticized the majority for the "noncoercive" test it used to analyze the free exercise claim at issue, arguing that the distinction it created between "governmental actions that compel affirmative conduct inconsistent with religious belief, and those governmental actions that prevent conduct consistent with religious belief" lacked merit.[107] Justice O'Connor's linguistic semantics did not impress Justice Brennan, who called her reliance on the belief-action distinction one "without constitutional significance."[108]

Justice Brennan also faulted Justice O'Connor for her "noncoercive" analysis in *Lyng*, arguing that "[Native Americans] will not derive any solace from the knowledge that although the practice of their religion will become 'more difficult' as a result of the [g]overnment's actions, they remain free to maintain their religious beliefs."[109] The "noncoercive" test that Justice O'Connor articulated in Lyng took great pains to distinguish between the permissible government regulation of religious belief and that of conduct linked to religious beliefs, a distinction that Justice Scalia followed to the letter in *Smith*.[110] Justice O'Connor acknowledged in *Lyng*, citing the unemployment compensation cases decided under the free exercise clause, that the government still carried the burden of showing that the challenged regulations advanced a compelling state interest. The result reached in *Lyng*, though, with its attendant lack of concern about the consequences of state action and its willingness to depart from strict application of the compelling state interest test, provided the analytical foundation for the outcome in *Smith*. Despite her protests in *Smith*, Justice O'Connor's *Lyng* opinion gave Justice Scalia the plausible rationale he needed to write the opinion that he did. As discussed earlier, the votes to overrule *Sherbert* were in place when *Smith* was before the Court; Justice O'Connor's "noncoercive" analysis in *Lyng* added the necessary final ingredient for Justice Scalia to slam the door shut on the issue once and for all.

Reconciling Religious Rights with Secular Responsibilities

The Evolution of Judicial Guidelines

The Supreme Court has interpreted federal constitutional provisions and federal statutory law to allow religious observers special protection against employment discrimination not otherwise available to protected class groups under equal protection doctrine. Employers are required to make reasonable efforts to accommodate the needs of religious observers whose faith-compelled behavior interferes with their ability to meet workplace responsibilities unless such accommodation poses an "undue hardship" on regular business operations.[111] Moreover, individuals who refuse to accept employment or who are fired from their jobs for religious reasons are, in some cases, entitled to public welfare benefits and, in others, eligible for such benefits under federal and state statutes.[112] The Court has also ruled that the implied and enumerated provisions in the corpus of federal civil rights law that exempt religious institutions from its antidiscrimination requirements are constitutional,[113] even if the challenged discriminatory employment practices extend to nonfaith related jobs.[114]

Two core principles have animated the rationale for securing religious observers preferential treatment under federal civil rights law and exempting religious institutions from antidiscrimination requirements that are otherwise applicable to nonreligious employers. Congress has determined,[115] and the Court has so upheld,[116] that religion poses a special case in the enforcement of antidiscrimination guarantees in the workplace that prejudicial treatment on the basis of race, color, gender, and national origin do not. Because the free exercise clause creates a substantive constitutional right; and because religious conduct varies according to religious belief; and because faith-compelled religious conduct can result in job-based conflicts for reasons that attributes based on race, gender, or ethnic origin cannot, government must take special precautions to ensure that religious rights are protected. In addition, the Court has long recognized the rights of religious institutions having wholly or pervasively sectarian functions to decide their own doctrine and church practices and to order their internal affairs without interference from civil authorities.[117] The church autonomy doctrine mandates that churches remain free from governmental regulation because of the neutrality requirement of the establishment clause and because of the fundamental free exercise clause principle of removing civil jurisdiction over private religious affairs.[118]

But the Court has never declared the accommodation of religious rights in the workplace or through the public welfare system an absolute constitutional guarantee. *Smith* narrows the obligation of states to accommodate religiously-based claims to public welfare benefits[119] and eliminates it in others,[120] but leaves standing those cases that do not involve conflicts with generally applicable laws,[121] or involve what the Court now refers to as "hybrid" constitutional claims.[122] While it has ruled that employers must demonstrate reasonable efforts to accommodate the religious needs of their employees, the Court has also held that statutes entitling employees to an absolute right not to work on their Sabbath violate the establishment clause.[123] *Smith* means that government agencies will have far more discretion in their treatment of religious claims. But *Smith* will not relieve employers of their obligation to demonstrate reasonable accommodation of religious needs under the *Hardison* rule because it is not applicable outside the context of state action.

The Court has not always been so hostile to religiously-based claims for exemption from private and government policies that burdened religious conduct falling within the scope of the employment and hiring arena. In fact, the Court had been quite hospitable to the notion that exemptions for faith-compelled conduct that conflicted with secular obligations were entitled to constitutional and statutory protection. That doctrine stemmed from the foundational jurisprudential principles established in *Cantwell*. But the Court, after *Cantwell*, did not confront the relevance of the free exercise clause to the arena of private commercial enterprise until just over twenty years later. In the interim, several important cases were decided under the free exercise clause, but most of these involved challenges to government regulations that limited or prohibited religious speech in public places[124] and temporal statutes that required churches and their faithful to disavow certain beliefs in order to retain tax exemption.[125] During this period, the Court also liberalized the "ministerial exemption" requirement for individuals claiming conscientious objection from the federal selective service laws.[126]

In 1961, the Court decided four separate cases raising both establishment and free exercise challenges to Sunday closing laws, sometimes referred to as "blue laws," that adversely affected Saturday Sabbatarians. In the *Sunday Closing Cases*,[127] the Court heard arguments from four separate business owners in Pennsylvania, Maryland, and Massachussetts that these "blue laws" violated the establishment clause because they singled out Sunday, which for most Christian denominations constitutes the Sabbath, to regulate or forbid commerical activities in order to promote church attendance and religious observance, and violated the free exercise clause because it placed at a competitive disadvantage those religious denominations that observed the Saturday Sabbath. In each case, the Court reexamined the origin of Sunday closing laws against their contemporary purpose to determine if such statutes advanced religious goals or discriminated against religious minorities in violation of the First Amendment religion clauses.

In *Two Guys v. McGinley*[128] and *McGowan v. Maryland*,[129] the Court rejected the establishment clause attack on the Pennsylvania and Maryland Sunday closing laws. Chief Justice Earl Warren wrote for the Court in both cases, as he did in the two companion free exercise cases decided the same day, *Gallagher v. Crown Kosher Market*[130] and *Braunfeld v. Brown*.[131] The Court acknowledged in the two establishment clause cases that the origin of the Sunday closing laws was "strongly religious," but found the subsequent purpose of these laws was to secure a common day of rest and relaxation, a legitimate secular purpose designed to advance the general public welfare.[132] If individuals could show that these statutes constituted state aid to religion or demonstrated coercive power to force compliance with religious belief, then their secular orientation would be questionable. In *Two Guys* and *McGowan*, the Court held, with only Justice Douglas dissenting, that states could regulate commercial enterprise on Sunday as a valid exercise of its power to promote the public welfare. The establishment clause did not ban "state regulation of conduct whose reason or effect merely happens to coincide or harmonize with the tenets of some or all religions."[133]

Maryland's law permitted numerous exceptions to the ban on commerical activities. These included alcohol and tobacco sales, professional sporting events, movie theaters and other entertainment, and even the operation of bingo halls.[134] The Chief Justice concluded that these exceptions taken together formed the heart of common recreational weekend activities.[135] But Chief Justice Warren's opinion never addressed the consequences that these inconsistencies have for individuals whose business suffers as a result. Nor did the opinion explain the significance of the Christian Sabbath as the designated time for communal relaxation. On the other hand, it was difficult to show that, even with the knowledge of the Sunday closing laws' orgins, the state was unconstitutionally advancing the interests of majoritarian religion. Thus, the Court offers in *Two Guys* and *McGowan* a plausible if superficial defense of state police power to regulate in the public interest.

The Court's failure to find in favor of the Orthodox Jewish merchants who were forced to cease food and clothing sales under separate state Sunday closing laws was then and remains utterly indefensible. In *Braunfeld* and *Crown Kosher Market*, the Court did not find these statutes to violate the free exercise clause because their impact on the religious rights of Orthodox Jews was incidental when compared to the more compelling state interest of using state power to advance the legitimate secular objective of positive social welfare. Chief Justice Warren did not find that either Pennsylvania or Massachusetts had singled out Orthodox Jews and other Saturday Sabbatarians for discriminatory treatment under their laws, but instead had enacted laws of general application intended to benefit the population as a whole.[136] Such legislation carried presumptive validity unless an individual could demonstrate an unconscionable burden on religious liberty. Distinguishing between the constitutional protection given to religious belief and religious practice, the Court, minus Justices Douglas, who again dissented, and Justices Stewart and Brennan, who defected from the Court's establishment clause analysis in *McGowan* and *Two Guys*, held that "to permit the exemption might well undermine the State's goal of providing a day that, as best possible, eliminates commercial noise and activity."[137]

Justice Brennan and Justice Stewart filed separate dissents in *Braunfeld*. Justice Stewart wrote that forcing "an Orthodox Jew to choose between his religious faith and his economic survival" amounted to a "cruel choice" that "no State can constitutionally command."[138] For religious observers whose commitment to their beliefs placed them in this position, the consequence of upholding the Sunday closing laws was not "something that can be swept under the rug and forgotten in the interest of enforced Sunday togetherness."[139] Justice Brennan voiced similar dissatisfaction with the Court's opinion. In his view, the Court had "exalted administrative convenience to a constitutional level high enough to justify making one religion economically disadvantageous."[140] In future cases, Justice Brennan urged the Court to subject state statutes having general application to the population but which nonetheless burdened religious conduct to the compelling state interest test used to analyze laws having discriminatory intent.[141] Two years later, Justice Brennan made good on the chance to turn his dissent into law in *Sherbert v. Verner* (1963).[142]

In *Sherbert*, the Court articulated the constitutional standard that would govern its subsequent free exercise jurisprudence until *Smith* eviscerated it twenty-seven years later. Unlike *Braunfeld* and *Crown Kosher Market*, *Sherbert* did not involve the rights of business owners, whose decision to open or close on the Sabbath was their own choice.

Sherbert concerned the rights of employees, rather than employers, whose religious convictions prohibited them from working on their Sabbath.

Adell Sherbert, a Seventh-day Adventist, was fired from her job in a South Carolina textile mill because she would not work on Saturday, the Sabbath of her faith. Sherbert applied for jobs at several other mills in the area, but each time she was denied job offers because of her refusal to work on her Sabbath. Having failed to secure suitable employment because of her religious obligations, Sherbert applied for unemployment compensation with the South Carolina Employment Security Commission. She was turned down for such benefits because South Carolina's law did not allow disbursement of benefits to persons "able to work . . . available for work . . . [but] have failed, without good cause . . . to accept available suitable work offered. . . ."[143] Sherbert then filed an administrative appeal with the unemployment commission. It did not accept her position that refusal to accept work on religious grounds constituted "good cause." The commission's ruling was sustained in the South Carolina state courts.[144]

The Supreme Court, 7-2, reversed. Justice Brennan, writing for the Court, which included all but two Justices from the *Braunfeld* and *Crown Kosher Market* majorities of just two terms before, ruled that South Carolina's statutory scheme of unemployment compensation amounted to unconstitutional religious discrimination under the free exercise clause. Justice Brennan noted that "it is apparent that [Sherbert's] declared ineligibility for benefits derives solely from the practice of her religion."[145] The commission's ruling forced her, as Justice Stewart had phrased it in his *Braunfeld* dissent, to have to make the "cruel choice" between fidelity to her religious beliefs or to her economic livelihood. Justice Brennan also wrote that South Carolina's labor laws contained a discriminatory provision that placed religious minorities at an express disadvantage. South Carolina's labor laws authorized the state labor commissioner to order textile mills to operate on Sunday in times of national emergency, but exempted employees who refused to work on Sunday because of their religious obligations.[146] These laws made it illegal for companies to discriminate against such Sunday worshippers who invoked these statutory exemptions. Companies were prohibited from demoting and firing workers who objected to Sunday labor. However, the South Carolina regulations contained no such provisions for Saturday Sabbatarians.

Of more lasting significance was the Court's decision in *Sherbert* to adopt the compelling state interest/least restrictive means test in claims brought under the free exercise clause challenging generally applicable laws, not just statutes that imposed direct burdens on religious conduct.[147] Justice Brennan took the language of his *Braunfeld* dissent and turned it into the law of the land. In *Braunfeld*, Brennan, joined only by Justice Stewart, had written that, in cases involving impingments of First Amendment religious rights, the Court was

> not confined to the narrow inquiry whether the challenged law is rationally related to some legitimate legislative end. Nor is the case decided by a finding that the State's interest is substantial and important, as well as rationally justifiable. . . . This exacting standard has been consistently applied by this Court as the test of legislation under all clauses of the First Amendment. . . . For religious freedom has classically been one of the highest values of our society. . . . The honored place of religious freedom in our constitutional hierachy . . . must now be taken to be settled.[148]

In *Sherbert*, Justice Brennan applied the compelling state interest/least restrictive means test to the South Carolina unemployment compensation scheme and found that it failed on both counts. Six other Justices, including Chief Justice Warren, who wrote *Braunfeld* and *Crown Kosher Market*, agreed with Justice Brennan's holding that South Carolina had not asserted a state interest compelling enough to warrant the constitutional abridgement of Adell Sherbert's religious rights. The Court said that its holding "reaffirms a principle that we announced a decade and a half ago, namely that no State may 'exclude individual [religious believers] . . . or non-believers, or members of any faith, *because of their faith, or lack of it,* from receiving the benefits of public welfare legislation'"[149]

In dissent, Justice John Harlan, joined by Justice White, argued that *Sherbert* isolated if not "necessarily overruled" *Braunfeld* because little difference existed between the stated and applied objectives of the two regulatory schemes.[150] Neither Pennsylvania nor South Carolina had targeted religious denominations their adherents for discriminatory treatment, the standard under which such cases should be ajudicated. Justice Harlan believed that the Court's opinion in *Sherbert* constitutionalized compelled religious exemptions from state statutes otherwise applicable to the general population, a conclusion neither the text nor the intent of the free exercise clause commanded.[151] He remained alone in that view, except for Justice White. Twenty-seven years later, Justice White would be one of five Justices who, "necessarily overruled" the *Sherbert* rule on grounds quite similar to those expressed in Justice Harlan's dissent.

On one count, Justice Harlan was right; *Sherbert* and *Braunfeld* could not then and cannot now be reconciled. That did not appear to matter to the Court, which expanded the scope and application of the *Sherbert* rule in subsequent free exercise cases. The Court chose not to overrule *Braunfeld* directly, but rather to distinguish it, or, more conveniently, simply ignore it altogether from *Sherbert* onward. Justice Brennan denied that *Sherbert* made *Braunfeld* extinct, but that was most likely judicial statesmanship on his part because, until *Smith*, *Braunfield* had remained lifeless. In order to assemble the majority for *Sherbert*, Justice Brennan had to muster at least two more votes. He got three, plus newly appointed Justice Arthur Goldberg, who had replaced Justice Felix Frankfurter. Justice Frankfurter had voted with the *Braunfeld* majority. Along with Justices Stewart and Douglas, the other *Braunfeld* dissenters, that made seven votes. It is not clear what in *Sherbert* persuaded Chief Justice Warren and Justices Black and Tom Clark to depart from the *Braunfeld* holding. But whatever did spur this defection, it marked a turning point in the constitutional protection for religious minorities whose sincere but sometimes unorthodox practices often ran afoul of generally applicable laws.

Sherbert became the benchmark from which the Court built its next generation of free exercise clause jurisprudence. Contrary to the Court's assertion in *Smith*, the *Sherbert* rule did not create an absolute right to engage in religious conduct that conflicted with generally applicable civil and criminal laws. *Sherbert* did require the Court to draw meaningful and principled lines between the permissible and the impermissible. This meant the Court had to engage in the weighing and balancing of competing interests, with a presumption that only the most compelling state objectives could overcome an asserted constitutional claim in conflict with those provisions of the constitution securing preferred rights and liberties.[152]

But the Court did not create new or novel constitutional doctrine in *Sherbert*. It took an acknowledged and central method of modern constitutional interpretation, one that even the *Smith* majority conceded was "familiar from other fields,"[153] and held that it was applicable to religious free exercise. The Court reaffirmed *Sherbert* on numerous occasions before *Smith* renounced it.[154] For reasons that cannot be found in either the text or meaning of the free exercise clause, the Court in *Smith*, as it did in *Braunfeld*, decided that administrative convenience and political deference to lawmaking bodies were more important principles to uphold than enforcing constitutional protection for an enumerated constitutional right.

The Rise and Fall of the Compelling State Interest Test

The application of the *Sherbert* rule to free exercise cases involving the unemployment compensation field remained unchallenged and undisturbed until 1981, when the Court decided *Thomas v. Review Board of Indiana*.[155] In the interim, the Court had extended the compelling state interest requirement to other cases involving alleged governmental infringements of religious liberty.[156] It appeared resolute in its conviction that religious rights are preferred rights, and that constitutional jurisprudence in such matters required meticulous and exacting scrutiny of the asserted competing interests. *Thomas* gave the Court the chance to reassess the appropriateness of the compelling state interest test to generally applicable state statutes providing public welfare benefits. The Court could either affirm *Sherbert* or discard it. In an 8–1 opinion, written by Chief Justice Burger, the Court chose the first course.

Thomas arose when a Jehovah's Witness, who had quit his job because it resulted in a conflict with his religious beliefs, brought suit against the Indiana state agency responsible for reviewing unemployment compensation claims. Unlike Adell Sherbert, Eddie Thomas's conflict originated not from the inability to find an employer willing to accommodate a Sabbath exemption from work, but from his religiously-based refusal to accept an in-house job transfer to work as an assembler on war-related products. Thomas was denied unemployment benefits by the Indiana Review Board, which ruled that the state public welfare laws prohibited such compensation for persons "who quit work voluntarily for personal reasons" that were not "objectively job-related."[157] The Indiana Supreme Court affirmed.[158]

The Supreme Court reversed. In a routine opinion, Chief Justice Burger held that *Sherbert* applied to instances in which persons were discharged or forced to quit over religious reasons that placed them in the position of choosing between doing as their faith compels them and performing their work responsibilities. The free exercise clause did not require that an individual "be compelled to choose between the exercise of a First Amendment right and participation in an otherwise available public program [when] the infringement upon" religious liberty is substantial.[159] In more explicit language, the Court held that

[w]here the state conditions receipt of an important benefit upon conduct proscribed by a religious faith, or where it denies such a benefit because of conduct mandated by religious belief, thereby putting substantial pressure on an adherent to modify his behavior and to violate his beliefs, a burden upon religion exists. While the compulsion may be indirect, the infringement upon free exercise is nonetheless substantial.[160]

The Court found that Indiana had not demonstrated the compelling interest necessary to overcome the significant burden on Thomas's capacity to exercise his religious beliefs.

Justice Rehnquist disagreed. In the first of several dissents calling on the Court to overrule *Sherbert*, Justice Rehnquist argued that the Court had misconstrued the free exercise clause in *Sherbert*, and now in *Thomas*, to require what the establishment clause forbids. The free exercise clause prohibited government from punishing held or professed religious beliefs; it did not, according to Justice Rehnquist, entitle individuals to unemployment benefits because the state had not forced either Adell Sherbert or Eddie Thomas to work under religiously proscribed conditions.[161] In making individuals eligible for public benefits based on conflicts with generally applicable state laws, Justice Rehnquist argued that the Court was giving preferred treatment to religious over nonreligious exemptions from such laws.[162] Justice Rehnquist maintained that, absent *Sherbert*, this interpretation requires that a state do something it ought not do under the establishment clause—create a religious exemption—in order to satisfy an obligation under the free exercise clause.[163] Justice White, who dissented in *Sherbert*, did not find the same problem. In fact, Justice White signed the Court's opinion and felt no need to write separately to explain how *Thomas* differed from *Sherbert*, if indeed it did.

The Court faced another variation on *Sherbert*'s application to the employment and hiring arena six years later in *Hobbie v. Unemployment Appeals Commission* (1987). In *Hobbie*, the Court was asked to decide whether Florida's refusal to award Paula Hobbie, a Seventh-day Adventist, unemployment compensation for her refusal to work on her Saturday Sabbath violated the free exercise clause. In a sense, the issue was

identical to that in *Sherbert*, with one minor exception. Hobbie converted
to the Seventh-day Adventist faith after she had been working in her job
for several years. Thus, the Court had to decide whether an employee
who experienced a religious conversion after having worked for an
employer for some time qualified as a "good cause" exception to
Florida's unemployment compensation eligibility requirements.

The Court dismissed Florida's argument that Hobbie had declared
herself ineligible for state unemployment compensation because she had
acted as the "agent of change." Comparing *Sherbert* and *Thomas* to the
facts in *Hobbie*, Justice Brennan, writing for an 8–1 Court, found no
"meaningful distinction to exist" among the three cases, other than the
timing and manner of the religious objections proffered to the respective
employer policies.[164] The Court held that the "timing of Hobbie's conversion is immaterial to our determination that her free exercise rights
have been burdened. . . . The First Amendment protects the free exercise
rights of employees who adopt religious beliefs or convert to another
after they are hired."[165]

Justice Brennan also pointed out that the Florida Appeals Commission
did not even contend that its unemployment compensation eligibility
requirements could withstand the Court's strict scrutiny analysis triggered under the compelling state interest test.[166] The state had asked the
Court to reject *Sherbert*'s application in *Hobbie*, and to rely instead upon
the reasonableness standard it had used in *Bowen v. Roy*.[167] In *Roy*, the
Court ruled that the federal government did not have to grant an exemption to Native American compliance with social security regulations
because requiring such an obligation, "neutral and uniform in its application, is a reasonable means of promoting a legitimate public interest."[168]

In a four-sentence rejoinder, Justice Brennan rejected Florida's argument that reasonableness, rather than a compelling state interest, was all
that was required in order to sustain generally applicable a law that placed
a burden on individual religious freedom. Noting that Chief Justice
Burger's plurality opinion in *Roy* failed to muster a majority on the
appropriateness of applying a reasonableness standard in free exercise
cases involving generally applicable state statutes, Justice Brennan ruled
that Hobbie was squarely controlled by *Sherbert* and *Thomas*, not *Roy*.[169]
Justice Brennan suggested that *Roy* was aberrant, and would have little

application in the Court's future free exercise jurisprudence free exercise. Unfortunately, Justice Brennan turned out to be wrong.

Two terms later, the Court again affirmed the *Sherbert* rationale employment-related free exercise clause claims in *Frazee v. Illinois Department of Employment Security* (1989).[171] Like *Thomas* and *Hobbie*, *Frazee* presented an unremarkable fact-pattern, one almost identical to *Sherbert*, except in one regard. William Frazee, who refused on several occasions to accept jobs secured for him by a temporary hiring agency because he would not work on Sunday, did not profess membership in a recognized church or religious denomination. Frazee claimed that his Christian beliefs prohibited him from engaging in profitable labor on his chosen Sabbath. The Illinois authorities denied his application for unemployment compensation because Frazee lacked the requisite "good cause" necessary to qualify for state benefits. Like state appellate courts in the previous unemployment compensation cases, the Illinois Court of Appeals affirmed the agency's decision, ruling that Frazee's religious beliefs had no roots in a "tenet, belief, or teaching of an established religious sect,"[172] and therefore was illegitimate.

A unanimous Supreme Court reversed. Justice White, a *Sherbert* dissenter, found the issue of religious affiliation irrelevant. The fact that Frazee did not belong to an established religious denomination had no bearing on his individual status under the free exercise clause. Justice White found *Sherbert* controlling; no concurrences were forthcoming to distinguish *Frazee* from the prior unemployment compensation cases. No one, not even Chief Justice Rehnquist, who had argued in *Thomas* that *Sherbert* should be overruled, and Justice Scalia, who would author *Smith* the next term, disagreed with Justice White's opinion holding that "the notion . . . [that] to claim the protection of the Free Exercise Clause, one must be responding to the commands of a particular religious organization."[173]

Frazee solved none of the inconsistencies that plagued the Court's free exercise decisions after *Sherbert*. As we have seen, the Court hesitated to extend the compelling state interest test to generally applicable statutes outside the unemployment compensation arena.[174] Instead, the Court utilized an *ad hoc* balancing scheme in most of its confrontations with the free exercise clause,[175] which contributed little to establishing a principled, coherent jurisprudential underpinning in future religious liberty cases. But these problems plague much of its jurisprudence in the other areas of constitutional doctrine involving preferred freedoms, including freedom of speech,[176] race-based equal protection,[177] and abortion rights.[178]

Perhaps it was the Court's inability to reconcile its contradictory approaches to resolving religious claims against generally applicable secular statutes that led it to use *Smith* to overrule *Sherbert*.[179] Perhaps it was the Court's professed discomfort in assessing the "centrality" or "seriousness" of religious-based claims to legal exemptions, a task it said in *Smith* that judges were not competent to perform.[180] Or perhaps the Court's desire to exorcise what remaining demons exist of liberal Warren Court precedent is driving its enthusiasm for political deference with nary the blink of a skeptical judicial eye. Whatever its motives, whether all or none of the above, the Court in *Smith* ushered in a new era for religious rights under the free exercise clause.

In *Employment Division of Oregon v. Smith* (1990),[181] the Supreme Court held that Galen Black and Alfred Smith, who were fired from their jobs as counselors for a drug rehabilitation clinic because they ingested peyote in violation of company policy, were not eligible for unemployment compensation under *Sherbert* and its progeny, even though use of the drug was a long-standing ritual of the Native American church. Justice Scalia, writing for himself, Chief Justice Rehnquist, and Justices White, Stevens, and Kennedy, wrote that since the Oregon law criminalizing the possession and use of peyote applied to the general population and was not specifically directed at religious practices per se, the state was not required under the free exercise clause to demonstrate a compelling interest for failing to grant a religious exemption to followers of the Native American church, even though the prospect of criminal penalties imposed a substantial burden on their religious obligation. Justice Scalia held that *Smith* could be distinguished from the *Sherbert* line of cases because, "as we have observed [before], the conduct at issue in those cases was not prohibited by law," a distinction the Court claimed was "critical."[182]

Had it wanted, the Court could have reached the same outcome under the compelling state interest test. Justice O'Connor's concurrence is quite clear on this matter. Conceding that the "question is close," Justice O'Connor nonetheless would have concluded that "uniform application of Oregon's criminal prohibition is 'essential to accomplish' its overriding interest in preventing the physical harm caused by the use of a

Schedule I controlled substance."[183] Controlling the harmful effects of illegal drug use overrode the case for a religious exemption to such a law. The state's interest in prohibiting drug possession was similar to its interest in enforcing compliance with legislation requiring the vaccination of children against small pox: to prevent physical harm.[184] This is a questionable analogue, but it at least reflects a principled method for resolving such vexing, competing claims for constitutional moment.

Justice Scalia did not think so. Without prodding or warning, the Court held that the *Sherbert* test was an inappropriate rule under which to review free exercise claims brought against generally applicable laws. An "across-the-board criminal prohibition on a particular form of conduct" does not require the state to demonstrate any more than reasonableness, even if such conduct accompanied by religious convictions. Justice Scalia held *Sherbert* to be no longer applicable in such challenges; government power to "enforce generally applicable prohibitions of socially harmful conduct, like its ability to carry out other aspects of public policy, 'cannot depend on measuring the effects of a governmental action on a religious objector's spiritual development.'"[185] Justice Scalia reached this conclusion, despite acknowledging that the compelling interest test is "familar from other fields."[186] To that, Justice Scalia wrote:

The "compelling government interest" requirement seems benign, because it is familiar from other fields. But using it as the standard that must be met before the government may accord different treatment on the basis of race . . . or before the government may regulate the content of speech . . . is not remotely comparable to using it for the purpose asserted here. What it *produces in those other fields—equality of treatment, and an unrestricted flow of contending speech—are constitutional norms; what it would produce here—a private right to ignore generally applicable laws—is a constitutional anomaly.*[187]

We cannot afford the luxury of deeming *presumptively invalid*, as applied to the religious objector, every regulation of conduct that does not protect an interest of the highest order.[188]

Justice Scalia was not satisfied with just discarding *Sherbert*. Consistent with his stated objective of reducing the judicial role to one that defers all policy determinations to the political process, Justice Scalia said:

It may fairly be said that leaving accommodation to the political process will place at a relative disadvantage those religious practices that are not widely engaged in; but that unavoidable consequence of democratic government must be preferred to a system in which each conscience is a law unto itself or in which judges weigh the social importance of all laws against the centrality of all religious beliefs.[189]

There is no explanation for what led Justice Scalia to determine that refusing to grant religious exemptions from generally applicable laws is an "unavoidable consequence of democratic government" when just one term before he had joined the Court's opinion in *Frazee*, which relied directly on *Sherbert*. Even more difficult is reconciling Justice Scalia's dissenting opinion in *Texas Monthly v. Bullock*, (1990) handed down one month before *Frazee*, in which the Court held that exempting religious publications from a state sales tax violated the establishment clause.[190] In *Texas Monthly*, Justice Scalia argued that such exemptions were constitutional under the establishment and free exercise clauses because they served to promote the dissemination of religious beliefs without affirmative state support.[191]

Justice Scalia said the Court's "long line of cases in which we have recognized that 'the government may (and sometimes must) accommodate religious practices'" permitted and even required religion-based exemptions from generally applicable laws.[192] *Walz v. Tax Commission* (1990)[193] allowed such permissive accommodation under the establishment clause, said Justice Scalia. But there was more:

> In such cases as *Sherbert*, *Yoder*, *Thomas* and *Hobbie*, we held that the Free Exercise Clause of the First Amendment *required* religious beliefs to be accommodated by granting religion-specific exemptions from otherwise applicable laws.[194]

He added:

> I dissent because I find no basis in the text of the Constitution, the decisions of this Court, or the traditions of our people for disapproving this longstanding and wide-spread practice.[195]

But in *Smith*, Justice Scalia took another view of the Court's precedents and his own opinions on the matter:

> Respondents urge us to hold, quite simply, that when otherwise prohibitable conduct is accompanied by religious convictions, not only the convictions but the conduct itself must be free from from governmental regulation. We have never held that, and decline to do so now.[196]

In *Texas Monthly*, Justice Scalia congratulated the Court for its impressive "judicial demolition project."[197] But in *Smith*, Justice Scalia ignored both the Court's precedents in this area and his own written opinion published just one term before to conduct a judicial demolition project of his own—one that eliminated thirty years of settled free exercise jurisprudence! His opinion in *Texas Monthly* arguing that the failure to grant religious exemptions from generally applicable tax laws was inconsistent with the historical recognition and approval "our people" have granted to such practices somehow got tossed aside in *Smith.*

Nor did Justice Scalia account for the internal weaknesses of *Smith.* For example, there is no reason given as to why the Court relied so heavily on *Minersville v. Gobitis* (1940),[198] which was overruled three years later in *West Virginia v. Barnette* (1943),[199] or *Braunfeld*, "effectively overruled" in *Sherbert*,[200] or insisted that *Reynolds v. United States* (1879),[201] the Mormon polygamy case, and not *Sherbert, Thomas* and *Frazee*, controlled *Smith.* Nor did Justice Scalia explain what led him to repudiate the foundation of his *Texas Monthly* dissent, or his votes in *Hobbie* and *Frazee.* Chief Justice Rehnquist did not explain how *Frazee*, which he joined, differs from *Hobbie* and *Thomas*, from which he dissented. The Chief Justice also joined Justice Scalia's dissent in *Texas Monthly*, as did Justice Kennedy, who was part of the unanimous *Frazee* Court.

Dissenting, Justice Blackmun, joined by Justices Brennan and Marshall, accused the majority of "effectuat[ing] a wholesale overturning of settled law concerning the Religion Clauses."[202] Calling the Court's interpretation of its free exercise precedents "distorted," Justice Blackmun wondered why the judicial obligation to review free exercise claims under strict scrutiny had suddenly become a "'luxury' that a well-ordered, democratic society could no longer afford."[203] To require government to demonstrate a compelling interest when justifying laws burdening religious free exercise does not mean *a fortiori* that all religion-based exemptions are mandated; it simply means that the state cannot engage in the repression of unfamiliar or obnoxious religious practices, whether tangentially or directly, without accomplishing an objective of the "highest order."[204]

The *Smith* dissenters did not believe that Oregon had met the compelling state interest requirement to justify denying Alfred Smith and Galen Black unemployment compensation. In order to deny a religious exemption on compelling state interest grounds, Oregon was required to provide an evidentiary record proving that sacramental peyote ingestion had caused substantial harm among Native Americans, or had been abused by members of the Native American church for nonreligious reasons.

Instead, Justice Blackmun charged in his dissent, the state's concern that permitting sacramental peyote use within the "carefully circumscribed ritual context" would lead to irresponsible drug use and a flood of religious claims for similar exemptions was "purely speculative."[205] Pure speculation as to the potential harm that religious exemptions cause in the administration of generally applicable laws did not, as the Court had ruled before, satisfy the compelling state interest requirement.[206]

Religious organizations and secular constitutional liberties organizations reacted to *Smith* with amazement. An unprecedented coalition of religious and civil liberties organizations petitioned the Court immediately after the decision was announced for rehearing in order to brief the issues raised and decided in *Smith*, but were denied the opportunity.[207] Since then, this extraordinarily diverse coalition of organizations, from the American Jewish Congress to the National Association of Evangelicals, from the National PTA to Americans United for the Separation of Church and State, have lobbied Congress to pass the Religious Freedom Restoration Act.[208] The legislation would require courts having proper jurisdiction to review free exercise challenges raised against generally applicable statutes under the compelling state interest/least restrictive means standard. Justice Scalia was right on one count: Full protection for "those religious practices not widely engaged in"[209] will depend upon whether the legislative process is willing to implement what the Supreme Court had said for years was not a constitutional choice, but a constitutional imperative.[210]

The Status of Religious Exemptions under Federal Civil Rights Law

In 1964, Congress, after several ineffectual and transparently false starts,[211] passed the first sweeping federal civil rights law designed to eliminate discrimination on the basis of race, color, religion, sex, or national origin in the private sphere of American life.[212] The Civil Rights Act of 1964 marked the first concerted use of federal power to prohibit discrimination in privately owned "public accommodations" by recipient institutions of federal monies and in the employment and hiring arena. For reasons that were self-evident, Congress was fundamentally concerned with the elimination of segregated public facilities that for so long had subjugated black Americans to inferior-class status and with the removal of discriminatory policies that had served as artificial barriers to equal opportunity in education and employment. But Congress also sought to—and did—extend the promise of equal protection and nondiscrimination to all individuals without regard to gender, national origin, or religion.

Organized American religion recognized that sweeping reform of federal civil rights law was long overdue and supported passage of the Civil Rights Act of 1964. Several national religious organizations and their denominational affiliates, such as the National Council of Churches, the American Jewish Congress, the National Conference of Catholics for Interracial Justice, and the Union of American Hebrew Congregations, took active and visible roles in pressuring Congress to pass civil rights legislation.[213] Ecumenical religion provided an essential moral foundation within the broader civil rights coalition calling for the reform of American race relations, but its enthusiasm for equal rights in the secular world masked some genuine worries about the status of religious institutions under the new civil rights legislation. Would religious institutions retain their status as autonomous bodies independent of government regulation? Would Congress force religious employers to comply with the antidiscrimination provisions of the legislation in their hiring of nonministerial staff? Could religious and religiously-affiliated schools use religious criteria to discriminate in hiring math, science, or social studies teachers or in admitting students? Could such institutions use racial or gender criteria?

Churches and the Right to Discriminate

In its original form, the Civil Rights Act of 1964 provided clear answers to just some of these questions. For example, Congress did not consider churches, synagogues, and other congregational bodies "public accommodations" under Title II of the 1964 Civil Rights Act and the courts have interpreted that provision accordingly.[214] Neither did the legislation give governmental authorities power over religious bodies in their selection of congregants, ministerial staff, or other individuals who perform ecclesiastical duties.[215] Under Title VII, church and church-affiliated institutions can discriminate against all protected class individuals when hiring, promoting, or firing employees who perform functions related to the religious mission of the institution.[216]

In Title VII, the provision of the Civil Rights Act that bars discrimination in employment and hiring, Congress crafted an exemption that
permitted religious employers to discriminate on the basis of religion,
but not race, color, gender, or national origin, in such matters. Religious
discrimination was permissible "with respect to the employment of
individuals of a particular religion to perform work connected with the
carrying on by such corporation, association, educational institution, or
society of its activities."[217] In 1972, Congress amended Title VII of the
1964 Civil Rights Act to permit religious employers to discriminate on
religious grounds against persons who perform duties not related to
ministerial or other faith-related responsibilities.[218] This broadened scope
of protection from federal antidiscrimination law did not include discrimination based on race, gender, color, or national origin. The statute
covered "pervasively sectarian" institutions (churches, synagogues, parochial schools, and theological seminaries), but did not reach church-
related or affiliated employers (religious colleges, hospitals, and social
service agencies).[219]

This last grouping of religious exemptions under federal antidiscrimination law has proved the most problematic to resolve both
legally and morally. Nondiscrimination is a universal, redemptive principal of human dignity; citizenship status in the secular state should not
and cannot rise or fall depending upon the color of one's skin or one's
place of origin. Conversely, increasing the regulatory power of government over religious affairs, even to promote the compelling societal
interest of racial or gender nondiscrimination, risks compromising the
rights of congregational bodies under the free exercise clause. Neither
principle is more or less attractive than the other.

In *Corporation of the Presiding Bishops v. Amos* (1987)[220] the Supreme Court was asked to decide the constitutionality of the amended
provisions of Title VII that permit religious institutions to discharge or
discriminate against employees in nonministerial capacities who are not
adherents to the faith. *Amos* began when six employees of three separate
Mormon church-owned companies were fired because of their religious
affiliation. One employee worked as a truck driver; three others were
seamstresses; one was a janitor; and another worked in the personnel
services division of the church's clothing manufacturer. In their lawsuit,
the discharged employees claimed that Section 702 of Title VII was
unconstitutional under the establishment clause because it exempted

religious institutions from general antidiscrimination law for reasons not related to the church's religious mission, enabled religious employers to coerce religious obedience from nonreligious employees and violated the equal protection principles of the Constitution in favor of advancing religious objectives.

Justice White, writing for a unanimous Court, rejected those arguments *in toto*. In reversing the lower court's decision that held Section 702 to be constitutionally infirm under the "effect" prong of the *Lemon* test,[221] the Court held that the statute advanced the permissible legislative purpose of "alleviating significant governmental interference with the ability of religious organizations to define and carry out their religious missions."[222] Unlike the Connecticut statute that it found unconstitutional two years before in *Estate of Thornton v. Caldor* (1985),[223] which *required* Title VII employers to relieve employees of work on their chosen Sabbath, the Court ruled in *Amos* that Section 702 did not compel religious institutions to engage in religion-based discrimination, but instead protected them from governmental regulation. The Court held that the broad discretion which Congress granted to religious institutions in the civil rights legislation to control their internal affairs was intended to allow religion to remain out from under the sometimes oppressive cast of large, bureaucratized administrative agencies, and best served the noble aspirations of the church and the state.

Reasonable Accommodation for Religious Practices

While the Civil Rights Act of 1964 made religion an illegal factor upon which nonreligious employers could base hiring and promotion decisions, the legislation remained silent on the question of whether employers were obligated to accommodate employees whose religious practices interfered with their work responsibilities. Since Congress sought to ban invidious workplace discrimination, it was reasonable to assume that employers who accommodated employee schedules and other job-related responsbilities for religion-based reasons were acting within the spirit of Title VII. Since religion-compelled conduct also cut across racial, ethnic, and gender lines, it was difficult to conclude that such accommodation represented anything more than good-faith compliance with Title VII, rather than a misinformed understanding of it.

In 1968, the Equal Employment Opportunity Commission issued regulations that interpreted the antidiscrimination provisions of Title VII to include an employer's refusal to make reasonable efforts to accommodate employees whose religious practices created conflicting obligations between faith-compelled conduct and their job responsibilities.[224] Employers were now *required* to make "reasonable accommodations" to the religious practices of an employee when such conflicts arose. In 1972, Congress, to alleviate potential confusion over the EEOC interpretation, amended the language of the 1964 Civil Right Act to require through statute the "reasonable accommodation" of employee religious practices, with the stipulation that such requests not pose an "undue hardship" on employer business operations.[225]

The Supreme Court considered its first constitutional challenge to the "reasonable accommodation" requirement of the 1972 congressional amendments in *Trans World Airlines v. Hardison* (1976).[226] Trans World Airlines argued that requiring an employer to reasonably accommodate employee religious needs was objectionable on establishment clause grounds, since the provision amounted to preference for religious over nonreligious personnel. The Court, 7–2, rejected the establishment clause attack on the reasonable accommodation provision, but interpreted the "undue hardship" language to require no more than a *de minimus* effort on the employer to satisfy an employee's religious needs.[227] Justice Marshall, dissenting, wrote that the *de minimus* interpretation of Title VII flouted congressional intent and undermined the nation's historic commitment to honoring diverse religious traditions in public and private life.[228]

The Court has still not provided a clear definition of what constitutes "undue hardship" under the reasonable accommodations provision of Title VII, other than the vague *de minimus* standard articulated in *Hardison*. In two cases interpreting Title VII since *Hardison*, the Court has failed to breath additional life into the "reasonable accommodation" requirement.

In *Estate of Thornton v. Caldor* (1985),[229] the Court heard an establishment clause challenge to a Connecticut statute forbidding employers to require individuals to work on their chosen Sabbath. The case centered on the misfortune of Donald Thornton, who was employed by the Connecticut-based department store chain, Caldor, Inc. Thornton informed his employer that he no longer would work on his Sabbath. Caldor gave him two choices: Thornton could either work at another store, which would require a much longer commute, or accept a demotion that would not require relocation. Thornton quit, and filed suit under the Connecticut statute's provision protecting Sabbath observers. Caldor defended its attempts at "reasonable accommodation," but also argued that the Connecticut Sabbath law violated the establishment clause because it compelled the employer to confer a benefit upon religious workers not otherwise available to all employees.

The Court, in an 8–1 opinion written by Chief Justice Burger, agreed with Caldor that the Connecticut statute violated the establishment clause. Chief Justice Burger ruled that the absolute nature of the Sabbath exemption advanced an impermissible religious objective under the establishment clause because it compelled the endorsement of a "particular religious practice."[230] Concurring, Justice O'Connor agreed with the Court that Connecticut's Sabbath exemption had "an impermissible effect" of advancing religion.[231] But Justice O'Connor, joined by Justice Marshall, wrote at length to defend the "reasonable accommodation" language of Title VII as required to effectuate the statute's anti-discrimination guarantees. Wrote Justice O'Connor:

> [A] statute outlawing employment discrimination based on race, color, religion, sex, or national origin has the valid secular purpose of assuring employment opportunity to all groups in our pluralistic society. Since Title VII calls for reasonable rather than absolute accommodation and extends that requirement to all religious beliefs and practices rather than protecting only the Sabbath observance, I believe an objective observer would perceive it as an antidiscrimination law rather than an endorsement of religion or a particular religious practice"[232]

In *Caldor*, several religious and secular organizations that are traditionally staunchly separationist in establishment clause matters, such as Americans United for the Separation of Church and State, the American Jewish Committee, and the American Civil Liberties Union, filed *amicus* briefs in support of Thornton's claim. The American Jewish Congress and the National Jewish Commission on Law and Public Affairs, which had appeared on the same side of an establishment clause case just once before in *Walz v. Tax Commission* (1970), represented Thornton in the Supreme Court. Together, the plaintiff and his *amici* argued that the Connecticut Sabbath law represented no more than a reasonable legislative attempt to relieve religious employees of the choices that emerged in such cases: either accept a job that paid less and entailed fewer responsibilities or quit and receive unemployment compensation. The Court did not accept that argument, but at least it reaffirmed the constitutional firmness of the "reasonable accommodation" requirements.

One term later, the Court continued its pattern of crabbed interpretation of Title VII. In *Ansonia v. Philbrook* (1986), the Court, overruling the Second Circuit Court of Appeals, ruled that Title VII did not require employers to accept an employee's "reasonable accommodation" proposals, but only that whatever arrangements were worked out satisfied the "reasonableness" standard outlined in *Hardison*.[233] As in *Caldor*, the Court appeared sympathetic to the difficulties imposed upon employees facing such agonizing choices. Writing for a 7–2 Court, Justice Rehnquist wrote that "where the employer has already reasonably accommodated the employee's religious needs, the statutory inquiry is at an end. The employer need not further show that each of the employee's alternative accommodations would result in undue hardship."[234]

Even in *Wards Cove v. Atonio* (1989)[235], which reordered without warning an eighteen-year-old evidentiary rule required of employers and employees in "disparate impact" cases brought under Title VII,[236] the Court held that in cases involving race or national origin discrimination, individuals could still demonstrate discrimination by proving the existence of alternative business practices that fulfilled the employer's requirements, but affected racial minorities less adversely. The same is not true for employees charging their employers with religious discrimination.[237] The Court's Title VII decisions since *Hardison* turning down repeated requests from a wide range of religious organizations and civil liberties groups for expansion of federal antidiscrimination protection for religious employees in the secular workplace have demoted religious rights under the law to less-protected status. On that matter, the Court is clear.

Conclusion

Freedom of religion, once considered sacrosanct among the fundamental freedoms entitled to vigorous judicial protection against majoritarian rule, enters the 1990s relegated to the unaccustomed and unforseen position of second-class stature in our constellation of constitutional values. The historical evolution of the First Amendment free exercise clause in the modern judicial era had breathed real life into the parchment promise of religious freedom for religious minorities, and further strengthened the rights of all individuals to believe and practice their religious beliefs free from government intrusion. But the preferred position of religious rights under the Constitution has vanished. The *Smith* decision demolishes the constitutional protection that, for the better part of four decades, had shielded unorthodox religious conduct from the legislative will of intolerant majorities. This result is not simply unfortunate; it is tragic.

The Court did not undercut the minimal constitutional protection extended to religious minorities in the workplace through the religious accommodation provisions of Title VII of the Civil Rights Act of 1964. The Court's interpretation of Title VII's guarantees protecting the rights of religious observers in the workplace remains crabbed. But the Court did not indicate that a desire to expand or contract the *Hardison* rule occupies a significant place among its immediate or future concerns. Given the new, uncertain direction of the religion clause jurisprudence of the Court, the likelihood that religious minorities stand to benefit from innovative legal doctrine broadening their rights in the workplace is minimal.

The Court's decision in *Smith* must not be underestimated for the consequences it will have for religious minorities. Justice Scalia's opinion for the Court did not mince words. Religious minorities that do not possess the political power to influence legislative outcomes will have their fate left to the dominant forces of majoritarian poltics. The Court's new understanding of the free exercise clause drains it of any real substantive meaning. For religious minorities, religious freedom no longer means the right to exercise an enumerated substantive liberty. Instead of enforcing the free exercise clause to ensure religious minorities meaningful insulation from majoritarian whims, the Court now views religious conduct as subject to reasonable regulation. Such is the status of religious liberty in the current constitutional moment, its once exalted place toppled by a Court no longer animated by a concern for individual rights, but instead by a blind fidelity to the smooth order of the majoritarian paradigm.

Notes

1. *Employment Division of Oregon v. Smith*, 110 S.Ct. 1595, 1599 (1990).
2. Id.

3. E.g., *Smith*, 110 S. Ct. at 1599; *Lyng v. Northwest Indian Cemetery Protective Association*, 485 U.S. 439 (1988); *Cantwell v. Connecticut*, 310 U.S. 296, 303–04 (1940).
4. E.g., *Wooley v. Maynard*, 430 U.S. 705 (1977) (upholding right of Jehovah's Witness to cover offensive state slogan on license plate on free speech and free exercise clause grounds); *Wisconsin v. Yoder*, 406 U.S. 205 (1972) (free exercise clause and unenumerated right of parents to direct their children's education permits exemption for Amish from state compulsory education laws); and *West Virginia v. Barnette*, 319 U.S. 624 (1943) (free speech and free exercise clauses prohibit state from compelling dissenting individuals to affirm or acknowledge repugnant beliefs).
5. *Smith*, 110 S.Ct. at 1606.
6. On this point, see Douglas Laycock, "Formal, Substantive and Disaggregated Neutrality Toward Religion," 39 *DePaul Law Review* 993 (1990); Michael McConnell, "Neutrality Under the Religion Clauses," 81 *Northwestern University Law Review* 146 (1986); Stephen Pepper, "Some Thoughts on Perspective," 4 *Notre Dame Journal of Law, Ethics and Public Policy* 649 (1990). But see, Ellis West, "The Case Against A Right to Religion-Based Exemptions," 4 *Notre Dame Journal of Law, Ethics and Public Policy* 591 (1990).
7. See, generally, Michael McConnell, "The Origins and Historical Understandings of Free Exercise of Religion," 103 *Harvard Law Review* 1410 (May 1990); McConnell, "Free Exercise Revisionism and the Smith Decision," 57 *University of Chicago Law Review* 1109 (1990). But see West, "The Case Against Religion-Based Exemptions."
8. 310 U.S. 296 (1940).
9. Id. at 303.
10. Id. at 303–4.
11. Id. at 304.
12. Id.
13. *Wisconsin v. Yoder*, 406 U.S. 205, 215 (1972).
14. E.g., *Frazee v. Illinois Department of Employment Security*, 489 U.S. 829 (1989); *Hobbie v. Employment Commission*, 480 U.S. 136 (1987); *Ansonia v. Philbrook*, 479 U.S. 60 (1986); *Thomas v. Review Board of Indiana*, 450 U.S. 707 (1981); and *Sherbert v. Verner*, 374 U.S. 398 (1963).
15. 319 U.S. 624 (1943).
16. Id. at 638.
17. 450 U.S. 707 (1981).
18. Id. at 718, quoting *Wisconsin v. Yoder*, 406 U.S. 205, 215 (1972).
19. 455 U.S. 252 (1982).
20. 406 U.S. 205 (1972).
21. Justice Powell and Justice Rehnquist took no part in the consideration or decision of the case.
22. 268 U.S. 510 (1925).
23. *Yoder*, 406 U.S. at 214.
24. *Lee*, 455 U.S. at 259.
25. *Yoder*, 406 U.S. at 241 (Justice Douglas, dissenting).
26. Id. at 237 (Justice Stewart, concurring).
27. *Sherbert*, 374 U.S. at 423 (Justice Harlan, dissenting).
28. Id.
29. *Lee*, 455 U.S. at 262 (Justice Stevens, concurring).

30. *Sherbert*, 374 U.S. at 418.

31. 485 U.S. 439 (1988).

32. 110 S.Ct. 1595 (1990).

33. E.g., *Bowen v. Roy*, 479 U.S. 6O (1986); *O'Lone v. Shabazz*, 482 U.S. 342 (1987).

34. E.g., *Frazee v. Illnois Department of Employment Security*, 489 U.S. 829 (1989).

35. See note 6, but also *Wisconsin v. Yoder*, 406 U.S. 205 (1972) (ruling that the refusal of Amish children to comply with compulsory state education laws requiring school attendance until the age of sixteen did not violate the free exercise clause).

36. E.g., *Goldman v. Weinberger*, 475 U.S. 503 (1986) (holding that free exercise clause neither required nor prohibited statutory religious exemptions to uniform military dress code). Soon afterward, Congress passed legislation granting a religious exemption to the challenged Air Force regulation. See Department of Defense Directive No. 1300.17 (3 Feb. 1988); *Bowen v. Roy*, 476 U.S. 693, 715–16 (1986) (a majority ruled that, had the plaintiffs survived a mootness challenge, the federal government could not assign Native Americans social security numbers if doing so violated their religious beliefs) (Justice Blackmun, concurring).

37. *Smith*, 110 S.Ct. at 1603–6.

38. E.g., *Patterson v. McLean Credit Union*, 485 U.S. 617 (1988); *Illinois v. Gates*, 459 U.S. 1028 (1982); *Miranda v. Arizona*, 384 U.S. 436 (1966); *Brown v. Board of Education*, 347 U.S. 972 (1953).

39. The Religious Freedom Restoration Act of 1991, H.R. 2797, proposed in the 101st Congress.

40. See *Payne v. Tennessee*, 111 S.Ct. 2597, 2609–10 (1991) ("*Stare decisis* is not an inexorable command; rather, it 'is a principle of policy and not a mechanical formula of adherence to the latest decision.' This is particularly true in constitutional cases, [while] [c]onsiderations in favor of *stare decisis* are at their acme in cases involving property and contract rights, where reliance interests are involved") (citations omitted) (Justice Rehnquist, for the Court); Id. at 2613–14 ("That [*stare decisis*] doctrine, to the extent it rests upon anything more than administrative convenience, is merely the application to judicial precedents of a more general principle that the settled practices and expectations of a democratic society should generally not be disturbed by the courts. It is hard to have a genuine regard for *stare decisis* without honoring that more general principle as well.) (Justice Scalia, concurring); see also, *Ohio v. Akron Center for Reproductive Health*, 110 S.Ct. 2972, 2984 (1990) ("I continue to believe, however, as I said in my separate concurrence last Term in *Webster v. Reproductive Health Services* [citations omitted] that the Constitution contains no right to abortion. . . . Leaving this matter to the political process is not only legally correct, it is pragmatically so. . . . The Court should end its disruptive intrusion into this field as soon as possible") (Justice Scalia, concurring); *Wallace v. Jaffree*, 472 U.S. 38, 106–7 (1985) ("There is simply no historical foundation for the proposition that the Framers intended to build the 'wall of separation' that was constitutionalized in *Everson*. . . . The 'wall of separation between Church and State' is a metaphor based on bad history, a metaphor which has proved useless as a guide to judging. It should be frankly and explicitly abandoned") (Justice Rehnquist, dissenting).

41. E.g., *I.N.S. v. Cardoza-Fonseca*, 480 U.S. 421–55 (1987) (Justice Scalia, concurring); *Wallace v. Jaffree*, 472 U.S. 38, 91–114 (Justice Rehnquist, dissenting).

42. *Smith*, 110 S.Ct. at 1606 (Emphasis added).

43. For historical accounts of religious prejudice directed against nonmainstream religion in America and legal efforts to overcome such discrimination, see David

Manwaring, *Render Unto Caesar: The Flag Salute Controversy* (Chicago: University of Chicago Press, 1962).

44. For legal, historical, and social science analyses of the efforts of disenfranchised religious minorities to secure their constitutional rights through the legal process, see, for example, Gregg Ivers, "Organized Religion and the Supreme Court," 32 *Journal of Church and State* 775 (1990); Leo Pfeffer, "Amici in Church-State Litigation," 44 *Journal of Contemporary Problems* 83 (1981); Frank Sorauf, *The Wall of Separation* (Princeton, N.J.: Princeton University Press, 1976); Richard E. Morgan, *The Politics of Religious Conflict* (New York: Columbia University Press, 1968).

45. E.g., *Niemotoko v. Maryland*, 340 U.S. 268 (1951); *Murdock v. Pennsylvania*, 319 U.S. 105 (1943); *Cantwell v. Connecticut*, 310 U.S. 296 (1940).

46. *Simmons v. U.S.*, 348 U.S. 397 (1955); *Dickinson v. U.S.*, 346 U.S. 389 (1953).

47. *Sherbert v. Verner*, 374 U.S. 398 (1963).

48. *Wisconsin v. Yoder*, 406 U.S. 205 (1972).

49. The NAACP's litigation campaign to dismantle Jim Crow and the *de facto* discrimination more common in the Northern states served as the model for several other organizations that successfully used the courts to advance their policy interests. For further discussion, see Clement Vose, *Caucasians Only* (Berkeley, Calif.: University of California Press, 1959).

50. 475 U.S. 503 (1986).

51. Id. at 505 (statute cited in text).

52. 530 F.Supp. 12 (D.D.C. 1981).

53. *Goldman v. Secretary of Defense*, 734 F.2d 1531 (D.C. Cir. 1984).

54. *Goldman*, 475 U.S. at 508.

55. Id. at 509.

56. Id.

57. Id. at 509–510 (Justice Stevens, concurring).

58. Id. at 513.

59. Id.

60. Id. at 514 (Justice Brennan, dissenting).

61. Id.

62. Id. at 516.

63. Id.

64. Id. at 521.

65. See *Chevron U.S.A. Inc. v. Natural Resources Defense Council, Inc.*, 467 U.S. 873, 842–43 (1984) ("If the intent of Congress is clear, that is the end of the matter; as well as the agency, must give effect to the unambiguously expressed intent of Congress").

66. 482 U.S. 342 (1987).

67. *Shabazz v. O'Lone*, 595 F.Supp. 928 (D.N.J. 1984).

68. Id. at 934.

69. Id.

70. *Shabazz v. O'Lone*, 782 F.2d 416 (3rd Cir. 1986).

71. Id. at 420.

72. *O'Lone v. Shabazz*, 482 U.S. 342, 353 (1987).

73. Id.

74. Id. at 356 (Justice Brennan, dissenting).

75. Id. at 368.

76. 108 S. Ct. 1319 (1988); *Lyng v. Northwest Indian Cemetery Protection Association.* 485 U.S. 439 (1988).
77. Id. at 442.
78. Id.
79. *Northwest Indian Cemetery Protective Association v. Peterson,* 565 F.Supp. 586 (N.D. Cal. 1983).
80. *Northwest Indian Cemetery Protective Association v. Peterson,* 795 F.2d 688 (9th Cir. 1986).
81. Justice Kennedy did not hear or take part in the case.
82. *Lyng v. Northwest Indian Cemetery Protective Association,* 485 U.S. 439, 442 (1988).
83. Id. at 450.
84. Id. at 452.
85. Id.
86. See *Lyng,* 485 U.S. at 449–51.
87. On this point, see Douglas Laycock, "The Remnants of Free Exercise," *The Supreme Court Review* 1, 33–36 (1990).
88. *Smith,* 110 S.Ct. at 1606–15.
89. Id. at 1606.
90. Id. at 1613.
91. See *Goldman,* 475 U.S. at 528 (Justice O'Connor, dissenting)
92. Id. at 530 (Justice O'Connor, dissenting) ("There is no reason why . . . general principles should not apply in the military, as well as the civilian, context").
93. Id. at 533.
94. 476 U.S. at 727.
95. 455 U.S. 252 (1982).
96. 485 U.S. 660 (1988).
97. 452 U.S. 640 (1981).
98. 479 U.S. 60 (1986)
99. 110 S.Ct. 688 (1990).
100. See *Shabazz,* 482 U.S. at 353.
101. See *Lyng,* 485 U.S. at 451.
102. 450 U.S. 707 (1981).
103. 480 U.S. 136 (1987).
104. 489 U.S. 829 (1989).
105. *Lyng,* 485 U.S. at 458 (Justice Brennan, dissenting).
106. Id. at 459.
107. Id. at 468.
108. Id.
109. Id. at 477.
110. Compare *Smith, supra,* at 1603–6, especially fns. 2, 3, 4 and 5, in which Justice Scalia replies to the criticisms of his opinion offered in Justice O'Connor's concurrence.
111. E.g., *Trans World Airlines v. Hardison,* 432 U.S. 63 (1977).
112. E.g., *Frazee v. Illinois Department of Employment Security,* 489 U.S 829 (1989); *Hobbie v. Unemployment Appeals Commission,* 480 U.S. 136 (1987); *Thomas v. Review Board of Indiana,* 450 U.S. 707 (1981); *Sherbert v. Verner,* 374 U.S. 398 (1963).
113. See *Estate of Thornton v. Caldor,* 472 U.S. 703 (1985).

114. See *Corporation of the Presiding Bishop of the Church of Jesus Christ of Latter Day Saints v. Amos*, 483 U.S. 327 (1987).

115. The Equal Opportunity Employment Act of 1972, 86 Stat. 104–05, 42 U.S.C. 2000e(j) (amending the Civil Rights Act of 1964 to require that religious observers are entitled to "reasonable accommodation" from their employer if their religious obligations conflict with job requirements before they can be dismissed or demoted).

116. See *Amos*, 483 U.S. at 339; *Hardison*, 432 U.S. at 85.

117. See *Watson v. Jones*, 13 Wall. 679 (1872) (recognizing this rule of deference under federal common law); *Presbyterian Church (U.S.A.) v. Hull Memorial Presbyterian Church*, 393 U.S. 440 (1969) (holding that the First Amendment barred civil authorities from deciding internal church disputes); cf., *Jones v. Wolf*, 443 U.S. 595 (1979) (ruling that, as a matter of civil law, civil courts must defer to ecclesiastical bodies the power to decide church disputes involving religious or theological doctrine, but could apply neutral principles doctrine to matters such as property disputes).

118. E.g., *Jones v. Wolf*, 443 U.S. 595 (1979); *Serbian Eastern Orthodox Diocese v. Milivojevich*, 426 U.S. 696 (1976); *Kedroff v. St. Nicholas Cathedral*, 344 U.S. 94 (1952).

119. *Smith*, 110 S.Ct. at 1601–5.

120. Id.

121. Id.

122. Id. at 1601–2.

123. *Thornton v. Caldor*, 472 U.S. 703 (1985).

124. See note 45, *supra*.

125. E.g., *First Unitarian Church v. Los Angeles*, 357 U.S. 545 (1958) (declaring church compliance with county loyal oath requirement to retain tax exemption to violate free exercise clause); *Witmer v. U.S.*, 348 U.S. 375 (1955) (upheld conscientious objection claim of a Jehovah's Witness on "ministerial exemption" grounds that made all Witnesses ineligible for military service).

126. E.g., *Dickinson v. U.S.*, 346 U.S. 389 (1953).

127. *Gallagher v. Crown Kosher Market*, 366 U.S. 617 (1961); *Braunfeld v. Brown*, 366 U.S. 599 (1961); *Two Guys v. McGinley*, 366 U.S. 582 (1961); *McGowan v. Maryland*, 366 U.S. 420 (1961).

128. 366 U.S. 582 (1961).

129. 366 U.S. 420 (1961).

130. 366 U.S. 617 (1961).

131. 366 U.S. 599 (1961).

132. *McGowan*, 366 U.S. at 444–45.

133. Id. at 442.

134. Id. at 448.

135. Id.

136. *Braunfeld*, 366 U.S. at 605.

137. Id. at 608.

138. Id. at 616 (Justice Stewart, dissenting).

139. Id.

140. Id. at 615–16 (Justice Brennan, dissenting).

141. Id. at 614–15.

142. 374 U.S. 398 (1963).

143. Id. at 400, 401.

144. 240 SC 286 (1962).

145. *Sherbert*, 374 U.S. at 404.

146. Id. at 406.

147. Cf., *Cantwell v. Connecticut*, 310 U.S. 296 (1940).

148. *Braunfeld*, 366 U.S. at 611–13 (Justice Brennan, dissenting).

149. *Sherbert*, 374 U.S. at 410, citing *Everson v. Board of Education*, 330 U.S. 1, 16 (1947).

150. Id. at 421 (Justice Harlan, dissenting).

151. Id. at 423.

152. *Braunfeld*, 366 U.S. at 613, citing *U.S. v. Carolene Products*, 304 U.S. 144, 152, n.4 (1938) ("There may be narrower scope for operation of the presumption of constitutionality when legislation appears on its face to be within a specific prohibition of the Constitution, such as those of the first ten amendments, which are deemed equally specific when held to be embraced within the Fourteenth") (citations ommited).

153. *Smith*, 110 U.S. at 1604.

154. E.g., *Frazee v. Illinois Department of Employment Security*, 489 U.S. 829 (1989); *Hobbie v. Unemployment Appeals Commission*, 480 U.S. 136 (1987); *Thomas v. Review Board of Indiana*, 450 U.S. 707 (1981).

155. 450 U.S. 707 (1981).

156. E.g., *McDaniel v. Paty*, 435 U.S. 618 (1978); *Wisconsin v. Yoder*, 406 U.S. 205 (1972); *Gillette v. United States*, 401 U.S. 437 (1971).

157. *Thomas*, 450 U.S. at 712.

158. 271 Ind. 233 (1979).

159. *Thomas*, 450 U.S. at 716.

160. Id. at 717–18.

161. Id. at 725 (Justice Rehnquist, dissenting).

162. Id.

163. Id. at 723.

164. *Hobbie*, 480 U.S. at 141.

165. Id. at 144.

166. Id. at 141

167. 476 U.S. 693 (1986).

168. Id. at 708 (plurality opinion).

169. *Hobbie*, 480 U.S. at 141.

170. Id. at 142, note 7.

171. 489 U.S. 829 (1989).

172. *Frazee v. Illinois Department of Employment Security*, 512 N.E.2d 789, 791 (1987). The Illinois Supreme Court denied a petition to hear an appeal. See id., 117 Ill Dec 224 (1988).

173. *Frazee*, 489 U.S. at 834.

174. But see *Wooley v. Maynard*, 430 U.S. 705 (1977) (holding that New Hampshire had not demonstrated a compelling interest to require Jehovah's Witnesses to display state motto, "Live Free or Die," on automobile license plate); *Wisconsin v. Yoder*, 406 U.S. 205 (1972).

175. E.g., *Lyng v. Northwest Indian Cemetery Protective Association*, 485 U.S. 439 (1988); *O'Lone v. Shabazz*, 482 U.S. 342 (1987); *Bowen v. Roy*, 476 U.S. 693 (1986); *Goldman v. Weinberger* 475 U.S. 503 (1986).

176. E.g., *Osbourne v. Ohio*, 110 S. Ct. 1691 (1990); *Ward v. Rock Against Racism*, 109 S. Ct. 2746 (1989); *Miller v. California*, 413 U.S. 15 (1973); *Bradenburg v. Ohio*, 395 U.S. 444 (1969).

177. E.g., *Metro Broadcasting, Inc. v. FCC*, 110 S. Ct. Z997 (1990); *City of Richmond v. J. A. Croson Co.*, 488 U.S. 469 (1989); *Regents of University of California V. Bakke*, 438 U.S. 265 (1978).

178. E.g., *Webster v. Reproductive Health Services*, 492 U.S. 490 (1989); *Roe v. Wade*, 410 U.S. 113 (1973).

179. On this point, see West, "The Case Against Religion-Based Exemptions," 600–13.

180. E.g., *Smith, 110 U.S.* at 1604 ("It is no more appropriate for judges to determine the 'centrality' of religious beliefs before applying the 'compelling interest' test in the free exercise field, than it would be for them to determine the 'importance' of ideas before applying the 'compelling interest' test in the free speech field").

181. 110 S.Ct. 1595 (1990).

182. Id. at 1598.

183. Id. at 1614 (Justice O'Connor concurring).

184. Id., citing *Jacobson v. Massachusetts*, 197 U.S. 11 (1905).

185. Id. at 1603, citing *Lyng*, 485 U.S. at 451.

186. Id. at 1604.

187. Id.

188. Id. at 1605.

189. Id. at 1606.

190. 489 U.S. 1 (1989).

191. Id. at 29–45 (Justice Scalia, dissenting).

192. Id. at 38.

193. 397 U.S. 664 (1970).

194. *Texas Monthly*, 489 U.S. at 38 (emphasis in original).

195. Id. at 33.

196. See *Smith*, 110 U.S. at 1602.

197. *Texas Monthly*, 489 U.S. at 29.

198. 310 U.S. 586 (1940).

199. 319 U.S. 624 (1943).

200. *Sherbert*, 374 U.S. at 421 (Justice Harlan, dissenting).

201. 98 U.S. 145 (1879).

202. *Smith*, 110 S.Ct. at 1616 (Justice Blackmun, dissenting).

203. Id.

204. See *Yoder*, 406 U.S. at 215.

205. *Smith*, 110 S.Ct. at 1618, 1620.

206. Id. at 1617.

207. *Employment Division of Oregon v. Smith*, petition for rehearing denied, 58 U.S.L.W. 3676, 24 April 1990.

208. See note 40, *supra*.

209. *Smith*, 110 U.S. at 1606.

210. The Court has made clear that it wishes to see Smith followed. See, e.g., *First Covenant Church v. City of Seattle*, 787 P.2d 1352 (Sup.Ct. Wash. 1990); *cert. granted, judgment vacated and remanded*, 111 S.Ct. 1097 (1991) (vacated a Washington Supreme Court decision that held the application of Seattle's Landmark Preservation Ordinance to churches violative of the free exercise clause and ordered the case to be reconsidered under the Smith rule); *St. Bartholomew's Church v. City of New York*, 914 F.2d 348 (2nd Cir. 1990); cert. denied, 111 S.Ct. 1103 (1991) (rejecting free exercise claim and permitting government to require church-owned buildings to comply with municipal landmarking ordinances); *Minnesota v. Hershberger*, 444 N.W. 2d 282 (Sup.Ct. Minn. 1990) (ordering Minnesota Supreme

Court to reconsider whether free exercise clause permits Amish to exempt their horse-drawn buggies from state statute requiring display of flourescent orange triangle on slow-moving vehicles. The Minnesota Supreme Court reheard the case and ruled on behalf of the Amish, but on state constitutional grounds.

211. The Civil Rights Act of 1957, 71 Stat. 634, 42 U.S.C. 1971; The Civil Rights Act of 1960, 74 Stat. 86, 42 U.S.C. 1971.
212. The Civil Rights Act of 1964, Pub.L. 88-352, 78 Stat. 241, as amended, 42 U.S.C. 2000e *et. seq.* Section 703, codified at 42 U.S.C. 2000-2(a) reads:
    [I]t shall be unlawful employment practice for an employer . . . to discriminate against any individual with respect to his compensation, terms conditions, or privileges of employment because of such individual's . . . religion.
213. See, for example, Robert Wuthnow, *The Restructuring of American Religion* (Princeton, N.J.: Princeton University Press, 1988), 145-48; A. James Reichley, *Religion in American Public Life* (Washington, D.C.: The Brookings Institution, 1985), 243-339.
214. *Heart of Atlanta Motel v. U.S.*, 379 U.S. 241 (1964); *Katzenbach v. McClung*, 379 U.S. 294 (1964).
215. The Civil Rights Act of 1964, 78 Stat. 255, as amended, 42 U.S.C. 2000e *et. seq.*
216. The Civil Rights Act of 1964, 78 Stat. 255, as amended, 42 U.S.C. 2000e *et. seq.*
217. The Civil Rights Act of 1964, 78 Stat. 255, 42 U.S.C. 2000e-1.
218. The Equal Employment Opportunity Act of 1972, Pub. L. 92-226, 86 Stat. 103, 42 U.S.C. 2000e.
219. The Equal Employment Opportunity Act of 1972, 86 Stat. 103-04, 42 U.S.C. 2000e.
220. 483 U.S. 327 (1987).
221. *Amos v. Corporation of the Presiding Bishop of the Church of Jesus Christ of Latter-Day Saints*, 618 F. Supp. 1013 (D. Utah 1985).
222. *Amos*, 483 U.S. at 339.
223. 472 U.S. 703 (1985).
224. 29 C.F.R. 1605.1(b) (1968).
225. The Equal Employment Opportunity Act of 1972, 86 Stat. 103, 104-05, 42 U.S.C. 2000e(j). Section 701 (j) reads:
    The term "religion" includes all aspects of religious observance and practice, as well as belief, unless an employer demonstrates that he is unable to reasonably accommodate to an employee's or prospective employee's religious observance or practice without undue hardship on the conduct of the employer's business.
226. 432 U.S. 63 (1977).
227. Id. at 84-85.
228. Id. at 88-91 (Justice Marshall, dissenting).
229. 472 U.S. 703 (1985).
230. Id. at 710.
231. Id. at 711 (Justice O'Connor, concurring).
232. Id. at 712.
233. 479 U.S. 60, 68-69 (1986).
234. Id. at 68.
235. 490 U.S. 642 (1989).
236. *Griggs v. Duke Power Co.*, 401 U.S. 424 (1971). Congress, after almost two years of fierce debate with the Bush administration, passed the Civil Rights Act of 1991 that overturned the *Wards* Cove ruling on statutory grounds and restored the *Griggs* standard in "disparate impact" cases.

237. *Ansonia v. Philbrook*, 479 U.S. 60 (1987), *infra*, (upholding dismissal of an employee whose suggested accommodations posed more than a de minimus burden on employer, but ruling that employee was entitled to unemployment compensation under the Sherbert rule); see also, *American Postal Workers Union v. Postmaster General*, 781 F.2d 772 (9th Cir. 1986) (ruling that dismissal of two Post Office employees for refusing to hand out selective service registration forms on religious grounds, despite requests of employees for alternative work arrangements, not to violate the *Hardison* rule).

Epilogue

The Court is not the Constitution, as Louis Fisher reminds us, but an equal participant in the ongoing constitutional dialogue between the different branches of government and government and the people.[1] The executive and legislative branches of government, at the national and state levels, are the political institutions responsive and accountable to the electorate and thus retain the primary responsibility to make and enforce laws. The Constitution explicitly affords the legislative and executive branches the power to make and enforce laws that reflect the preferences of political majorities to rule. But the power to make law does not mean that political institutions can bypass constitutional commands. The Constitution permits constitutional majorities to rule; it does not, however, give license to tyrannical majorities. Constitutional rights do not depend on political will. The political branches are equal participants in constitutional dialogue, but this does not enable them to ignore or degrade the constitutional rights of individuals or minorities too powerless to influence the political process.

The extent to which the political process has affirmative constitutional power to make and enforce laws that implicate individual rights and liberties and when the courts possess the requisite power to invalidate such action through judicial review has anchored the debate in constitutional law from time immemorial. The Constitution makes the resolution of this question impossible to avoid. But disagreement over what the Constitution means, how it should be interpreted and who should enforce its provisions will continue as long as the document endures, and it will remain passionate, emotional and subject to irreconcilable opinion. The reason is simple. In the legal, political science, and historical scholarship, we often talk about the Constitution in the abstract, as if resolution of intellectual disagreements is the sole end of constitutional dialogue. But, as Erwin Chemerinsky has written, constitutional interpretation is ultimately about defining and protecting society's most cherished values and determining the relationship of those values to the higher law.[2] How these values are defined and determined in the real world determines the constitutional relationship of people to their government. And when we take constitutional rights and liberties and turn them over to the political process for resolution, we risk subverting the integrity of these values and this relationship.

This book has focused on one of the most fundamental of our constitutional rights, religious liberty, and argued that it no longer occupies a preferred position in the Court's religion clause jurisprudence. The Court, remade to comport with and extend the political agenda of President Reagan and, to a lesser extent, President Bush, has redefined the constitutional relationship between religion and public life. Consistent with President Reagan's distaste for the Court's landmark decisions of the 1960s amd 1970s that constrained state power to promote majoritarian religious values and elevated religious minorities from political and constitutional subjugation to equal status in the American religious milieu, the Court has now returned broad power to the political process to legislate on religious matters and enforce these policy choices.

Considerable implications flow from the Court's religion clause jurisprudence. On a general level, religious organizations and allied interest groups possessing size and political clout are better positioned than ever before to exercise their influence in the popular branches of government and determine how they will resolve constitutional issues. The Court's deferential posture to the policy choices of the political process cannot be equated with distaste for judicial activism, although the Court claims that judicial restraint, not substantive concerns over those choices, guides its approach to the exercise of judicial power. As I have tried to demonstrate, the Court has not balked at overruling or limiting decisions that it felt were wrong, sometimes for substantive reasons and sometimes for no reason at all. With the Court more and more unwilling to recognize and enforce the religion clauses, smaller religions, religions that lack political sophistication and unpopular faiths are now dependent on the political process to secure their rights.

On a more specific level, the Court's refusal to enforce the fundamental rights secured by the religion clauses means that religious individuals and communities whose faith-compelled conduct conflicts with generally applicable laws will find themselves unable to practice their religion. More children will find themselves marginalized and outcast in public schools that choose to make prayer an inclusive part of their day. Citizens will be required to pay taxes to support religious schools and social institutions. Government can and will use tax dollars to display religious symbols on public land. In sum, the power of temporal political majorities to exercise their discretion over and on behalf of religion will continue. This cannot be right. But, for now, it is the law.

Notes

1. Louis Fisher, *Constitutional Dialogues* (Princeton, N.J.: Princeton University Press, 1988).
2. Erwin Chemerinsky, "The Vanishing Constitution," 103 *Harvard Law Review* 44, 47 (1989).

Table of Cases

Corporation of the Presiding Bishops of the Church of Jesus Christ of Latter Day Saints v. Amos, 483 U.S. 327 *(1987)*
County of Allegheny v. ACLU, 109 S.Ct. 3086 (1989)
Dickinson v. U.S., 346 U.S. 389 (1953)
Doe v. City of Warren, 889 F.2d 1987 (6th Cir. 1989)
Doe v. Ferguson, 934 F.2d 743 (7th Cir. 1991)
Edwards v. Aguillard, 482 U.S. 578 (1987)
Employment Division of Oregon v. Smith I, 108 S.Ct. 1444 (1988)
Employment Division of Oregon v. Smith II, 110 S.Ct. 1595 (1990)
Engel v. Vitale, 370 U.S. 421 (1962)
Epperson v. Arkansas, 393 U.S. 421 (1968)
Estate of Thornton v. Caldor, 472 U.S. 703 (1985)
Everson v. Board of Education, 330 U.S. 1 (1947)
First Covenant Church v. City of Seattle, 789 F.2d 1352 (10th Cir. 1990)
First Unitarian Church v. Los Angeles, 357 U.S. 545 (1958)
Florey v. Sioux Falls School District, 619 F.2d 1311 (6th Cir. 1980)
Frazee v. Illinois Department of Employment Security, 109 S.Ct. 1514 (1989)
Gallagher v. Crown Kosher Market, 366 U.S. 617 (1961)
Garnett v. Renton Area School District, 874 F.2d 608 (10th Cir. 1989)
Gideons Int'l v. Tudor, 100 A.2d 857 (1953)
Gillette v. U.S., 401 U.S. 437 (1971)
Goldman v. Weinberger, 475 U.S. 503 (1986)
Grand Rapids v. Ball, 473 U.S. 373 (1985)
Green v. Connally, 330 F.Supp. 1150 (D.D.C. 1971), *aff'd per curiam sub nom, Coit v. Green,* 404 U.S. 997 (1971)
Hazelwood School District v. Kuhlmeier, 484 U.S. 260 (1988)
Hefron v. ISKCON, 452 U.S. 640 (1981)
Hobbie v. Unempolyment Appeals Commission, 480 U.S. 136 (1987)
Hunt v. McNair, 413 U.S. 734 (1973)
I.N.S. v. Cardosa-Fonesca, 480 U.S. 421 (1987)
Jager v. Douglas County School District, 862 F.2d 824 (11th Cir. 1989)
Kaplan v. City of Burlington, 891 F.2d 1024 (1st Cir. 1989)
Karcher v. May, 484 U.S. 72 (1987)
Karen B. v. Treen, 653 F.2d 897 (5th Cir 1981)
Keith v. Department of Education, 553 F. Supp. 295 (M.D. La. 1982)
Kunz v. New York, 340 U.S. 290 (1951)
Larkin v. Grendel's Den, 459 U.S. 116 (1982)

Index